IN THE HEART OF WARSAW

Corner of Nalefky and Gensha, Warsaw, Poland, 1937.

In the Heart of Warsaw

AN AUTOBIOGRAPHICAL NOVEL BY

Szloma Renglich

TRANSLATED FROM
THE YIDDISH BY
ZIGMUND JAMPEL

Véhicule Press

EDITED FOR THE PRESS BY ZIGMUND JAMPEL

The publisher and the translator wish to thank
Ida Renglich for her special assistance.

Published with the assistance of The Canada Council.
Printing: Imprimerie d'Edition Marquis Ltée
Photo on page 2: Corner of Nalefky and Gensha streets, Warsaw,
Poland, 1937. Courtesy of the YIVO Institute for Jewish Research.

CANADIAN CATALOGUING IN PUBLICATION DATA
Renglich, Szloma, 1912-
In the heart of Warsaw

ISBN 1-55065-037-8

1. Jews--Poland--Fiction. I. Title.

PS8585.E6716 1993 839'.0933 C93-090227-0
PR9199.3.R4616 1933

Published by Véhicule Press, P.O.B. 125, Place du Parc Station,
Montréal, Québec, Canada H2W 2M9

Printed in Canada on acid-free paper

Contents

In the Heart of Warsaw

I DRIFTED AIMLESSLY from street to street. From Gensha to Twarda, from Smotcha to Nalefky, late into the night, I covered the heart of Warsaw's Jewish Quarter with uneven footsteps as I thought of the drunkard's story. It made me sick to believe even a word out of Itzhak Copperstein's mouth, but how else could I explain what I had seen that afternoon?

It was the bitter cold of the night that finally brought me back to my senses. I was frozen by the wind blowing through my threadbare jacket and pants. My teeth chattered as I began to hurry back to my boss's house.

Dluga Street was deserted. I knocked on Nagil's door with fingers raw from the icy air. I waited a long time before I heard the shuffle of footsteps inside the house. Mrs. Nagil, her coat wrapped tightly over her nightgown, finally looked out through a crack in the door.

"Oh, it's you? Come in quickly," she said, pulling me in by the arm.

"What a miserable night," she whispered in the dark hallway. "We thought you wouldn't be back until the morning. Where've you been?"

"At my Aunt Liebe's," I lied. "I left her house late."

"Do you want something to eat?"

"I'm not hungry."

"Then go to sleep." Mrs. Nagil walked back to her bedroom.

From behind the kitchen door I pulled out the folding cot. As quietly as I could, I dragged it to the middle of the floor and set it up. I turned off the light in the kitchen, took off my shoes, and still wearing all my clothes, I lay down.

My nightmares seemed to start before I was even fully asleep. Again I was walking up and down Stafke Street, hoping for a glimpse of my mother and feeling terrified of getting caught by Itzhak Copperstein.

A plump woman with a painted face appeared out of thin air and stopped me. I recognized her at once. She was one of Copperstein's wives. Laughing, she began to pull me by the hand. "Don't you want to see your mother?" she asked. "Roise'll be so glad that you're in Warsaw." I tried to pull free of her but her grip was too strong. The woman dragged me down a dark stairway to an open cellar door. In a room full of deformed beggars and criminals, I saw my mother at last. All life had been drawn out of her. She sat next to Itzhak Copperstein, her head bent, crying from shame. *"Mamme,"* I called to her. Without warning Copperstein lunged at me. I screamed and woke with a start.

I lay sweating under the cover in the cold kitchen afraid to go back to sleep. I was too exhausted, however, and soon I was thrown back to Otwock. In the bright sunlight of the resort town, I ran to save my life from the drunken Copperstein. Blood dripped from his head and chest as he chased me with a broken bottle. Suddenly, I tripped and fell. As I lay sprawled on the ground, Copperstein began to kick me. I rolled along the ground trying to escape until I felt the cot being shaken.

"Get up!" Mr. Nagil was shouting. "Get up! It's after seven already. It's freezing in here. Are the press irons ready? When are we going to start work? In the afternoon?"

I was still shivering. Mournful daylight pressed against the kitchen window. I threw the blanket off. The floor felt like ice to my feet. I slipped my shoes on but when I tried to stand up, I became so dizzy, I had to sit back down. After a while, my head stopped spinning. I stood up again. I folded the cot and pulled it behind the kitchen door.

"Are you up already?" Nagil called to me from the living room.

"Yes, Mister Nagil," I called back. "I'm lighting the stove right now."

I quickly opened the coal bin, grabbed handfuls of coal, a few sticks of wood, threw them into the stove, sprayed the coal with naphtha and lit a match to it. As the fire began to burn, I washed my hands in the sink.

The short, bowlegged tailor charged into the kitchen scowling. "Go in. See what Mrs. Nagil needs from the grocer. Everybody's late today because of you."

"Mister Nagil, I'm not feeling well."

He thrust his big head and flapping ears into my face. "'*I'm not feeling well,*'" he mimicked me. "You stay out all night at parties. What do you want from me now? I have work to get done!"

"Don't scream, Kalmen," Mrs. Nagil said, entering the kitchen with money in her hand. Her thick red hair was tied up in a kerchief and she was wearing a fur coat to keep warm. Her green eyes reminded me at once of my mother.

"Here are five zlotys," Mrs. Nagil said. "Go to the grocer on Shwentoyearska and buy a loaf of white bread, a half pound of butter, a dozen eggs, and four apples. Don't take too long. Yankele has to eat breakfast before he goes to school."

The kitchen was just beginning to warm up, my bones ached, and I left with great reluctance. The moment I stepped out of the building I began to sneeze and cough. I had never seen such a miserable Sunday.

The quickest way to Shwentoyearska was through Krashinsky Square, an area I usually avoided because hoodlums gathered there. Now as I rushed across the square, I didn't care what happened to me. I only wished I had a cigarette to calm me down. I fished out the few coins in my pockets and counted twenty groschen, enough for ten cigarettes.

On the way back from the grocer's, I smoked a Wanda. The cigarette, instead of calming me down, made me sicker.

"The irons are cold!" Mr. Nagil screamed as I opened the front door. "You forgot the press irons!"

I ran back into the kitchen, put the groceries down on the table, and immediately placed the two press irons on the metal sheet on the stove.

"I don't know where my head is this morning," Mrs. Nagil said. She had taken off her fur coat now that the house had warmed up and was wearing a black dress with red and yellow flowers. "I forgot we don't have any milk. Could you please run back to the grocer?"

I was feeling chilled even in the warm kitchen. I bent down under the work table where I kept my sack of belongings and took out my sweater. The small sack of gray cloth, my grandmother's gift to me before I left Lublin, reminded me of Babbe's frightened, wrinkled face when I told her that I was traveling to Warsaw to look for my mother. I hadn't seen my grandmother and my sister in over six months. I knew that when I wrote to Babbe and Ruchele I would have to protect them. I couldn't tell them what I had found out.

The brown sweater had grown small on me. I pulled my jacket over the sweater and I left the house once more.

On the street I lit another Wanda. The smoke made me nauseous. I remembered that I hadn't eaten since lunch the day before.

When I returned with the liter of milk, Chaim Friedman, Nagil's young, stylish assistant had already come in and was busy working at his sewing machine.

"There's your breakfast," Mrs. Nagil said as she took the bottle of milk and change from me. She poured the milk into a pan and set it on the stove to boil.

On a corner of the work table, I saw the breakfast Mrs. Nagil had prepared for me: a slice of buttered bread, a piece of marinated herring, a tomato and onion salad, and a glass of hot tea.

"Did you enjoy your day of freedom, Schloime?" Mr. Friedman asked in his playful manner.

"He had himself some party last night," Mr. Nagil said from where he sat working. "He came back in the middle of the night."

"A party?" the assistant tailor asked me with a smile. "Have you found yourself a girl friend?"

"No," I said, as I ate. "I was at my aunt's house. We were talking and it got late."

"Well, don't talk so much now," Mr. Nagil blurted over his shoulder. "You have to go to Mendel's on Nalefky and get supplies."

As soon as Nagil's wife stepped out of the kitchen to get her son ready for school, Mr. Friedman said, "You have such a kind-hearted boss, Schloime, I hope you remembered him in your prayers yesterday. I sure did."

"Chaim, don't start up so early," Mr. Nagil said. "Let's get some work done today. And you," my boss turned to me, "are you eating?"

I began to eat quickly. When I was done, Mr. Nagil handed me a list of supplies, ten zlotys, and I left the house again.

The day had grown colder and grayer. The early morning looked like late afternoon. My sweater was useless as the chill wrapped itself around my bones. But I was soon flooded with memories of the previous day and the pain made me insensitive to the cold. I couldn't erase the image from my eyes of my mother as she sat in that cellar among beggars and thieves, holding a baby wrapped in rags while a small boy tugged at her skirt. My poor mother, who had been such a beautiful, decent, and honest woman, how could she have allowed herself to be dragged down so low? For four years I tried to find out what had happened to her. I followed her from Lublin to Otwock to Warsaw. Finally, here, in a slum in Warsaw's Jewish Quarter, I learned the truth. My mother had abandoned us, my sister Ruchele, me, and her own mother, out of shame. Mamme had been deceived into marrying a man who was a drunkard and a thief, a man who had three other wives. And with such a man our mother now had two children.

Nalefky Street, enclosed by tall apartment buildings, with rows of clothing stores at street level, was already packed with tradesmen and shoppers. At No. 18, I walked up a flight of dark, dusty stairs to Mendel's. Tailors and errand boys were standing at the long counter being waited on. Soon one of Mendel's sons, a short, round boy, recognized me. Nuttem grabbed Mr. Nagil's list from my hand and a few minutes later returned from the back with a package. I paid him, Nuttem thrust the parcel into my hands, gave me my change, and I left.

The supplies, no more than what I usually bought at the start of every week, felt heavy today. I wished I had another cigarette, but I had smoked them all and I had no money left to buy more. I hoped Nagil would have a finished suit for me to deliver. A delivery usually meant at least a half-zloty tip. When I returned to the kitchen, however, I didn't want to leave. I just wanted to go to sleep.

"Before you put the supplies away," Mr. Nagil said, "I have to press a suit."

There was a hot iron on the stove. I unhooked the wooden handle from the cold iron, slipped the metal tips into the handle holes of the hot iron, picked it up, and set it down on the table.

While Mr. Nagil pressed the suit, I untied the package of supplies and laid out the thread, buttons, chalk, seam binding, and lining material in their proper places. I finally sat down to rest a moment. At once my eyes began to close.

"Schloime, what's the matter?" asked Nagil's assistant.

"I'm sick."

"Well, maybe you need to go on vacation?" Mr. Nagil asked. "How about a health spa for a few weeks to recuperate?"

"A golden heart," the assistant tailor muttered sarcastically without looking up from his machine.

One of the irons had been left on the pressing table. I put it back on the metal plate of the stove to heat up again. I sat down near the stove to warm up. The tailor and his assistant were both so busy they left me alone. My head felt heavy and I dozed off.

I woke up with a start as Mr. Nagil kicked the leg of my chair. "Next time you stay out until the middle of the night, don't bother coming back. If you want parties, go work somewhere else."

Under my breath, I wished him the same party that I had gone to the night before.

"You have to make a collection," said my boss. "Do you still remember where Glazer lives?"

"On Djika Street, No.12."

"He has to pay you forty zlotys. And don't take all day."

I was disappointed that the errand wasn't a delivery. At least on a delivery I could expect a tip. No one was ever pleased to see me when I came to collect money. Once a customer had given us the wrong address and I had to go chasing from courtyard to courtyard, asking tenants and janitors, until I tracked him down.

On the street, the cold wind sliced right through me. After ten minutes, I was so cold and tired that I walked into an apartment building, sat down on the stairway, and dozed off.

"What are you doing here?" an elderly man asked me as he shook my shoulder. "Is something wrong?"

I stumbled back to my feet and started to walk again, but I couldn't go on. I wasn't far from Muranovska Street. I decided to go to Frau Liebe's.

I entered through the black iron doors into the courtyard of Liebe's building. Only two boys were out playing in the cold. I walked down the steps to the basement.

"Mama, look who's here," Elke said. Liebe's pretty sixteen-year-old daughter was in the kitchen helping her mother cook.

Frau Liebe turned around from the stove. "Schloimele, what's wrong?" Her careworn, gray face filled with concern. "Are you sick?"

"I'm freezing. I can't stop shaking. Can I lie down for a while?"

"Of course, you can," Liebe said. She took a pan off the fire and moved it aside. "But tell me what is the matter. Do you have a fever?" Liebe wiped her greasy hands on her wide apron and put her palm to my forehead. "Elke, he's on fire. Maybe Doctor Feinberg's still home. Come with me."

Liebe pulled off her apron. I followed her up the stairs. We crossed the courtyard and entered the opposite building.

"I hope he hasn't left yet," Liebe said as she knocked on the doctor's door. She put her arm around my shoulder to keep me warm.

The door was opened by a bald man in his middle forties with a clean-shaven face. He was dressed in a white shirt, gray pants, and was holding a newspaper in his hand.

"Doctor Feinberg, you must help me," Liebe pleaded. "This boy is burning up."

The doctor took a close look at me and opened the door. "Come into my office."

The apartment was warm and neat. The walls were chalk white. The wooden floor was polished. The doctor opened two glass doors to his consultation room and told me to sit on the examining table.

"How did you get so sick?" he asked me as he washed his hands at the white porcelain sink.

"I caught a chill yesterday," I said trembling.

"After you left our house?" Liebe asked.

"I think so."

"But it wasn't so cold when you left," Liebe said.

"Open your mouth," said the doctor.

After the examination, the doctor sat down at his desk to write out a prescription. "He has to stay in bed until this fever is gone," he said to Frau Liebe.

"I have to go back to work," I said, getting off the table. "I'm going to lose my job."

"You can't go anywhere," said the doctor.

"Don't argue," said Liebe as she held my hand and led me back to her basement apartment.

"He's very sick," Liebe said to Elke as we entered the kitchen. "He has to go straight to bed. Come, Schloimele."

"But I have to collect money from a customer."

"Heaven forbid!" said Liebe firmly. "You heard the doctor."

Reluctantly I followed Liebe to the bedroom. There were two beds in the dark room. On one of the beds lay Hertzke Schneidleider, Liebe's elderly, sick husband. His head was propped up on two pillows. Hertzke woke up when we walked in.

"Is this Schloimele?" he asked weakly, opening his sunken eyes. His beard was no more than a few strands of straw.

"Yes," Liebe said to her husband. "He has a high fever. Doctor Feinberg says that he has to stay in bed."

"Lie down, Schloimele," Hertzke said, closing his eyes again. "We'll be sick together for a while. God willing, you'll get better soon. But I don't think I can ever get better again."

Frau Liebe pulled away the covers on her bed and whispered to me, "Get undressed and lie down. I'm going to buy your syrup and then I'm going to talk to Nagil. I'll tell Elke to bring you some hot soup."

I did as she told me. As soon as I was under the covers, I began to warm up and fell asleep. I woke up briefly when Elke brought me soup and later when Frau Liebe gave me two spoonsful of syrup. I slept until the night when it was time for Frau Liebe herself to go to bed. Her son prepared a cot for me in the kitchen.

In the morning, I was moved back to Frau Liebe's bed. On the second night of my illness, my fever shot up so much that I began to hallucinate. Dr. Feinberg came to the basement and said that I should be in the hospital but I was too sick to be moved. He gave an injection and asked someone to watch me during the night and call him if I began to hallucinate again. Frau Liebe's children took turns staying up.

My high fever lasted almost three days. After the fever had gone down, I was still too weak to go out. I lay in bed, awake, listening to Frau Liebe and Elke talk as they prepared the little fish which Liebe sold in the market. The smell of the frying fish made my mouth water.

One afternoon, when Frau Liebe brought me some food, she sat down at the edge of the bed. "Tell me something, Schloimele," she asked while I ate. "When I went to see Mr. Nagil, he said that you got sick because you were out until the middle of the night at some party. Is that true?"

I hated to lie to her but I couldn't tell her what had really happened. I was too ashamed. Liebe had been my mother's best friend ever since we had lived together in the same building on the Tchurtick in Lublin twelve years earlier.

"I wasn't at any party," I said without looking at Liebe. "I was walking around the streets thinking how much I miss my family."

Liebe seemed to understand at once and didn't ask me anything else. "I thought Nagil was talking foolishness," she said. "I know how hard you work." She was silent for a few moments and then said, "I don't want to scare you, Schloime, but I want you to realize how important it is for you to take better care of yourself. Dr. Feinberg said, Heaven forbid, that you could have died."

Frau Liebe's words shook me up. I had wished deep down that I were dead and my wish had almost come true. Finally, after another week of rest, I felt well enough to go back to work.

Early on Sunday morning, after crossing the snow covered streets, I knocked on the door at No. 8 Dluga Street. Mr. Nagil himself answered.

"Well, look who is here?" said my boss, with a crooked smile. "The party boy is finally back."

"I've been in bed with fever," I said.

"Wait here," he said.

He returned with my sack of belongings. "I had to hire another boy. Take your things," he said, shoving the bag into my hands, "and go back to your parties."

The Madman and His Cat

WHEN I CAME OUT on Dluga Street the morning had grown so bright, the glaring whiteness of the snow made me squint. With every gust of wind the fine snow dust flew up, caught the sun, and shimmered in the air. There was even a fresh smell to the cold. As I began to walk slowly, I realized that I would have to rely on Frau Liebe's kindness again. I couldn't go back to Lublin. No matter how difficult life was in Warsaw, the thought of going back to live in Uncle Yankel's cramped kitchen was unbearable. I still remembered my uncle's curses on days when he didn't earn enough to feed his wife and six children; and for Uncle Yankel, who was a porter, those days weren't few. At times, as I sat in the kitchen with my grandmother and sister, I overheard Uncle Yankel in the other room threaten his wife that if she didn't get rid of us he would break her jaw. But how could Aunt Simke throw her eighty-year-old mother and her sister's two children into the street? The only thing my aunt could do was curse her fate and cry.

As usual, the door to Liebe's basement apartment was open. The market was closed on Sunday and Liebe and Elke were at home. I found them at the kitchen table peeling potatoes.

"What happened?" asked Liebe.

"I lost my job. Nagil hired another boy."

"Don't look so sad. It's not the end of the world," Liebe said with a kind smile. "Sit down with us."

I put my sack down in a corner of the kitchen. The coal stove was burning and the warmth felt comforting.

Elke threw a peeled potato into the pot of water in the middle of the table and said, "There are plenty of tailors looking for apprentices to take advantage of." Elke herself had recently been laid off from her job as a sales girl and was having trouble finding work.

15

"That Nagil didn't seem like such a treasure anyway," said Liebe. "Was he teaching you anything?"

"No."

"So," Liebe continued, "maybe it's better this way."

It was already too late in the morning to start looking for a new job. I spent the day with Liebe and Elke, listening to their stories as they cooked.

In the evening, when Liebe's son came home from his job at the leather factory, he was outraged. "What is a man supposed to be now, a machine that never breaks down? That bastard Nagil wouldn't get away with this if you belonged to a strong union. They would have sent in a few men and he would have changed his mind quick or they would have broken his head." Leibel, who was already in his late twenties, had been involved with trade unions for many years. His words gave me courage.

The next morning I woke up early. On the street the sky was just beginning to pale. I ran to the newsstand on the corner of Muranovska and Zamenhoff. Since I couldn't afford thirty groschen for the whole newspaper, I paid five groschen to look through the page with the "Employment" section. As I read the short notices, I suddenly saw, "Wanted a boy to learn tailoring. Full upkeep. Chaim Goldwasser, No. 13 Franciskaner Street, apartment 6." There was no mention that the boy had to be from a province as Nagil had specified in his advertisement. Perhaps it was a good sign that this tailor wasn't just looking for someone to exploit. Leaning against the wall of the newsstand, I copied the name and address. I returned the page of *The Express* and ran off to Franciskaner Street. Everything depended on my being the first one there.

I made my way quickly up Zamenhoff and turned right at Gensha, a wide street of cobblestones, lined with peddlers selling fruits and vegetables from two-wheeled carts. Franciskaner turned out to be a residential continuation of Gensha, and No. 13 was a well-kept, three story building. I ran up the stairway to the first floor. I was glad to see there were no other boys waiting in the hall. I caught my breath and knocked on the door of apartment 6.

A short man of fifty, with rounded shoulders, opened the door. Pieces of thread clung to his gray suit.

"Did you advertise for a boy?" I asked.

"Have you ever worked for a tailor before?" he asked as he let me in.

I walked into the kitchen, a large, empty-looking room with a white cupboard, icebox, stove, table and two chairs. While the tailor asked me, Who are you? Where do you live? and so on, I noticed that the stove, on which two pots of clothes were boiling, used gas instead of coal—a welcome sight. It meant that if I got the job, I wouldn't have to drag sacks of coal up from the basement as I had done at Nagil's. I also noticed that the tailor wasn't wearing a skullcap, which meant he wasn't religious and wouldn't make me say prayers every morning as Nagil had done and then order me to light a fire and make him tea on the Sabbath.

"Can you handle a needle and thread?" the tailor asked.

I assured him I could.

Suddenly the door to the kitchen opened and a thin woman in her late thirties entered carrying a bag of groceries. Her black hair was tied back severely in a bun, adding to her gloomy expression. The tailor and the woman didn't even glance at each other.

"Let's see if you can help me," said the tailor, leading me into another room.

The workshop, also the tailor's bedroom and living room, was as barren as the kitchen. There was a sewing machine, a table with an ironing board and press-cushions, a small clothes rack, and the tailor's large bed. What caught my eye, however, was a wide folding bed with a metal frame and a real mattress. It was pushed up against the wall near the kitchen. If I got the job, that bed would most likely be mine. After the cots I had been sleeping on, it looked simply luxurious.

The tailor handed me a needle and thimble, a spool of brown thread, and laid four pieces of striped brown fabric across my lap. "Sew me a border seam," he said.

I kept my stitches small and even. Except for the noise of the sewing machine now and then, there was a deep silence in the apartment. No one spoke and even the woman in the kitchen never seemed to rattle a dish. I worked as fast as I could. When I had finished the first piece of cloth, the tailor checked it. "The stitches don't have to be so small," he said.

I continued with the other three pieces of cloth. I became so absorbed in my work, I lost all sense of time. When I looked up, half a day had flown by. I was hungry. I hoped lunch would be served at any moment.

As soon as I was done with the pants, the tailor sat next to me with the unfinished lapel of a suit and showed me how to stitch the stiff linen to the underlay of the fabric. I followed his instructions.

When I had finished that, Chaim Goldwasser said, "Now your stitches could be a little smaller. But not bad."

Next the tailor put me to work on pressing. The iron was electric, the first such iron I had ever used. It was a pleasure not to have to keep on running back and forth to the stove.

Late in the afternoon, when it grew dark out, the tailor turned the light on in the apartment. I wondered whether he had completely forgotten about lunch. I hadn't eaten the whole day. But since the tailor hadn't stopped to eat either, I decided to say nothing.

I kept pressing until the woman suddenly came in from the kitchen and announced, "Food is ready."

"Go in and eat," the tailor told me.

I switched the iron off.

On the table in the kitchen I saw only one plate. It had a mound of kasha, a boiled potato, a piece of dark bread, and next to the food was a glass of tea. I sat down to eat at once.

The woman joined the tailor in the other room. While I ate I could hear their murmuring. Finally the tailor reappeared.

"My wife, Dvoire, and I have talked it over," he announced, "and if you're willing to work hard, I'll take you on. Where are your things?"

"At my aunt's on Muranovska."

"Go and get them," he said. "But come right back. You'll sleep here in the kitchen on the folding bed."

The wide folding bed with the thick mattress was to be mine.

Running against the cold wind to Liebe's apartment, I kept thinking how good it would feel to lie down on that soft bed.

The tailor was still working when I returned. I threw my sack under the table and went back to pressing. I continued until the tailor got up from his chair, and told me it was time to go to sleep.

"Take the folding bed into the kitchen," he said, "and have a good night."

The bed rolled easily on its little wheels. The tailor's wife said good night, and closed the door between the bedroom and the kitchen.

I opened the bed carefully. Folded inside I found a large blanket and under it two pillows. A fresh white sheet covered the mattress. I undressed quickly and turned off the light. A pleasant drowsiness overtook me as soon as I lay down. I was as comfortable as a king. I was fast asleep when I was suddenly jolted awake by someone trying to break into the apartment. I jumped out of bed, ran into the dark room where the tailor and his wife were sleeping, and slammed shut the door to the kitchen.

"Who's there?" shouted the startled tailor in the darkness.

"A thief!" I whispered in a panic. "Breaking in!" I heard footsteps in the kitchen. I couldn't move for fright.

"Chaim, put a stop to this!" the tailor's wife ordered her husband.

A chilling caterwauling came from the kitchen.

"The cat," moaned the tailor. "It's back!"

"So it's back!" shouted the wife. "Are you blaming me?" She stormed out of bed and stumbled in the darkness. "Where's my robe?"

"I'm not blaming you for anything," the tailor tried to appease her. "Don't upset yourself."

"Don't upset myself?" she continued to scream. "Everything falls on my head! "Come here!" she said suddenly grabbing my shoulder and flinging open the door.

In the flood of the kitchen light, I saw a tall, well-dressed man of forty, in a black suit and tie, overcoat, and wide brimmed hat. He was holding a fat gray tomcat with a string around its neck.

"That's my brother," the tailor's wife blurted as an introduction. "He sleeps in the kitchen, too."

"Sruel, listen to me," she said as if speaking to a child. "This is the new boy."

The man, who seemed embarrassed to meet me, looked away.

"He won't hurt you," the tailor's wife assured me.

"Go to sleep, Sruel," she ordered and went back to her bedroom, slamming the door shut behind her.

I was left alone with the strange man. I didn't know what to do. The two pillows had not been put there for me, after all. I took one and lay back down. The man undressed. Finally the kitchen light was turned off. I was tired and wanted to sleep but the man kept fidgeting. I wondered what he was up to but I was afraid to turn around. Suddenly I heard the cat growl. The man had brought the animal to bed and was playing with it.

In the middle of the night the cat's screeching woke me with a start. A violent struggle was going on the other side of the bed. Suddenly, the madman jumped up. In the dark, I heard a chair fall as he chased the cat around the kitchen. At last he caught it and brought it back to bed, where the struggle continued.

In the morning, when I opened my eyes, the only other person in the kitchen was the tailor's wife. She was pouring water into a kettle. I had slept very little. As soon as Dvoire had set the kettle on the stove to boil and left the room, I got dressed. I folded the bed, pushed it up against a wall, and ran down to the courtyard to use the toilet.

I returned as the tailor's wife was preparing breakfast. From the bread box on top of the icebox, she took a small loaf of rye. She cut it into quarters, thinly buttered two pieces and put each piece on a plate next to a sliver of salty herring. The water boiled. She poured a glass of tea for me and one for the tailor, who joined me in the kitchen for breakfast.

"How did you sleep?" my boss asked me after his wife had put on her coat and left.

"Not well," I said honestly. "He was playing with that cat all night. What's wrong with him?"

"Who knows? Anyway, he won't be here much longer. He's going to an insane asylum. That's where he belongs. It's hard to believe he was a wealthy man. Made a fortune in furs. But he couldn't stay away from the horses. Played until he lost everything, including his mind."

"I'm afraid to sleep in the same bed with him."

"Where else am I going to put you? He's harmless, believe me."

"I'd rather sleep on the table," I suggested.

"You want to sleep on the kitchen table?" My boss stared at me as if I were crazier than his brother-in-law. "Go ahead, if that's what you want," he finally agreed.

My second day was just as busy as the first. I couldn't help wondering where the work came from since no customers showed up at the tailor's apartment. I soon found out. At noon, a heavy man, chewing an unlit cigar, swept into the shop with a large bundle of cut cloth. He flung the material on the table, strode up to the rack and with a sweep of his arms gathered the finished garments, threw a cord around them, and left.

There would be no deliveries to customers and no tips. I wouldn't even earn an extra two groschen for a cigarette. What bothered me most, however, was my hunger. The tailor and I worked straight through the morning and afternoon. It wasn't until early evening that his wife called me to the kitchen to dinner. On my plate I found a mound of mashed potato, a boiled chicken wing, and a piece of bread. It wasn't enough food to fill me, and as soon as I had eaten, the tailor called me back to work.

When it was time to go to sleep my boss told me to wait in the workshop while he spoke to his wife in the kitchen.

"On the kitchen table?" I heard her shriek. But the tailor calmed her down. From a trunk at the foot of her bed, she took out two blankets and handed them to me.

"Take the pillow from the folding bed," she said coldly.

I rolled the folding bed into the kitchen, opened it, and took a pillow. I folded one of the blankets in half and made my bed on the table.

I hadn't seen the tailor's crazy brother-in-law the whole day. I hoped he had gotten lost. But the moment I lay down on the table, the outside door opened and in came the madman carrying the gray cat. This time I didn't jump up. I hid my head under the cover and waited. Soon enough he got into bed and began to fight with the cat.

In time I got used to sleeping on the kitchen table. I got used to the madman and his cat, to the hissing and fighting, even to the chases in the dark for half of each night. But I simply couldn't get used to the hunger. Every morning the tailor's wife fed me a quarter of a small rye bread, sometimes with a bite of herring, most often with only a glass of tea. On that bit of food I was supposed to work a whole day. The tailor's scheme, I soon figured out, was to get as much work out of me for as little food as possible. I began to wonder how much longer I could bear it.

One afternoon the tailor noticed that he was low on supplies. Chaim Goldwasser checked boxes of buttons, rolls of seam binding, lining, spools of thread and prepared a list. When he was done, the tailor handed me the list, the samples of buttons, ten zlotys, and sent me to the supplier.

If my boss had had an inkling of how hungry I was, he would have thought twice before putting a grosch in my hand much less ten zlotys. I myself didn't realize what temptations await a starving person who has suddenly been handed so much money. The moment I stumbled across a bakery and smelled the hot bread, I was a lost man. Between the threshold of the bakery door and the counter, I had feverishly hatched a plan to swindle the tailor out of five groschen. From the hundreds of buttons that Chaim Goldwasser had ordered me to buy, I would simply buy a few buttons less.

The baker, a giant with a face spotted by flour, looked at me suspiciously.

"A roll with seeds, please," I croaked, certain my voice was betraying my crime.

The baker picked up a roll and held it across the counter. "Five groschen," he said.

I handed him the ten-zloty bill.

21

"A big spender." The baker glared at me. "Don't you have anything smaller?"

Too nervous to speak I shook my head.

The baker handed me the roll as he took my money. I turned at once for the door.

"Come back here!" called the baker.

Discovered! I considered running away.

"Don't you want your change?" he asked.

I shoved the money into my pocket without counting it. On the street, I tried to enjoy the taste of the sesame seeds on the freshly baked roll as long as possible, but with each bite the roll melted away in my mouth. I wasn't far from the bakery when the last morsel was gone. I began immediately to hatch a scheme to swindle the tailor out of another five groschen. My new plan, along the lines of my first, was to buy less of the seam binding.

The second roll finally restored me to reason. I walked quickly to Gensha Street. At the supply store, I asked for five buttons less of each of the six samples. I watched as the store keeper took a small cardboard box, counted out the buttons on the counter and scooped them into the box. Then I took a meter off the order of seam binding.

On my way back I regretted taking the ten groschen from my boss, but there was nothing I could do.

My heart was pounding as I put the bundle down on the table and gave the tailor his change.

"Good," he said after counting the money. "Now you can go back to work."

My hands shook as I picked up the iron. Whenever I could, I stole a glance at my boss.

Chaim Goldwasser opened the package and put away the small carton of pins, the chalk, lining, and spools of thread. I was relieved to see him hang up the seam binding. My boss opened the box with the buttons and spilled the contents out on the sewing machine table. He separated the buttons into six small mounds, which he carefully swept one by one into the little boxes in which he kept the buttons.

I watched with relief as he put the boxes away. I promised myself that no matter how hungry I felt, I would never steal from my boss again.

"Where's my list?" asked Chaim Goldwasser.

I reached into my pocket and gave it to him.

He looked it over and asked, "How many buttons did you buy?"

I became confused. I didn't know what to say.

"Well?" asked Chaim Goldwasser, growing annoyed. "How many buttons did you buy?"

"Whatever's on the paper," I stammered.

"Do you think I can't count?"

"I don't know what the store keeper gave me."

"There are exactly five buttons missing from each sample. That's not a mistake. That's a little thief at work."

I had been caught.

"Mr. Goldwasser, I was hungry," I pleaded with the angry tailor. "I bought myself two rolls."

"Take your things and get out," he said. "Out and quick! Before my wife comes back!"

"I'll pay you back," I offered.

"You're a thief," he said. "I can't have a thief working for me. If you don't get out before my wife comes back, she'll tear your eyes out."

I picked up my small sack of belongings from under the table. The tailor walked behind me.

At the open door, I stopped, looked the tailor in the face, and said, "What I did was more your fault than mine. If you make a person work from morning to night you should at least know enough to feed him."

He didn't answer me, but as soon as I had stepped out of his apartment, the tailor locked his door.

The Dead Delivery Boy

I LIED TO FRAU LIEBE and her family. I told them that I had been laid off because the tailor ran out of work. I felt more ashamed of that lie than for the money I had stolen, but my situation was desperate. If Liebe had thrown me out for being a thief, I would have been lost. I didn't have a grosch to my name; I couldn't go back to Lublin; I couldn't turn to my mother for help; and as for my father, he had gone off to war when I was two years old, and that was the last we saw of him.

Again I slept on a folding cot in Liebe's kitchen. Early every morning, I rushed to the corner of Zamenhoff and Muranovska with five groschen, borrowed from Leibel, to check the advertisements in *The Express*. But the next job was not easy to find. For three days there was nothing in the newspaper. I began to despair. On the fourth day, the only advertisement was from a tailor of boys' suits. Even though I knew nothing about that specialty, I rushed off to apply for the job.

The worst of that terrible winter was over, and the streets were no longer covered with snow and ice. I ran as fast as I could. I was afraid that other boys who could afford the five groschen for the trolley, or who didn't have a limp to slow them down, would get to the tailor's house ahead of me.

When I finally reached the front gates of No. 30 Novalypia Street, I was drenched in sweat. The women and children in the courtyard stared at me as I dashed past them.

The impressive lobby of the building I entered had marble walls decorated with gild-edged mirrors. I raced up the stairs to the third floor. On the landing, I heard the noise of sewing machines coming from an apartment. I opened the door and saw five men and one woman, working in a large room which looked like a factory. Six sewing machines were lined up against two walls; a cutting table, piled with layers of material, stood against the third wall; and against the fourth wall there was an ironing table.

"What do you want?" asked the cutter over his shoulder. He was a tall man in his fifties with yellow teeth and a balding head.

"I'm looking for work," I said.

"Motte!" the cutter yelled into the air. "A boy for the job!"

"Send him in!" answered a man's voice from deep inside the apartment.

"Go through that door," said the cutter, pointing to the other side of the room.

I crossed the workshop and walked into a corridor. To the right, I saw a small bedroom with a large bed; to the left, a bathroom with a white porcelain bathtub, sink, and toilet. These were obviously wealthy people. Finally I came to a spacious living room where a thickset man in his thirties was poring over open ledgers. The red-wood table at which he sat had massive legs carved with leaves and flowers. The chairs were upholstered in green velvet. Behind the man there were two large china cabinets filled with fancy dishes and figurines; the cabinets stood one on each side of an arched entry with glass doors.

"What's wrong with your leg?" asked the man as he continued to write.

"Nothing. I have a small limp."

He put down his pen and looked at me. He had blue eyes, a dark complexion, thick, black hair, and fleshy cheeks and lips. "I need a boy to make deliveries."

"I've always made deliveries."

"No, no," he said, waving me away with his hand. "I can't use you. I don't want anymore trouble." He turned back to his ledgers.

"Let me just work until you find someone else then," I blurted out.

"No."

"I'll show you what a good worker I am."

"What is this? I can't get rid of you?"

"What do you have to lose?"

He laughed. "You're worse than a beggar." He asked me where I lived and when I told him that I lived on Muranovska at my aunt's, he wanted to know why not with my parents. It hurt me to say it, but I told him that I was an orphan.

"I'll try you for a few days," he finally gave in. "But if you don't work out, you leave. Understood?"

I agreed at once.

"Well, do you want to sleep here or go home every night?"

"Here. It's crowded at my aunt's."

"Then you'll have that room," he said, pointing to the small bedroom with the large bed.

I wasn't happy with my new quarters. I had learned my lesson at Chaim Goldwasser's. I wondered with how many people I would have to share that large bed, and what madness I would have to put up with. I would have preferred a folding cot in a corner of the kitchen where I could sleep undisturbed.

"Have you eaten breakfast yet?"

"No."

"Go into the kitchen and tell the maid to fix you something. Helena!" he bellowed. "I've hired a new boy. Give him breakfast."

"Right away, Mr. Zisslof." These words, spoken in Yiddish by a woman with a heavy Polish accent, came from another room. I followed the sound of the voice through the arched passage into a corridor, past a storage room with shelves filled with rolls and rolls of fabrics. The next room was the kitchen, where Helena, a plump woman in her mid-thirties, with a pock-marked face, short blonde hair, was waiting for me with a welcoming smile.

"Sit down and tell me what would you like to eat," she said. "I have everything."

"Eggs."

"Just eggs?"

"With bread and butter," I added.

Helena's eyes narrowed—not enough.

"And milk, with honey. And a small piece of herring. And a salad, onions and tomatoes."

Helena smiled. "That's better. Sit." She began to bustle about the kitchen, and soon I had a feast set on the table before me.

Helena sat down next to me. "Eat as much as you can," she said softly. "Nissele, the last delivery boy, the Good Lord protect you, died."

The eggs stuck in my throat. "What happened?"

"He was making a delivery to the store, and he collapsed on the street and died. They said it was his heart. But I think he was working too hard and not eating enough. Anytime you're hungry just tell me."

This news frightened me, but I couldn't give up the job. As I wiped the plate clean with my last piece of bread, Mr. Zisslof looked into the kitchen.

"So," he asked me, "did Helena take good care of you?"

"Very good," I said.

"Helena, my darling," Mr. Zisslof chuckled, "why can't you take care of me like that?"

"He's talking nonsense again," I heard her mutter. She got up at once and began to clear the table.

As Helena passed by Mr. Zisslof, he gave her bottom a pat.

The maid swung around furiously. "I'll tell your wife," she snapped. "Keep your hands to yourself!"

"Come, Schloime," said Mr. Zisslof, laughing, "let's get out of here before she really gets mad and poisons everybody with her *pyrogen*."

"We need supplies," said my new boss as he led me away, a heavy arm over my shoulder. "Leibish will give you a list. Leibish!" Mr. Zisslof yelled as we approached the noisy workshop. "Schloime's going for supplies."

A young man in his mid-twenties, with red cheeks and a small pot-belly, put down the boy's coat he had been sewing.

Mr. Zisslof gave me a twenty-zloty bill and returned to the living room.

Leibish took the list out from his shirt pocket. He looked at the back of the tall, spinsterish woman, and pulled me away from her as if she were an enemy. In a whisper, he asked, "Do you know about Nissele?"

I nodded.

"Then I don't have to say anything else. The supplies are heavy. Don't rush." He handed me the sheet of paper. "I wrote down the address of the supplier. Just be back before lunch."

I didn't believe that buying supplies could be such backbreaking work.

The supplier was a large store on the Nalefky. I had a long walk there and a much longer walk back carrying a package that must have weighed over fifteen kilos. In spite of Helena's and Leibish's warnings, I was afraid that if I took too long Mr. Zisslof would blame my limp and let me go. After I had dragged myself up the two sets of stairs, I felt exhausted.

"You ran," Leibish said as if accusing me of a crime. "I can tell from the way you're sweated up. Don't be such a hero. I don't want your death on my conscience." He took the package from me and set it down on a table. "Give the boss his change, and then maybe you can do us a favor and get us a few things."

Mr. Zisslof was not in the living room. As I walked through the glass doors into the hallway to look in the kitchen, I suddenly heard my boss's voice coming from the small storage room. The door was partly open; I pushed it and there he was with the spinster.

"Is this the color you had in mind for the little suits?" she asked, holding the swatch of material against a roll of fabric on the shelf.

"Genya darling," said Mr. Zisslof, "look what the wind blew in."

The woman gave me a tight-lipped smile. I took a good look at her face, at her painted red cheeks, her thin nose, sharp chin, the small dark eyes under the long lashes, the deep lines where the makeup caked up. All the paint on her face couldn't cover up that she wasn't a spring chicken.

I handed Mr. Zisslof the change. He shoved it into his pocket without a glance.

The moment I returned to the factory, Leibish asked, "Did you find the boss?"

All the men seemed to be waiting for my answer.

"Of course," I said.

The cutter laughed as he rubbed his hands. "Each of you owes me a zloty," he said. "Pay up."

"You got lucky this time," said Leibish, handing his zloty to the cutter.

"Shah!" one of the men whispered as we heard footsteps in the living room.

"Who needs cigarettes?" asked Leibish to cover any suspicions. "Who wants food?" He gave me pencil and paper to write down the orders as I collected money.

When I was about to leave, Leibish asked, "How about yourself, Schloime, do you smoke?"

"Yes, but I haven't been able to afford a cigarette in weeks."

Leibish took out his pack of Wandas, the cutter himself lit a match for me, and I left enjoying a good smoke, feeling like one of the men.

After my lunch, I helped out in the factory. I was kept busy until the evening. After all the workers had left, I asked Mr. Zisslof if I could go to my aunt's house to pick up my clothes.

When I returned, it was already night. In the living room I ran into my boss and his wife, a heavy woman with a beautiful face. Mrs. Zisslof, I was told, ran the store in the Woller Market where all the clothes produced in the factory were sold.

After I had eaten, Mr. Zisslof led me back to the workshop.

"You must clean the sewing machines every night," he said. "If you don't they'll be in the garbage in a few months."

I watched as my boss unscrewed the body plates of a Singer, brushed out the lint and small pieces of cloth from the fine mechanism, oiled it, and screwed the plates back on. I worked on the next machine as my boss watched.

It was after ten o'clock when I finally dragged myself to the small bedroom. I pulled off my clothes and sank into the softness of the large mattress. I fell asleep wondering when a mad relative of the Zisslofs would show up to claim his portion of the bed.

In the morning, incredibly, I was still alone in the room. I felt more rested than in a long time. As I pulled my pants on to go down to the toilet in the courtyard, I remembered that across from my room there was an indoor bathroom.

I soon heard the sewing machines starting up in the factory. After my breakfast, Mr. Zisslof sent me to see Leibish. All the workers were already in their seats when I walked in. "Did they tell you where the store is?" asked Leibish.

"Woller Market, on Leszno."

"You have to deliver coats to Mrs. Zisslof," he said. "You'll have to make two trips. Take your time."

From under the press table, Leibish pulled out a worn red blanket and piled ten children's winter coats on it. He tied the blanket tightly around the coats with a rope, and thrust the bulky bundle into my arms. "Don't be a Nissele," Leibish warned me under his breath.

The spring morning lay like a golden crown over the busy streets of Warsaw. In spite of Leibish's warnings, I walked quickly. The coats were heavy, but not unmanageable. I was rested and well fed. After a few blocks, however, I began to feel that I was carrying lead. I was afraid to put the expensive merchandise down and get it dirty. I moved the load to my head, and balancing it with my hands, I continued to walk slowly. Sweat poured down my back. A painful strain gripped my neck and shoulders. By the time I reached the Woller Market my legs were trembling. Luckily, Mrs. Zisslof, sitting outside the children's clothes store, saw me. Together we carried the coats to the counter in the store.

"Sit down," said Mrs. Zisslof. She gave me a towel to wipe off the sweat. Outside the store an old woman with a shawl over her head was selling baked goods from a wicker basket. Mrs. Zisslof went out and bought me three cookies. As I munched on them, my boss's wife untied the bundle and hung up the children's coats.

When I was ready to leave, Mrs. Zisslof held me back. "Rest a little longer," she said and sat herself down next to me. "I hope you're happy with your bed and food."

"Very much."

"Good," she said. "And how has Mr. Zisslof been treating you?"

"Very well."

She thought carefully awhile and finally asked, "Tell me, Schloime, is Mr. Zisslof home the whole day? I mean, supervising the factory, of course, or does he go out sometimes?"

"He's always in the house," I said at once. "He works on the books a lot."

Mrs. Zisslof seemed relieved by my answer. "Please don't mention to anyone that I asked you this."

"Don't worry, Mrs. Zisslof," I reassured her.

"You're a good boy," she said. "My husband told me that he hired you only for a trial, but I can tell that you're going to work out."

When I returned to the factory, I found the men leaning back in their chairs, smoking cigarettes.

"Thank God, you're back. The boss wants to see you at once," Leibish said. "He has to give you ten zlotys. I have the list of supplies. Look at this, everybody paralyzed because we ran out of brown thread."

I marched into the living room and found it empty. Without giving it a second thought, I went to the storage room. The door was closed so I knocked. Inside I heard a sudden scrambling and grumbling. Finally Mr. Zisslof opened the door just enough to stick his head out. His face was red and sweated as if it had been boiling in a pot of water for an hour.

"Can't you see that I'm busy?" he asked. "What do you want?" He made a great effort to speak as if nothing was wrong, but he was obviously out of breath and enraged.

"Leibish sent me," I stammered, realizing the embarrassing situation in which I had caught my boss. Through the crack in the door, I saw that he was holding his pants up with one hand. "The men can't work. I need ten zlotys for supplies."

When Mr. Zisslof pulled his head in, I caught a glimpse of Genya inside, leaning against the shelves. Her face was so streaked with paint, she looked like a sad circus clown.

"Here," said my boss, shoving his fist out with a ten zloty-bill.

Boiled Beets

I GRABBED THE MONEY from my boss's hand and hurried away from the storage room.

"What took you so long?" Leibish asked, trying not to laugh. The other men couldn't stop themselves.

"You know what took me so long," I said, angry at the joke they had played on me. "I had to wait for him to open the door."

"Why?" asked Leibish, innocently. "Did you interrupt something?"

"Leave me alone. You want to get me fired."

"Don't get so sore," said Leibish. He took out his pack of cigarettes and offered me one. "You won't lose out on this deal. Trust me. Tell us what you saw?"

As one of the tailors lit my cigarette, all of them moved closer to hear what I had to say. I looked behind me to make sure Mr. Zisslof wasn't nearby. "He only stuck his head out," I whispered, "but I saw that he was holding his pants up with one hand. They looked like two boiled beets."

The men laughed.

"Can you believe that she's getting married in three months?" the cutter said to his co-workers.

"Someone should do her Chaiml a favor and tell him what a bargain he's getting," said another tailor.

"Why?" asked the cutter. "He's getting a good woman. What could be better than a piece like her? Every time a man invites her to sit, she lies down."

"Did you get the money?" Leibish asked me.

I pulled out the ten zlotys. Leibel slapped my back as if I had performed some heroic act. "Here is the list of what we need, and the receipt," he said, handing me two slips of paper. At the same time he reached under the table and pulled out a wrapped package which he quickly shoved into my hands.

"What're you doing?" I asked looking at the receipt. It was from our supplier and was filled out for five zlotys and forty groschen.

"Don't ask so many questions," Leibish said as he pushed me out the door. "Come back in a half hour with four zlotys and sixty groschen in change. Now, get out of here."

My heart was beating violently as I walked down the steps. I had already been fired from my last job for stealing ten groschen for food. If the boss caught me stealing five zlotys, he would have me arrested.

On the street I tried to think of what to do but I had no choice. The wrapped package was already in my hands. My only hope was that the boss wouldn't be in the workshop when I returned.

I stopped in a grocery store and bought myself a pack of Wandas. Four zlotys and sixty groschen I set aside to give back to Mr. Zisslof. The five zlotys, which were left over, I decided to hide. I put three zlotys inside one shoe, and two zlotys into the other.

As soon as I opened the door to the factory, I felt doomed. There was Mr. Zisslof waiting for me. Genya had fixed her make-up and was back at her sewing machine. Leibish threw me a warning glance.

I moved to give the wrapped parcel to Leibish but Mr. Zisslof stopped me. "Come here," he said. "Give me that." He took the package to the cutting table and untied it. "What happened to the change?" he demanded.

I handed it to him with the receipt which Leibel had given me.

"Now, where's the list?"

Was this was another of Liebish's jokes, I wondered, setting me up to be caught stealing? As I handed the list over to our boss, I decided that if I got fired, I would make sure that Leibish was also fired.

Mr. Zisslof looked at the piece of paper, at the open package, and asked "What's all this brown thread? Didn't we just buy it last week?"

"We did," Leibish began to explain.

"Don't give me excuses!" Mr. Zisslof snapped. "If I find that you're wasting time sending him out for supplies we don't need, I pity both of you!" He stalked to the wooden cabinet where all the thread was kept, flung open the doors, and began to rummage through the spools.

"You won't find any," said Leibish. "We used it all up."

Mr. Zisslof, disgusted with the whole business, finally gave up. As he went back to the living room, he said, "Don't forget the second shipment."

"Well, I'm glad you finally decided to come back," Leibish chided me in mock anger. "Because of you we almost had to stop working."

I couldn't help grinning with relief, although I made sure my back was turned to Genya.

Leibish pulled out the worn blanket from under the cutting table. He wrapped it around ten children's coats and I left with the heavy bundle. I had learned my lesson on the first trip to the Woller Market. I walked slowly, stopping often to rest. When I arrived at the store, two hours later, Mrs. Zisslof welcomed me as if I were her long lost son.

On Friday evening after my first full week on the job, Mrs. Zisslof called me into the living room. Under her husband's glare, she paid me five zlotys and said that I would get paid every Friday. I went to my room. The salary was an unexpected bit of good luck. With the five zlotys I had already made that week and the tips from the tailors, I now had over twelve zlotys. As I sat on the bed counting my money, I overheard an argument break out between my boss and his wife.

"Why do you do this to me!" Mrs. Zisslof cried suddenly. "You know I can't go, it makes me sick!"

"Is that my fault?" her husband shouted. "Am I a prisoner here?"

A little later, Mr. Zisslof walked by my room swinging his walking stick. As soon as he had closed the apartment door, Mrs. Zisslof, in tears, ran into my room.

"Schloime, you must help me," she cried. "My husband says that he's going to a movie, but I don't believe him. He knows that I can't go with him because the flickering makes me sick. I want you to follow him for me."

Sorry as I felt for Mrs. Zisslof, I wasn't eager to follow her husband.

"I'm begging you!" she pleaded. "I must know for sure. I'll give you five zlotys if you do this for me."

Then, again, I reconsidered, maybe I could do both her and myself some good. "All right," I said, pulling on my jacket.

"Don't let him see you," Mrs. Zisslof pleaded. "I'm so ashamed. Please don't ever tell anyone."

I ran down the steps. I had no intentions of spying on my boss. If he caught me following him, Mr. Zisslof would kill me. All I wanted to do was to reassure Mrs. Zisslof that she had nothing to worry about. And as for my boss, I just wanted to stay out his way. I looked down Novalypia Street, now lit by pale lamplight. Just as I had suspected, I saw Mr. Zisslof turning the corner, headed in the opposite direction of the movie theater.

I looked up at the building. Above me, Mrs. Zisslof was leaning out a window. I decided to walk in the direction of the movie theater, the only place I was certain Mr. Zisslof was not going.

On the corner of Djelazna and Leszno Streets, I glanced at the middle of the block and under the lights of the Leszno Theater I saw Genya. I was so baffled by the sight of the skinny spinster, that I didn't notice Mr. Zisslof walking towards her from the other end of the street. As soon as I saw him I turned around and ran away.

On my walk back to Novalypia, I decided that it would be best to spend the night at Frau Liebe's. I wasn't sure whether Genya or my boss had seen me but just in case they had, I wanted my boss to think that I had been out for my own reasons and not to spy on him.

Mrs. Zisslof was waiting at the door of her apartment as I came up the steps. "Did you catch up to him?" she asked me at once in the darkened factory. "Did you see where he went?"

"He went exactly where he told you he was going," I said, "to the movie on Leszno Street."

"Are you sure?" she asked.

"Absolutely," I reassured her.

"You must think that I'm a foolish woman," Mrs. Zisslof said, smiling with relief at last. She gave me five zlotys and again begged me to keep "our secret."

I felt terrible for not telling her everything, but since she hadn't ask me whether her husband met another woman at the movies, I figured that in a way I was telling the truth.

"If you don't need me anymore," I said, "I would like to sleep over at my aunt's house tonight."

"Of course," said Mrs. Zisslof. "You can do as you please."

On the street, walking towards Liebe's apartment, I wondered why a man with such a beautiful wife and children would want to get involved with such an ugliness as Genya.

I received a friendly welcome at Frau Liebe's basement apartment, and I spent the night there on a folding cot in the kitchen.

The next morning, Saturday, I returned to Novalypia Street. Helena told me that Mr. Zisslof was out at the store with his wife. From the kitchen, I could hear the children playing in their bedroom. As Helena prepared breakfast for me, there was a knock on the front door. I went to answer it.

"Good morning," Genya greeted me with a friendliness I had never heard from her before.

I was amazed to see her and mumbled my good morning.

"I couldn't find my blue shawl," she continued in her friendly tone, "and since I was in the neighborhood, I said to myself let me see if I didn't leave it here." She went to her sewing machine. "Just as I thought, here it is, right on my chair."

"I'm glad you found it," I said.

In a casual voice, Genya asked, "Have you seen the movie playing at the Leszno Theater?"

"No," I said, trying to hide my nervousness.

"You must see it before it changes. It's wonderful. I saw it last night with Chaiml. Isn't that strange? I was waiting for him to show up and I thought I saw you pass."

"I went to my aunt's house. I slept over there."

"Oh? I must've been mistaken. Let me tell you," Genya said, "Chaiml and I thought that was the best movie we ever saw. Well, thanks for letting me pick up my shawl."

I closed the door after her and went back into the kitchen.

"Who was that?" Helena asked.

"Genya."

My breakfast was on the table. I sat down to eat.

"What did she want?"

"She was looking for her blue shawl."

"That one was looking for more than that," Helena said as she sat down next to me with her cup of coffee. "What's the matter, Schloime? You seem upset."

I could barely contain myself from talking over the whole complicated situation with Helena. "Can you keep a secret?" I asked.

"All my life I've kept secrets."

"I think Genya was trying to find out if I saw her and the boss going to the movies last night."

Helena was shocked. "I thought you went to your aunt's house?"

"I did. But first Mrs. Zisslof asked me to follow her husband when he left the house."

"Heaven save us," Helena said, crossing herself. "What did you tell her?"

"That he went to the movies."

"With that tramp?"

"Mrs. Zisslof never asked me if he went with anyone else, so I didn't say anything about it. Besides, Genya just told me that she was waiting for her fiance last night."

"Do you believe her?"

"No," I admitted. "She was just trying to find out if I saw her and the boss. Do you think I'll get fired now?"

"Mrs. Zisslof wouldn't let him fire you."

"Do you think I should have told her the truth?"

Helena thought a long while and finally said, "I don't know. What good would it do to upset her?"

I was glad for the talk with Helena. I trusted her judgement and she reassured me that I had done the right thing. As for Mr. Zisslof I didn't know what he was thinking. On Monday, he sent me out with a long list of supplies. When I returned, he was too busy to take the change and told me to hold on to the money and that he would go over the bill when he had time. A few days later, the same thing happened. For the next two weeks, every time I brought Mr. Zisslof change, he told me to hold it until he had time.

Finally, one Friday evening, after I had eaten dinner, Mr. Zisslof stopped me as I walked through the living room.

"What is going on here, Schloime?" he asked. "I must have given you over sixty zlotys these past few weeks and I haven't seen a receipt or a zloty change."

Mrs. Zisslof, who had been sitting on the sofa listening to music on the radio, picked up her head and gave me a questioning look. "Sixty zlotys? Schloime, how can you leave so much money unaccounted for so long?"

"Mr. Zisslof, you've been too busy to check my receipts," I reminded him.

"Just listen to that *chutzpa!*" Mr. Zisslof said to his wife. "Has this world been turned upside down? Do I have to go chasing after you now to get back my change?"

"That's not what I meant—"

"I need to know exactly how much you spent," Mr. Zisslof interrupted me, "and I want to see the change. Right now! Did you think you could just walk off with so much money, no questions asked?"

I began to pull out receipts from my pockets for all the purchases I had made. As I stood across the table, I gave Mr. Zisslof an accurate accounting of every grosch he had given me, including the extra five zlotys that I had to put in of my own money to cover the last purchase.

Mr. Zisslof was stunned. "Give me the receipts," he grumbled. "Let me check them out."

Mrs. Zisslof got up from the sofa and joined her husband at the table. She looked over his shoulder as he added up the receipts and twice came up with the same total I had reported to him.

Mrs. Zisslof opened her handbag. With a smile she said to me, "Here are the five zlotys we owe you, five zlotys for your salary, and five more zlotys for being such a conscientious worker."

After that incident, I was sure that if Mrs. Zisslof had not been protecting me, her husband would have fired me.

With the extra money, I bought myself a new jacket, a pair of pants, a shirt, and shoes. In spite of all benefits I enjoyed at the Zisslofs, I wasn't happy with my job. I bought supplies, maintained the sewing machines, made deliveries, but I never did a stitch of work with needle and thread. I was almost seventeen years old and yet I was no better than an errand boy. I had hoped to become a tailor so I could earn a decent living. I missed my grandmother and sister, who were still in Lublin, and only as a tailor could I earn enough to rent a room and bring them to Warsaw to live with me. Without a profession, I would have to depend on employers like Mr. Zisslof forever. I had even begun to forget the little tailoring that I had picked up so far.

On a Saturday morning, when I was alone in the house with Helena, I talked to her about my career. She agreed that I would never learn a thing working for Mr. Zisslof. Helena suggested, however, that I wait a few months to look for something new. Every summer the Zisslofs' rented a house in the country. Helena and the children spent the whole summer there, but Mr. and Mrs. Zisslof visited as often as they could. That would be the time, Helena said, when I would be able to come and go as I pleased. I decided that for my next job, I would only accept real tailoring work.

In June, as the first heat of summer embraced Warsaw, Helena and the children were sent to Otwock, a resort town outside of Warsaw. I knew the place. It was in Otwock, four years earlier, that I had first discovered my mother living in what she herself called a Hell. Those memories were so painful I tried not to think of them.

Without Helena, I felt lonely in the house. Every Saturday night Mr. and Mrs. Zisslof took the train to Otwock and stayed there until Sunday night. While Helena had predicted well and I was able to come and go as I pleased, she hadn't taken into account that the summer was the slow season and almost no tailor was hiring.

One evening, towards the middle of July, I overheard Helena's name mentioned as Mrs. Zisslof and her husband talked in the living room.

I moved closer to the door of my room.

"She could infect the children," Mr. Zisslof said.

"Nonsense," said his wife. "Helena doesn't have consumption. She has a bad cold, and if she didn't have a fever I wouldn't even be concerned."

"Then close down the store," Mr. Zisslof said, "and go to Otwock until she gets better."

"We can't afford to close the store," said Mrs. Zisslof. "We have to hire a woman."

"And pay another salary?" said Mr. Zisslof. "I have a better idea. Let's send Genya."

"Genya? She's not a maid."

"Every woman can do that kind of work. Besides, I'm paying her anyway."

"I can't believe she'll agree," Mrs. Zisslof said. "She's about to get married. Is her boyfriend going to let her go away for a week?"

"We'll ask her tomorrow," said Mr. Zisslof.

I was tempted to tell Mrs. Zisslof not to send Genya to Otwock. But I was afraid of creating an even greater mess. I hoped that Genya would refuse to go.

On Monday morning, however, when Mr. and Mrs. Zisslof spoke to her, Genya accepted at once. "You know how I love your children," she said.

"What about your boyfriend?" Mrs. Zisslof asked. "Don't you want to ask him first?"

"Chaiml?" Genya laughed. "Chaiml always agrees with me."

Genya took the train to Otwock that same morning.

For a whole week I heard no other news from Otwock. Helena must have been quite sick because at the end of eight days, Genya still hadn't returned to Warsaw. A week later, Mr. Zisslof wound up business at the shop and gave all the workers two weeks vacation. I had nothing to do except watch the apartment. On Saturday night, Mr. and Mrs. Zisslof took the train to Otwock.

Sunday night, Mrs. Zisslof returned alone. Her husband had remained in Otwock for a week's vacation. Mrs. Zisslof would take her week of vacation when her husband returned to take care of the store. I asked her how Helena was doing. Mrs. Zisslof told me that Helena was beginning to feel better but that Mr. Zisslof had insisted that Genya stay on to help keep the house running smoothly.

"I can hardly believe it," Mrs. Zisslof said, "Genya is entertaining the children as if she were their nanny. She takes them on hikes, picnics, swimming. I'm surprised that she doesn't mind leaving her boyfriend for such a long time. She's not so young. She should be looking to getting married and settling down."

I said nothing, but I guessed that Genya was staying in Otwock because of Mr. Zisslof.

Early next morning, after Mrs. Zisslof left for the store, I bought a copy of *The Express* and began to look for another job. The advertisements didn't interest me, but now that I could afford to buy the whole newspaper, I took it back to my room and spent the rest of the morning reading it. In the afternoon I dozed off until a frantic knocking on the front door woke me up. I jumped off my bed and ran to the door. "Who is it?" I asked.

"It's me!" Helena stumbled in carrying her valise. "Mr. Zisslof fired me!" she sobbed. Her face was blotchy from crying. "Genya has twisted the children's minds!"

I took the valise from her hand. "He only fired you so that he could be alone with Genya," I said.

"What am I going to do now?"

"Wait until Mrs. Zisslof gets back. Tell her what happened."

In the evening, when Mrs. Zisslof came home, she was shocked to see Helena in the kitchen in tears. "Helena! What are you doing here?"

"Your husband has let me go," Helena said and started to cry again.

"But why?"

"The children say that I beat them. They say the food I cook is bad. Someone threw sand in the soup and they said that I did it on purpose."

"I can't believe this!" Mrs. Zisslof said. "You're as faithful to me as a sister. What is going on out there! Does Genya have anything to do with this?"

Neither Helena nor I said anything. Mrs. Zisslof looked at us and suddenly she seemed to understand our silence.

"My God!" Mrs. Zisslof cried out. "Is my husband playing around with that woman?"

"Yes!" Helena said. "Yes! I can't stand it anymore!"

"No," Mrs. Zisslof gasped. "It can't be. It can't!" She buried her face in her hands and started to cry.

Helena and I waited until Mrs. Zisslof calmed down.

"Are you sure, Helena?" Mrs. Zisslof asked, wiping her eyes. "This is a terrible thing to accuse my husband of."

"I'm sure," Helena said. "Ask Schloime."

I suddenly felt sick. Mrs. Zisslof turned to me. Reluctantly, I told her that I had seen her husband meeting Genya at the Leszno Theater.

Mrs. Zisslof was deeply hurt. "How could you lie to me?"

I looked to Helena for help.

"He told me about it," Helena admitted. "We were afraid to tell you. I was hoping it would end when Genya got married."

Mrs. Zisslof looked at her wristwatch and said, "Helena, let's dry our eyes and wash our faces. We can still catch a train to Otwock."

No one returned that night. Early the next morning, however, I heard an angry beating on the front door.

"Open up, Schloime!" a woman shouted. "Open up!" This time it was Genya.

"Go away," I said from behind the locked door.

"Open up or I'll scream until the police comes!" Genya threatened hysterically.

I didn't want to alarm the neighbors. I opened the door and Genya flew into the factory in a rage. "It's your fault!" she screamed. Her hair was disheveled; her makeup was smeared. "What lies did you tell Mrs. Zisslof!"

"I did nothing to you," I said. "You did it all to yourself!"

"You spied on me! You followed me around like a dog!"

Suddenly the door opened and we saw Mrs. Zisslof. "What is all this noise? What are you doing here, Genya? Didn't I tell you last night that I never wanted to see you in my house again?"

Genya was struck dumb. She looked at Mrs. Zisslof and me, and then she clasped her hands and fell to her knees in front of Mrs. Zisslof. "Forgive me, Mrs. Zisslof!" she began to cry. "Please forgive me! Don't fire me!"

"Stop it," Mrs. Zisslof ordered. "Get off the floor at once. Schloime, get a chair for Genya."

I pulled a chair over and Mrs. Zisslof and I helped Genya to her feet and to sit down.

"Don't fire me!" Genya kept wailing. "I beg you, don't fire me! I don't want Chaiml to find out! We're going to be married and I don't want to lose him. Let me stay on just until I can find something else. Please, Mrs. Zisslof, please, have pity on me…"

Mrs. Zisslof was silent a long while, and then she said, "We will keep this a secret. It won't go any further. You can stay until you find another job, but start to look right away… Heaven knows, I have two girls of my own, may the Lord protect them from your fate, Genya."

18 Twarda Street

GENYA WAS GONE within a week after everyone returned from vacation. To replace her the Union sent Baile Tsopp, a simple, middle-aged matron shaped like a barrel of herring. Her coarse hair was twisted into one thick braid. She seemed to know our boss's reputation with women and came prepared to guard her treasures. The first time Mr. Zisslof asked Baile to help him select fabrics, she looked at him as if he had asked her to join him in bed. "I'm not moving from this chair," she snarled. "All fabric selection and matching will be done in full view of my co-workers."

The men could hardly contain their laughter as Mr. Zisslof, who was in no position to bargain, ran back and forth to the storage room carrying bolts of cloth.

In my spare time, I kept looking for other work. Since I could afford to wait, I remained determined to accept only a job which involved tailoring. I searched without any luck throughout the fall and winter. One morning in April, after a delivery to Mrs. Zisslof at the store, I stopped at a newsstand. As I checked the "Employment" section in *The Express* I found an advertisement for a novice tailor of boy's suits. I immediately pulled out my pencil stub and paper and copied the name and address: Arele Blumenstein, No. 18 Twarda Street.

That same evening, as soon as I could free myself, I took the long walk to see this Mr. Blumenstein.

Twarda Street, in the southern part of the Jewish Quarter, swung in an arc from Grzybowski Square to Chmielna Street. At No. 18, I found a small tailor shop, which by nine o'clock was already closed. I was about to leave when I noticed a flicker of light in the back of the store. I knocked on the glass. A stooped man looked out from behind a curtain and came to open the door.

"We're closed," he said, "but I can take your measurements. Let me just turn on the light."

I saw at once in his smooth, pasty face that he was a young man. "I'm not here for a suit," I said. "I saw your advertisement in *The Express*."

"Are you a tailor?" he asked.

I would have lied and said yes if I could have gotten away with it. "I have some experience," I said, instead. "Didn't you ask for a beginner?"

"Come with me." He turned off the light and locked the door. He walked ahead of me, hunched as if a sack of sorrows was slung over his shoulder.

The small tailor shop, filled with pale light from a street lamp, was divided by a narrow counter. In front of the counter, leaning against the wall, stood a full length mirror and a low footstool. Against the opposite wall there was a chair for a waiting customer. Behind the counter there was a small rack for finished work on which hung a few boys suits.

"Arele?" a woman called softly from behind the curtain. "Who is it?"

"A young man answering our advertisement," said the tailor. He pulled aside the curtain and I stepped into the back room. "This is the whole workshop," he continued, "myself and my Natachale."

The tailor's wife was a slight a woman, not much older than I. She gave me a quick, bird-like glance and returned to the pair of pants she was sewing. A bare light bulb hung from the ceiling. It shone on a sewing machine, a small table, an electric stove, three chairs, and a folded cot propped against the back wall.

"We need help," the tailor said, "but we can't afford to pay a tailor." He stopped and waited to hear what I would say.

"I've been an apprentice since I was twelve years old and I can do many things."

The tailor and his wife looked at each other. He raised his eyebrows as if to ask her, What do you say? She gave half a nod with her head as if to answer, What do you have to lose? And he shrugged his shoulders as if to say, All right, and began to ask me about my background. I was getting used to lying about my parents and I said that neither of them was alive.

When I had answered his questions, Arele looked again to his wife for a sign. She pressed her lips and creased her forehead.

"Why don't you come over tomorrow night for a trial," suggested the tailor, "and let's see how it works out?"

The next evening as soon as I had finished cleaning the sewing machines at the Zisslofs, I told them that I was going to visit my aunt Liebe.

I ran to Twarda Street. The small tailor shop was closed but I knocked on the glass and Mr. Blumenstein let me in. As he led me to the back, the tailor explained that he specialized in making school uniforms for boys. In the workshop, I greeted his wife, who was busy at the sewing machine. Without wasting a moment, the tailor asked me to sew pockets on a pair of pants. When I had finished, he checked my work, and gave me three pairs of pants to press. The tailor asked me to come back the following night for another trial. I left after 10 o'clock.

As I walked across the darkened Jewish Quarter, I was tired but hopeful that Arele Blumenstein would hire me, and that with my salary as a tailor I would be able to rent a room and send for Babbe and Ruchele. The gates at No. 30 Novalypia Street were already locked. Luckily, the janitor's son was still hanging around the entrance to let the latecomers in. He opened the gate for me and I gave him a twenty-five groschen tip.

At the end of a week of evening trials, Mr. Blumenstein said to me, "You have a little experience. You could help us out. But you still have a lot to learn." His talk, I knew at once, was meant to lower my wages as much as possible. "For now," he continued, "I can offer you ten zlotys a week."

My heart sank. I told him that I wouldn't even be able to rent a room and buy myself food for that salary.

Again the husband and wife consulted each other with quick looks, shrugs, and nods, until they reached a silent agreement.

"We have a solution," said the tailor. "We can let you sleep here."

"We wouldn't trust just anyone," he added quickly. "But you seem to be a decent boy. You can sleep on that folding cot, and you can cook on the electric stove. If you make your own food instead of eating in restaurants all the time, you'll save a lot of money. And you'll keep an eye on the shop when we're not here."

I realized that if I went to work for Blumenstein my hope of bringing Babbe and Ruchele to Warsaw would continue being just a hope. And yet this was the best offer I had and a chance to keep gaining experience. I accepted.

"We want you to start as soon as possible," Mr. Blumenstein said as he shook my hand.

I found Mr. Zisslof and his wife playing cards in the living room when I returned. I told them that I had been offered a tailoring job. Mrs. Zisslof was sorry to lose me, but her husband smiled and said that he would put an advertisement in the newspaper in the morning and I could leave the moment he hired a new boy.

The next day at breakfast, I told Helena about my new job. She was truly happy for me. "One day you'll meet a girl and want to get married and have a family," she said. "Without a trade, how would you take care of a wife and children?"

Mr. Zisslof found a boy to replace me within three days. On the morning the boy started, I said my goodbyes to Helena, Leibish and the workers, packed my small sack, and carried it to Twarda Street.

My new boss was happy to see me. I put my small sack into a corner of the workshop, next to the folding bed, and I began to work at once.

I enjoyed being with the Blumensteins. The husband and wife sewed quietly next to each other, exchanging a look or a sigh now and then. During the day, the curtain which separated the back from the front of the store was kept open, letting light into the workshop. Whenever the front door opened, Arele got up from his chair and sang out, "Be right with you!" After putting up with Mr. Zisslof and all the craziness that went on in his factory, it was a sheer pleasure to be around the peaceful Blumensteins.

At lunch time, Natacha unwrapped two sandwiches of dark bread and meat cutlets and shared their lunch with me. In the evening, Arele paid me two zlotys. I went to the grocery around the corner from the tailor shop and bought myself milk, bread, and a piece of cheese. Natacha showed me how to operate the electric stove and which pot to use for warming up milk. At night, after our work was finished, Arele gave me the key to the store. I walked the Blumensteins to the door and locked it after they left.

I hadn't seen Frau Liebe and her family for a whole week and I was looking forward to surprising them with my change of jobs. On the Sabbath, however, when I visited them, it was they who had a surprise waiting for me.

"There's a letter for you, Schloime," Frau Liebe said as I walked in. "It came just a few days ago."

I knew at once that it was from Babbe and Ruchele. They were probably angry with me for not having written and curious if I had found our mother yet. I would have to write to them; but what could I say? Elke went into the bedroom and came back with a thin envelope which had Uncle Yankel's name and address in the left corner. I opened it and pulled out a one page letter.

"Dear Schloime," I read, "I have sad news. Babbe caught a terrible cold last winter and had to be hospitalized. She came home after a few weeks. She seemed to be feeling better, but a week ago Babbe got sick again and died, may she rest in peace. She remembered you to the end. I feel very lonely without her. I need your help. Uncle Yankel wants me to marry Heniach. I'm not even sixteen years old yet and I don't want to get married. I've been so desperate, I went to see Aunt Khumale. I never felt so unwelcome in my life. She couldn't wait to get rid of me. I have no one else but you. Please help me move to Warsaw. I can't bear it in Lublin anymore. Please don't forget me. Your sister, Ruchele."

I put the letter down. I tried to control myself, but I couldn't, and I began to cry.

"God protect us," Liebe said. "It's bad news."

I collected myself and said, "Babbe Zlate died."

"May she rest in peace," Liebe said. "How that good woman suffered in her life."

I suddenly remembered Babbe's words to me on the day I left Lublin, the last time I saw her. We were in the kitchen. The small sack, which she and Ruchele had sewn for me, was packed. Babbe looked at me with alarm in her eyes. "I'm so old already," she said. "I will soon die and I won't even know where you've disappeared."

I began to cry again. Frau Liebe, her children, and her husband's three grandsons waited quietly.

"I need a favor," I said when I could speak. "Ruchele says that she has to leave Lublin. Uncle Yankel wants her to marry one of his sons, she doesn't want to get married, and Uncle Yankel is making her life miserable."

"Write and tell her that she can come here," Liebe said at once. "She is as dear to us as you are."

I thanked Liebe, then I excused myself and left.

On the street, I thought with bitter resentment how I had lost those I loved—my father when I was two years old; my mother when I was twelve; and now Babbe. Only Ruchele was left. As I walked, I became angry at my sister for not writing to me as soon as Babbe got sick. Maybe if I had gone back to Lublin in time, I could have saved Babbe's life. I didn't even say my last goodbye to her, my Babbe, who had been so devoted to me.

I let myself into the store. In the workshop, I turned on the light, made myself a glass of tea, and sat down to write a letter to my sister. I told Ruchele that she couldn't stay with me because I didn't have my own room, but I had asked Frau Liebe and she had agreed to help us.

The next morning, when Arele and Natacha came to work, they asked me at why I looked so sad. I told them that my grandmother had died. The tailor and his wife were sorry to hear that. "May she rest in the brightness of the Garden of Eden," said Arele. His wife added, "Amen." And they never mentioned my Babbe again.

My Mother's Voice

IT WAS PAST NOON on the Sabbath when I locked the store and began my long walk across the Jewish Quarter to Frau Liebe's apartment on Muranovska. The grayness of the clouds seemed to have settled over the houses. The streets were quiet, as if they too had been given a day of rest. Even though I was hoping to find a letter from Ruchele at Liebe's, I was worried about how we would manage after her arrival in Warsaw. Liebe had always treated me like family, but the basement apartment was crowded. Liebe and Hertzke slept in the small bedroom, which left only one room, a combination living room and kitchen, for Liebe's son and two daughters, and her husband's three grandsons. The times I had been forced to live in Liebe's basement, I had never stayed for more than a week or two. I had always managed to find work and a place to live quickly. With Ruchele, the situation would be different. She was still a young girl; she had never lived on her own; and even though she had been apprenticed to a seamstress in Lublin, I suspected that it would be years before she could earn her own living. And who knew how long it would be before I could support her?

These thoughts were dancing in my head as I walked down the steps to Liebe's apartment. From the staircase I could already hear a lively political debate going on. When I opened the door, I was greeted as if I were the guest of honor at a party. Suddenly, I heard my name called by a strangely familiar voice—my mother's voice before years of suffering had made it a hollow sound. I turned to the kitchen and saw a young woman in a pale blue dress who looked so much like my mother before grief had ruined her beauty that I was left speechless: the same green eyes that shone like summer leaves; the same soft, black hair full of curls; the same pretty, round face.

"Schloime, don't you recognize me?" the young woman asked as she ran to embraced me.

It had been two years since I had last seen Ruchele. I couldn't believe how much she had changed. My little sister was taller than me. "I didn't think you'd come so soon," I said in a daze.

"I've been here two days already."

"Why didn't you let me know you were on your way? I would have met you at the station."

"I didn't have time. Uncle Yankel was driving me crazy."

"How did you get here?"

"What do you mean? By train. And when I got to Warsaw, I asked for directions."

"You're surprised?" Liebe said. "Your sister isn't the little girl you left in Lublin."

"Everyone's been so nice to me," Ruchele said. "We went out last night and I saw so much of Warsaw. What a large city! So beautiful! All those lights! I could walk the streets here all night long."

Everyone laughed at Ruchele's innocence except me and Frau Liebe. We both knew how this beautiful city had ruined my mother's life.

"It may seem beautiful," said Liebe, "but you must be careful. There are many dangers for a young woman in such a big city."

"This is not Lublin," I added.

"Why're you scaring her?" Tsutel, Elke's older sister, piped up. Tsutel, who was tall, thin, and almost twenty-two years old, had her mother's plain, flat face. Tsutel, however, unlike her mother, knew how to use cosmetics and with red lipstick, a touch of pink powder on her cheeks and blue over her eyes, made herself look quite pretty.

"Don't listen to Tsutel, that great free thinker," said Elke to my sister. "Mother and Schloime are right. You have to watch yourself."

"You'll suffocate her," Tsutel scoffed.

Elke was ready to answer her sister when Leibel stopped her. "Enough," he said to his sisters. "Ruchele has a mind of her own. She'll take care of herself."

"Come children and sit down," said Liebe. "Now that Schloime is here, I can bring out the cake."

"Uncle Yankel and Aunt Simke send you regards," Ruchele said.

"How are they?" I asked, although my mind was on a more burning question.

"Much better, now that Heniach is working for a shoemaker. He can earn twice in a day what his father earns dragging those loads like a horse."

"Why didn't you write to me when Babbe got sick?" I asked unable to hold back anymore. "Maybe I could have helped."

Ruchele looked uncomfortable. "I wanted to write," she said, stiffly, "but Uncle Yankel wouldn't let me. He was afraid you would run back to Lublin and lose your job here."

"Afraid I would lose my job?" I flared up before I could control myself. "Babbe meant more to me than a hundred jobs!"

"What do you want from me!" Ruchele shot back. "Is it my fault that Uncle Yankel is so stubborn!"

Astonished eyes turned on us from everywhere in the room. I felt embarrassed for fighting with my sister in front of Liebe's family. No one knew what to say. Luckily, Frau Liebe walked in from the kitchen carrying a round sponge cake. It sat on the plate like a crown of gold. "Children," she said, putting the cake down on the table, "nothing can change what has happened. May your Babbe Zlate rest in peace. You're here now, together again, and for that you have to be thankful."

As soon as the cake was cut and the slices were passed around, the conversation turned to life in Warsaw and became very spirited. I ate my piece of cake, which tasted like sweetened air, and felt glad that attention had been taken off me and my sister. I could see that Hertzke's grandsons, Khiel, Nachme, and Yoinne, were taken with Ruchele. As they told her about the plays being performed in Warsaw, Ruchele listened with an open mouth. I followed the talk for a while but my mind wandered. I was overwhelmed with worry over how to take care of Ruchele, who was neither a child nor an adult.

"Can I see where you live?" my sister asked me suddenly.

"Now? It's a long walk."

"Take her out, Schloime," said Tsutel. "Show her around. It'll give you some time together."

"Let me get my coat and pocketbook," Ruchele said without waiting for my answer. She ran into Liebe's bedroom and returned a moment later wearing a long blue coat and carrying a brown shoulder bag. When I saw that coat I realized why Ruchele reminded me so much of Mamme; my sister was wearing clothes our mother had left behind in Lublin when she moved to Warsaw.

"Come," Ruchele said, taking my hand.

"Just be back before eight," Khiel said with a wink.

"What's he talking about?" I asked as we climbed up the basement steps.

49

"There's a dance tonight," Ruchele said. "Aren't you going?"

"No. And you shouldn't go either."

"Why not?"

"Because I'm telling you not to go. That's why."

"You can't tell me what to do."

"Who's going to look after you if not me? I don't like the people who go to these dances." Khiel himself had told me that these dances were organized by the Communist Party, and many who went were free thinkers, believers in free love. These were not things I could explain to my young sister.

"The dance is just a front for a political organization," I said.

"A what?"

"You see. I knew you wouldn't understand."

"But Tsutel and Elke are going. Frau Liebe wouldn't let her daughters go dancing if there was something wrong with it."

"Elke and Tsutel are older than you."

"I don't want to argue," Ruchele said, taking my arm.

The sky had cleared and the cloudy morning had turned into a warm April afternoon. I noticed that Ruchele looked at the buildings and the crowds of Jews in Sabbath dress with the same feeling of awe that I had when I first moved to Warsaw.

"I wish you had written as soon as Babbe got sick," I said.

"We did everything we could. Babbe Zlate was eighty-seven. She was old."

Ruchele continued to hold on to my arm as we walked without looking at each other.

"I never said goodbye to Babbe. I didn't even go to her funeral. I'll never forgive myself for that."

"Don't blame yourself," my sister said. "It's not your fault."

We continued to walk in silence. My vision was blurred by tears, and I let Ruchele guide me.

After a long silence, Ruchele asked, "Have you seen Mamme?"

My sister had finally asked the question I had dreaded most. For years, I had tried to protect Ruchele from the truth about our mother. Now, I didn't know what to say. "Why do you ask?"

"I miss her," Ruchele said. "I can't stop thinking about her. I want to see her."

"You wouldn't recognize her."

My sister stopped. "You have seen her?"

"Yes."

"Where?" Ruchele demanded.

"I can't tell you. It's for your own good."

"If you don't tell me, I'll look for her myself."

"Don't go near Mamme."

"Why?"

"*Because.* I can't speak to you about such things."

"Why not?"

"Why are you torturing me? Because you're a girl."

"I'll ask Frau Liebe. I bet she knows everything."

"Don't ever speak to Liebe or anyone else about Mamme."

Ruchele must have sensed that she had hit my weakest point. "I have no other choice," she threatened.

Even though it had been Liebe who had told me where Itzhak Copperstein's parents lived, she had never asked me if I had found our mother. Liebe was careful to spare my feelings. If Ruchele started to ask foolish questions, everyone at Liebe's would start to talk about our mother and the shame would be unbearable for us.

"All right," I was forced to agree. "I'll take you to her." I decided, however, to stall as long as possible.

"When?" asked my sister at once.

"I don't know. It can't be right away."

"Why not?"

"Because I don't even know where Mamme lives."

"But you saw her."

"All I know is where Itzhak Copperstein's parents live. She visits them sometimes."

"Take me there," Ruchele demanded.

"Itzhak and his parents are drunkards and thieves, do you hear me? They live in a cellar full of criminals and beggars. They're very dangerous people. Promise me that you won't go near them on your own."

"Only if you promise to take me to Mamme."

"I already said that I would."

"Tell me when?" Ruchele insisted. "So I know that you're not just trying to fool me?"

"As soon as I have time."

We walked in silence for a long while. I could tell that Ruchele was shaken by what I had told her of the people our mother had gotten involved with. At the tailor shop, I took out my key.

"What are you doing?" asked Ruchele.

"This is where I live. Come in."

We entered. I locked the door and took my sister to the back, behind the curtain.

"But this is a workshop," Ruchele said when she saw the sewing machine, the press table, and the tailor's dummy.

"Sit down," I said giving her one of the chairs. I sat down across the table from my sister. "I wish this were my own room so you could live with me."

"I don't mind sleeping in Liebe's kitchen for now," Ruchele said. "I was sleeping in Uncle Yankel's kitchen in Lublin. I'm much happier here in Warsaw."

"I don't know how long we can depend on Frau Liebe. She isn't a rich woman."

"I'm already looking for work," Ruchele said. "Everyone at Liebe's is helping me."

"What can you do?" I asked.

"I can sew. Don't you remember the seamstress on the first floor? I've been working for her since you left. She was paying me five zlotys a week."

"Do you have money?"

"No. I used all my savings for the ticket to Warsaw."

"I have eleven zlotys. You take five for now." I counted out the bills and gave them to my sister.

Ruchele thanked me as she put the money into her handbag.

"I almost forgot," she said reaching into her open handbag, "I have something to show you." My sister pulled out an envelope.

"What is this?" I asked.

"You'll never guess," Ruchele said. "Tatte's address in Russia."

I was astonished. "How did you get it?"

"From Aunt Khumale."

"I can't believe she gave it to you," I said. "I went to ask Khumale for help once. All she did was criticize Mamme for the divorce."

"She hasn't changed," Ruchele said. "She only gave me the address to get rid of me."

"Do you think it's the right address?" I asked, wondering what good that address might do us even if it were right. "Did you write to him yet?"

"I thought it would be better if you wrote," said Ruchele, handing me the envelope.

I looked inside it and found a small photograph. Above the jacket and tie was the face of a middle aged man with thick shock of hair, deep set eyes, a jutting nose, a wide mouth, and ears like jug handles. There could be no doubt that just as Ruchele had inherited our mother's features, I had our my father's. "Where's the letter?"

"Khumale didn't give it to me."

I put the envelope with the photograph into my sack of belongings.

By the time I brought Ruchele back to Liebe's apartment it was already after seven o'clock. Leibel had gone out with his girlfriend. The others, however, Tsutel, Elke, Khiel, Nachme, and Yoinne were in a cheerful mood, getting ready for the dance.

"How about a little spin around the floor?" Khiel said to Elke.

Khiel, who worked as a salesman in clothing store, was almost twenty. He was short and because of his bad legs he walked awkwardly. But Khiel loved pretty girls and couldn't keep his hands off Elke. He grabbed her around the waist and pulled her to him.

Nachme began to imitate a clarinet wailing a *frailich*, running his fingers up and down the body of the invisible instrument while Yoinne and Tsutel clapped in rhythm.

I felt embarrassed for Khiel. Even though the problem with his legs was far more severe than my limp, watching him made me self-conscious.

Elke laughed as she took a few clumsy steps with Khiel until she felt his hand slide from her waist down to her bottom. "Get away from me, you pig!" she squealed, as she pushed Khiel away.

"How about me, Elkele?" Yoinne asked with open arms. Yoinne, just a year older than me, was the handsomest of the three brothers. He worked in a factory that manufactured casual pants and jackets.

"You I can trust," Elke said smiling, and while the others continued to make the music, Elke and Yoinne skipped around the floor.

"Boys, boys," Liebe said, "your sick grandfather is trying to rest." But she was smiling, enjoying the horse play.

Ruchele's eyes were wide with pleasure and wonder. She had never seen this kind of carrying-on at Uncle Yankel's in Lublin.

"Let's get out of here," Tsutel said.

"Yes, what are we waiting for?" Khiel said. "Let's dance to a real band." He put his arm around Ruchele and said, "Come on, you two. Enough brother and sister talk."

"Come, Schloime," Ruchele said as Khiel pulled her out the door. "Come with us."

"Ruchele, I'm not going," I said firmly, "and I told you not to go, either."

"But I want to dance with you," said Tsutel, grabbing my hand and pulling me along. "I had my heart set on it."

"Set your heart on Khiel," I said. I had the sense that Tsutel who was much taller than me and five years older liked me.

"On that lecher, never!" Tsutel ran out laughing.

"I'm going," Ruchele said to me. "You can't stop me."

"Let her go, Schloime," Liebe said. "The children will be careful."

As Ruchele was being pulled up the steps by the crowd, she called to me, "Come and see me soon."

"Be careful!" I called back to her.

In a burst of laughter that grew fainter as the group floated up the stairs, they left.

"Why didn't you want to go?" Liebe asked me as she gathered the glasses and plates that had been left everywhere on the furniture.

"I don't like the organization that's behind the club," I said.

"Tsutel and Elke are the same Communists as you and I," said Liebe. "They just go to dance."

"I hope the police don't break in on them someday," I said. I couldn't tell Liebe, but I was more worried about the wild ideas of free love than the politics. I didn't want Ruchele to get involved in that dirty business.

I helped Liebe bring the plates and glasses to the bench in the kitchen where she washed the dishes. From under the bench I pulled out a pail with clean water and poured some into a wooden basin. Liebe put a few plates in the large basin and began to wash them.

When I was ready to leave, Frau Liebe tried to reassure me, "Don't worry about Ruchele. We're all looking out for her."

On the dark stairs, I lit a cigarette and held on to the burning match as I walked up the steps.

I crossed the courtyard. It was dark and quiet now except for the faint light and bits of conversations that fell softly from the open windows. The iron gates creaked as I opened and closed them.

A few steps away, leaning against the wall, I saw two young women.

"Here is a gentleman who can light my cigarette," one of them said holding up her cigarette. She had long dark hair and such a pretty face that she looked like a film actress. I approached her. As she leaned close to me to light her cigarette, my head was filled with the smell of her perfume.

"Thank you," she said blowing smoke in my face. "My friend says that I should cut my hair, but I think men like it long. What do you think?"

"It's beautiful just as it is," I said.

"What a lovely compliment," she said. "You must be quite a lover."

"Thank you," I mumbled as I continued to walk.

"Another time," she said and the two girls laughed behind my back.

On the Wings of an Angel

I RETURNED TO THE WORKSHOP and immediately put some water up to boil on the small electric stove. Instead of being comforted by Ruchele's arrival, I felt disturbed. I had never expected my sister to be so reckless. Warsaw was full of low-lifes looking for a foolish girl like Ruchele to take advantage of. Wasn't it here that Mamme had met Itzhak Copperstein? I had been powerless to save our mother, but I couldn't allow the same tragedy to destroy my sister.

While I waited for the water to boil, I took out a tablet of onionskin paper from my sack of belongings and the envelope with our father's address and picture. I spent a long time looking closely at his penetrating eyes, at the shape of his wide mouth, searching for a clue to the kind of man he was. But his expression was hard to read: not happy, not sad; not guilty, not innocent. After fourteen years, I was still angry at him for having abandoned us. I blamed him for what had happened to our mother. If Mamme's life hadn't been so hard, she would never have gone to Warsaw to look for a better job, and Ruchele and I wouldn't have lost her. And yet, I also desperately needed my father's help.

The water finally boiled. With a glass of hot tea at my side, I sat down at the table and in spite of my mixed feelings, I began to write.

'Dear Tatte, I hope you still remember your son and daughter, Schloime and Ruchele. We were babies when you left in 1914. Our life has not been easy without you. Mamme doesn't live with us anymore. I can't tell you what she has suffered. It's too painful. I only mention it because I want you to know how much we need your help.

'Ruchele has just arrived from Lublin and brought with her an envelope with your address. She got it from your sister Khumale. I would have written sooner if I had known where you live. Why did you stop writing to us? Why didn't you answer Mamme's letters? Why didn't you come back home after the war?

'To tell you the truth, I don't even know if you'll get this letter. The few times I went to Aunt Khumale for help she always turned me away, so I doubt that the address she gave Ruchele is still good. But if you do get this letter, could you please help us? Ruchele and I are alone now. Babbe Zlate died last month, may she rest in peace. I work for a tailor, but I earn very little. Ruchele is living with a very kind woman, Frau Liebe, an old friend of Mamme's from Lublin. Unfortunately, Frau Liebe is poor and has a sick husband. They live in a crowded basement with six grown children. I wish Ruchele could stay with me but I don't earn enough yet to rent a room. I sleep in the back of the store where I work.

Please write to me. Your son, Schloime.'

At the bottom of the sheet of paper, I wrote down Frau Liebe's name and address.

I folded the letter into an envelope and sealed it. Then I carefully copied the Polish letters of my father's name and address from the envelope which Ruchele had brought: Baruch Renglich, 25 Actiavetska Street, Fergana, Russia. I still had three of the stamps which I had bought to write to Lublin, and I pasted them now on my letter to my father.

I woke up early the next morning. On my way to the grocery, I dropped the letter into a mailbox.

By the time the Blumensteins came into the store, I had already eaten breakfast. Since the Polish Government forbid Jewish businesses from being open on Sunday, the store had to be kept locked and the curtain drawn.

Once they started to work, the Blumensteins almost never spoke to each other. Now and then, they would hum a song quietly. If Arele or his wife said anything to me, it was only to explain how a fold was to be sewed or how a cuff was to be finished. Silence filled my hours and in that silence fantasies filled my mind with the terrible things that had happened to our mother and which now threatened my sister. A few times during the day I had the urge to throw down my work and run to Liebe's to check up on Ruchele.

In the evening, however, after the Blumenstein's left, I felt torn about what to do. I knew that my sister wouldn't listen to me and I didn't want to have a fight.

I made tea, cut myself a slice of bread, and ate it with the piece of hard cheese left over from the morning. The food was tasteless. I tried to read an old newspaper, but I was too nervous. I slipped my jacket on and left the store.

On the dark stairs to Liebe's basement, I noticed that the apartment was unusually quiet. I hurried down the steps and opened the door.

Khiel, alone in the living room, looked up from the table where he sat reading a newspaper. "Schloimele, why are you running?"

"Where's my sister?"

"She found a lover and moved out," Khiel said and turned his eyes back to his newspaper.

With a sudden, painful jolt I remembered an evening four years earlier in Lublin when I came home from work and found Babbe and Ruchele crying in the kitchen. This memory sprang to life so vividly that for a moment I didn't know where I was. Babbe and Ruchele had been so upset neither could tell me what was wrong. I sensed at once that something had happened to my mother. I turned to Aunt Simke, who stood in the doorway to the kitchen. "Where's Mamme?" I asked. Simke, barely able to stop her own tears, embraced me and whispered, "Your mother has left for Warsaw." I tore myself out of Simke's arms. "Where is she?" I shouted. Simke tried to calm me down. "Your uncle just took her to the train station. Wait for Yankel to come back. He'll explain everything to you." I ran out of the apartment and didn't stop until I got to the station. But I was too late. My mother had vanished. When I returned to the apartment, Uncle Yankel was back. He looked at me with his crossed blue eyes and laughed. "Do you want to live in that stinking kitchen forever?" he asked. "Just let your mother settle down in Warsaw and start to earn a decent living. Then she's going to send for you and your sister and your Babbe." I couldn't believe him. I couldn't believe that our mother would leave us behind, even for a short time. A few weeks later Mamme's first letter came and seemed to confirm everything Uncle Yankel had said. We were overjoyed. She wrote that she was working in her cousin's store, and was soon going to start looking for an apartment for us. In her second letter, our mother even sent us twenty zlotys. But Mamme never wrote a third letter. Warsaw had swallowed her up into its underworld.

Khiel kept turning the pages, unaware of the effect his sarcastic remark had on me.

I slapped my hand down on his newspaper. "What the devil are you talking about? Tell me where my sister is?"

Khiel sat back in his chair. "What's the matter with you? Ever since your sister came you're like a worried hen with an egg. Believe me, your little sister can take her of herself. You should have seen her last night. At least five men were fighting to dance with her."

"Stop teasing him, Khiel." I heard Frau Liebe say. "Come in here, Schloime."

I walked into the kitchen where Liebe was drying dishes.

"What's Khiel talking about?"

"He's playing with you," Liebe said. "We have some good news for you. Ruchele has got a job and a place to live."

"Where? How could she find something so quickly?"

"Last night Ksiel came to visit his father after you left. When I told him about Ruchele and he heard that she had worked for a dressmaker, he said that maybe Lotte could use some help. She's so busy with the children that she's turning customers away. Well, tonight Lotte herself dropped by and spoke to your sister. Ruchele accepted the job and decided to move in with Lotte and Ksiel."

I heard Khiel's shuffling walk as he came into the kitchen behind me. He put his hand on my shoulder and said, "Everybody's at Ksiel's right now. They walked over with Ruchele."

Liebe, who understood my concerns, looked me in the eyes and said, "You can trust Lotte and Ksiel. Ruchele will be safe with them."

I thanked Liebe, but my words weren't enough to express my gratitude and sense of relief. I had met Ksiel and Lotte a few times and I liked them. Ksiel was in his thirties and worked in a factory which manufactured folding beds, and Lotte, I had heard, was a talented dressmaker.

Khiel gave me a little push. "What are you waiting for? Your little sister is at 30 Electoralna Street, in apartment 5."

Liebe's children suddenly poured into the basement.

"Look who's here!" Leibel said as he walked into the kitchen.

"Ruchele's all settled in," Elke said. "We just left her. Ksiel and Lotte gave her the small room all to herself."

"Ruchele's in heaven," Tsutel said.

"And so is Lotte," said Leibel. "With Ruchele's help, she expects to work up a big clientele again."

"I have to see Ruchele," I said.

"Tell her that we'll come tomorrow after work," Nachme said.

I was amazed at the stroke of good luck that had provided my sister with a room and a job. Not only were Ksiel and Lotte people I could trust, but Electoralna Street was much closer to Twarda. Ruchele was now living just a few blocks away from me and I could keep an eye on her more easily. I began to feel that maybe our situation was not so desperate after all.

At 30 Electoralna Street, I ran up the steps to the second floor. I pushed open the door of apartment 5 and startled Ruchele and Lotte, who were sitting in the kitchen at the sewing machine.

"Schloime, what a fright you gave me," Lotte said. "Come in." Lotte, in her mid-twenties, was a short, energetic woman. She was dressed in an elegant brown shirtwaist dress.

"You just missed everyone," Ruchele said.

"I saw them at Liebe's. They told me that you were here."

"Your sister's going to work for me, and live here," Lotte said. "What do you think of that?"

"And you were so worried about what I would do," Ruchele said.

"Go ahead, Ruchel, show him your room." Lotte got up from the machine. "We can talk about work tomorrow."

Lotte's two little girls burst into the kitchen as if they had just been waiting for their mother to say that work was done for the day. Lotte picked up the two-year-old, took the four-year-old by the hand, and said to them, "I bet your little sister needs her diaper changed."

"Come," said Ruchele and led me to a small room next to the kitchen. She lit a lamp with a pink lamp-shade on top of the chest of drawers.

"Well?" Ruchele beamed. "What do you think?"

"What can I think?" I said. "I'm very happy for you."

Besides the chest of drawers, there was a narrow bed and an old wardrobe. Ruchele's valise, tucked away on top of the wardrobe, had already been emptied. Since there wasn't a chair in the room, I sat down on the bed.

"I told you not to worry." Ruchele sat down next to me.

"You're very lucky. It's not easy to find such a good job."

"I don't think it's just luck," said Ruchele. "There are many opportunities here. I can't believe how many interesting people I met at the dance last night."

"Khiel told me how popular you were."

"What's wrong with that? I can't understand why you don't want to come out with everyone to the club."

"Because the people who go there are free-thinkers. I don't want to get mixed up with them. I have enough troubles."

"Maybe if you had more friends you wouldn't have so many troubles."

"Who taught you to talk like this, Khiel and Tsutel?"

"What difference does it make? Anyway, I agree with them."

I couldn't stand my sister's childish opinions. I didn't want to fight but it seemed that I couldn't say two words to her without getting into an argument.

"When are you taking me to see Mamme?" Ruchele began to harp again on the same subject.

"I told you, as soon as I have time."

"You'll never have time," Ruchele raised her voice, "because you don't want to take me!"

"Do you want them to hear you?" I whispered.

"I don't care," said my sister sharply. "You're lying to me."

"I said I'll take you and I will."

"When?" Ruchele demanded.

"I can't tell you exactly. I told you already." I was deathly afraid that Lotte and Ksiel would overhear our conversation. "I have to go back to the store now."

Ruchele walked me to the door. "Schloime, I'm begging you," my sister whispered as I was leaving, "please find her. Tell Mamme that I want to see her."

I ran out of the building. I had never imagined that having my sister close to me in Warsaw would bring so many aggravations.

For the rest of that week, I didn't go back to see Ruchele. On Friday night, as I sat at the work table under the bare bulb and read an old newspaper, I heard a knock on the glass of the front door. I looked around the curtain. Ruchele was standing at the store window, waving to me.

I immediately opened the door.

"Where've you been the whole week?" Ruchele asked as she stepped in.

"I've been busy." I locked the door and we walked to the back. "What're you doing here? Did you walk by yourself?"

"No, I flew over on the wings of an angel."

"How can you go out alone so late at night?"

"Nothing happened to me. You're worse than Babbe was."

"I know what I'm worried about."

"Warsaw is ten times more civilized than Lublin."

"It just looks that way."

"I don't want to fight. Take to me to see Mamme."

"I will, but—"

"No," Ruchele interrupted me, "not when you have time. Now."

61

"I can't. What do I have to do to convince you? I only know where Itzhak's parents live; Mamme's not there now."

Ruchele screwed her face into a grim, determined look. "Fine. Tomorrow I'm going to start looking for myself."

I had no doubt that Ruchele meant to carry through on her threat. "You're going to regret it," I warned her.

"And the first person I'm going to ask is Frau Liebe."

"Did you forget all the gossip about Mamme in Lublin? Do you want to start all of that here in Warsaw?"

"I just want to see my mother."

"Be patient."

"You've always lied to me about Mamme. Even in Lublin, when you came back from Otwock, you said that you hadn't found her."

"I had to protect Babbe. If she had known what I saw in Otwock, it would have killed her."

"I had to hear all that ugly gossip about Mamme from the neighbors' children. And even after I confronted you with your lies, you still didn't tell me everything that happened in Otwock."

"You were a little girl. I was trying to protect you."

"I never asked you to protect me." Ruchele stood up.

"Where are you going?"

"I'm leaving."

"Wait," I said, getting my jacket. "I'll walk you home."

I locked the store and offered Ruchele my arm. She looked away. I took her hand and put it under my arm. She left it there. As we began to walk, I realized that I would have to tell my sister the whole bitter truth. It would hurt her, but it was the only way to stop Ruchele from making a terrible mistake.

"You're right," I admitted. "I didn't tell you what had really happened in Otwock. I'll tell you everything now, but when I'm finished you're going to wish you didn't know. It'll give you nightmares and you'll hate me."

"I want to know," Ruchele said. "And I'll never hate you for telling me the truth.

"Remember your words," I said. "The first time I left to look for Mamme, I didn't even know that she was in Otwock. Uncle Yankel had information about her but he wouldn't tell me a thing. My plan had been to travel to Warsaw to speak with Frau Liebe. It wasn't until I was on my way to the train station that I heard someone call my name. I turned around and there was Uncle Yankel running after me.

When he caught up to me, he was crying. I didn't know what was going on. He embraced me, kissed me, then he pulled out a slip of paper. 'This is where you'll find your mother,' he said. It was Itzhak Copperstein's name and his address in Otwock, 33 Reimanta Street. I kept thanking Uncle Yankel, but he didn't want my thanks. He knew how I was going to suffer because of that address.

"When I got to Otwock and found 33 Reimanta Street, I saw two strange women there. Both were in their thirties and both were very pretty. One was kind of plump; the other was thin and had a cloudy coating over one eye. They were the only people in the house and I was sure that Yankel had lied to me again. They asked me what did I want. I told them that I was looking for my mother. As soon as they heard that, they asked me if I was Roise's son. They not only knew who I was, they started to ask me questions about you and Babbe. They wanted to know whether you were also on your way to Otwock. As for Mamme, they told me that I would have to wait for her to come back. I spent the whole day with these two women but I couldn't find out who they were.

"Late in the afternoon, the door to the house opened and a man came in with an old woman who was carrying a baby. I didn't recognize her at first but that old woman was Mamme. She couldn't speak a word to me; she couldn't even look at me. Every time our eyes met, Mamme immediately covered her face with her hands and started to cry."

I felt Ruchele's grip on my arm stiffen.

"At night, Itzhak took me out for a walk. He told me that Mamme was upset because she hadn't seen me for so long. He invited me to move in with them. He even wanted to send for you. I asked him who the two women were. He told me they were his sisters. I found that very strange because none of them looked like each other.

"The next morning, after the two women had left for work, Mamme spoke to me for the first time. She asked me if I wanted to go to the market with her to buy groceries. I immediately said yes. When we were ready to go, she asked Itzhak if she could leave the baby in the house with him. For some reason that made him angry and he yelled at Mamme to take the child. She wheeled out an old broken-down baby carriage that squeaked like a dying cat and we left. On the street we finally talked a little. I asked her why she looked so awful.

"'I've fallen into hell' she said, 'and I can't get out anymore.'

"'What do you mean you've fallen into hell?'" I asked her.

63

But she started to cry again and couldn't speak. I saw how upset she was and I thought I had better give her time.

"We shopped without saying a word and walked back. As we approached the house, Mamme became very agitated. She told me to wait on the sidewalk with the baby carriage. She crept up to the door, carefully pushed it open a crack, and spied in. I couldn't understand what was going on. She told me to come in quickly with the baby. I wheeled the carriage into the house. Itzhak wasn't there. As soon as we were inside Mamme said to me, 'Save yourself! Get away from here. Don't stay another minute.' She pulled out her last few zlotys and shoved them at me. 'Take it,' she said. 'Go!'

"'Come with me!' I told her.

"'No, I can't,' she said. 'I can never leave again.'

"'I'm not going without you,' I told her.

"'Please save yourself, Schloimele,' she begged me. 'Save yourself while you still can. My life is over. If you stay too long you won't be able to get away from this hell either.'

"'Why not?' I asked.

"At that moment the door to the house crashed open and Itzhak Copperstein stumbled in dead-drunk, carrying an empty bottle of vodka. His clothes were filthy and stank of vomit. He started to curse us. He was going to kill us, he shouted. We watched him without moving. Suddenly he threw himself at us. Mamme grabbed the baby out of the carriage and told me to run out. We only escaped because the drunkard stumbled over a chair and fell. I ran down the street, but Mamme had stopped in front of the house. 'Run!' I screamed to her. 'Get away from there!'

"'I can't,' she said.

"I ran back and started to pull her by the arm. 'He'll kill you!' I pleaded with her. But she wouldn't move.

"'I wish he *had* killed me long ago already,' she said.

"From the windows around us, people were staring. In the meantime, Itzhak had quieted down in the house. 'Let me see if he has passed out,' Mamme said. She crept up to the door, and I followed her. She opened it a crack. I couldn't believe what I saw. Itzhak was sitting on the bed beating his head against the wall, tearing at his own flesh, until blood was running down his face and chest. We walked away from the door. I asked her why was he doing that? 'He's got enough reasons,' Mamme said and she started pleading for me to run away. I told her that she had to come with me, that I couldn't leave her there with that

64

drunkard. Finally, she couldn't stand the people from the other houses staring at us. 'Maybe he has beaten his brains out,' Mamme said. She went back to look. I followed her again. This time Itzhak caught us spying on him. He stumbled to his feet, cursing, and he lunged at us with the bottle in his hand. Mamme and I ran from the door. Itzhak came raging out of the house like a madman and started to chase after me down the street. If he hadn't been so drunk he would have caught me in a few steps and murdered me. Bur even drunk, he was right behind me and I had to keep running as fast as possible to escape. Suddenly, I felt a sharp pain in my right knee, as if it had cracked, and I went sprawling to the ground. In a blink, I saw Itzhak above me, lifting his boot to trample me. I rolled to my side. He just missed me, lost his balance, and fell, and I was able to scramble back up on my feet."

"I can't believe it," Ruchele whispered, a ghastly paleness on her face.

It hurt me to see the disturbed look in my sister's eyes, but I had no choice.

"I ran around the corner and hid in the first house I came across," I continued. "It belonged to an elderly couple. They found me crouching in their hallway and wanted to know what I was doing there. I told them that a drunk had appeared out of nowhere and started to chase me.

"'It must be that human garbage on Reimanta Street,' the husband said.

"'Those people frighten me,' the wife said.

"'Don't worry,' the husband said, 'the police will soon arrest the whole rotten gang.'

"I couldn't tell them that my mother lived with that human garbage.

"I spent about twenty minutes with this couple, until it was safe for me to go out again. After I left their house, I decided that no matter what Mamme said, I had to find her and drag her away. I went back to Reimanta Street. A big crowd had gathered in front of the drunk's house. I approached carefully. Itzhak was standing at the door crying and yelling, 'Come back, Roise! Come back, my Roisele, my darling, my only love!'

"Mamme had run away. My first thought was that she had finally had enough of that hell and had gone to the train station. I started to run. I was praying that I would find her there and that we could leave this nightmare together. But she wasn't at the train station. I went back into town. I walked up and down Otwock looking for Mamme until it grew dark and the streets emptied of people. I was heading back to Reimanta when I suddenly saw a drunk under a lamppost. I wasn't sure if it was Itzhak Copperstein, but I was paralyzed by fear. He was cursing, yelling at the lamppost; suddenly he smashed his bottle against it, and he started to cry and kiss the lamppost. I was so frightened by this insanity, I started to run again. I felt as if I had seen the Devil. I knew suddenly that Mamme was right, that if I went back to Reimanta Street, I would never leave again alive. I ran back to the train station. The clerk at the ticket window told me that the next train to Lublin wouldn't leave until the morning. I was exhausted. I sat down on a bench and fell asleep at once. I don't know how long I slept, but all of a sudden I felt someone pulling at me. I woke up. There were Itzhak's two women, the ones he called his sisters. They wanted to know why I had run away; they wanted me to go back with them. I told them that I had to return to Lublin, but they wouldn't leave alone. They each took hold of one of my arms and started to drag me back to the house. I had to do something quickly. There was a toilet in the station. I told them that I had to use the pot badly. They let me go into the small room. I locked the door at once and looked for a way to escape. There was a window, but it was small and high above my head. I jumped up on the sink, pulled myself up to the window, wriggled through it, and fell out, head first, on the grass in the back of the station. I quickly got up and ran into a nearby woods. I spent the night hidden behind a large tree, sleeping on the roots.

"A train whistle woke me up in the morning. I ran back to the station. After I had gotten on the train, before it could leave, I heard someone calling me on the platform. I looked out the window. It was Itzhak Copperstein. He was running around, looking into cars and shouting my name. As soon as I saw him head towards my car, I slipped to the floor and lay there. The other passengers gathered around me. They thought I was sick and some wanted to put me off the train before it got going. But finally the train started to move and that's how I got away.

"Not only is Itzhak Copperstein a thief and a drunkard, he has three other women besides Mamme and they all live together."

Ruchele gasped. "I can't believe it," she repeated weakly.

"Those two strange women weren't his sisters. When I met him here in Warsaw, he himself told me that they were his wives."

"Wives?" Ruchele asked. "How can that be?"

"The devil knows what they really are."

"How did you find Mamme again?" Ruchele asked.

"When I got here, I asked Frau Liebe if she knew what had happened to Mamme. 'You mother has fallen into the clutches of a horrible gang,' Liebe told me. 'They must have bewitched her. I know Roise well. She's a kind and decent person. She would never have become involved with them of her own free will. If I hadn't seen it with my own eyes I wouldn't have believe it possible. Don't go near those people, Schloime. If you see one of them, run away, run as if from a wildfire!' Liebe didn't want to tell me anything else.

"I had to beg her to tell me everything she knew. I told her that ever since Mamme had left us I had no peace. Liebe was very reluctant but I kept pressing her, and finally she went on. 'I'm only telling you this, Schloime,' she said, 'because I don't want the same thing that happened to your mother to happen to you.

"'A few months after your mother came to Warsaw, I was standing in the market, selling my fried fish, when I suddenly saw your mother with a strange man. Roise hadn't visited us for sometime, and I was glad to see her again. 'Roise!' I called. 'Roise!' She must have heard me, but she ran away without even looking at me.

"'I began to ask my friends at the market if they knew the man who had been with her. They knew him all too well. One friend told me that he's a thief and terrible drunkard. Another friend said that he lives with four women and beats them. She also said that the women steal for him. I was astonished when I heard these things. Another friend told me that his father and mother live in a cellar at 46 Stafke Street. They're well known in the neighborhood as thieves and beggars, my friend said. She even mentioned that Copperstein often comes to visit his parents and brings his women with him.'

"As soon as I heard this from Frau Liebe, I knew where I had to go. I didn't say a word to anyone, but every Sabbath after I left Liebe's apartment, I went to Stafke Street. My plan was that when I saw Mamme, I would run up to her and try to get her away from Itzhak and his gang. Saturday after Saturday I went to Stafke Street but I never saw Mamme. A whole summer and fall went by like this. One evening at the beginning of winter, as I was going back to Mr. Nagil's, where I was working then, I passed a pretty, plump woman. Something about her struck me as familiar. She looked at me and smiled. 'Schloime?' she asked. At the same moment I realized that she was one of the two women who had been living with Itzhak in Otwock. 'Does your mother know that you're in Warsaw?' she asked me. 'Come with me and I'll take you to her.' After what had happened in Otwock and after everything Liebe had told me, I was afraid to go anywhere with this woman. I asked her to tell Mamme that I wanted to speak to her. 'I'll wait here on the street,' I said. The woman told me that if I didn't go with her, I wouldn't see my mother at all. I had no choice. She grabbed my hand at once and took me into No. 46 Stafke Street. It was a horrible, broken-down building, the worst slum I've ever seen. She led me down pitch black stairs to a cellar. When she opened the door to the Coppersteins' apartment, I almost fainted from the smell. In a dark room I saw about ten or fifteen people. Some of them looked like murderers and thieves, some of them, without arms and legs, looked like beggars. One of them wasn't even a full man, just half a body propped up on a little wooden platform with wheels. I immediately recognized Itzhak Copperstein. And in the middle of this gang, I saw Mamme. She looked even worse than in Otwock."

Ruchele was crying. I could barely continue to speak. I stopped to collect myself and went on.

"A little boy was clinging to Mamme's skirt. She also had a bundle of rags on her lap, another baby. As soon as she saw me, she started to cry. I asked her to come out. 'Mamme, I want to speak to you,' I said. 'Can you come out?'

'I can't come out now,' she said. 'Tell me where you live and I'll come to visit you.'

"I wanted to tell her, but I was afraid to let Itzhak and his gang know my address. I was sure that if they knew it, they would rob the house and kill me. When I saw that I wouldn't be able to speak to Mamme I told her that I would come back the next Sabbath. As soon as I started to leave, Itzhak Copperstein jumped up and said 'Wait. Where are you going?' I turned and tried to run up the step but I tripped and he caught my arm with a strong grip. I was doomed. He kept holding on to me as we walked up the steps. But when we were out on the street he let me go. I started to walk away. He followed me. He said he wanted to apologize for what had happened in Otwock. It wasn't his fault. He wanted to explain everything to me. I was convinced that he was trying to lure me into joining his gang, but I was also very curious. I stopped and I let him talk.

"He grew up in Lublin and became a shoemaker. He told me that when he was a young man, he couldn't find work because of his parents' reputation as thieves. When he got married to his first wife, he said, they were forced to steal to live. After a while they had a little daughter and he wanted to stop being a thief. But by then his wife had gotten used to stealing and she didn't want to stop. She had a partner, another woman, and the two of them kept on pulling off jobs. One day they slipped up. The partner managed to escape but his wife got caught by the police. She was arrested and sentenced to jail.

"His wife's partner came to Itzhak and offered to help take care of his child. She said that she felt guilty for what had happened and wanted to help him out. Soon he was living with this second woman. When his first wife came out of jail, the second woman wouldn't leave; so they decided to live together, all three of them. The women started to steal again. The next time they got caught both women ended up in jail. Itzhak got involved with a third woman. When the first two came out of jail, the third one wouldn't leave. Now, all three women decided to live with him. Eventually he left the three women and came to Warsaw. The women let him move. When he met Mamme, Itzhak was living alone and she had no idea of his past.

"He told me that he and Mamme fell in love and were going to get married. But when the other three women found out, they all came after him to Warsaw. By then it was too late for Mamme to leave him. She was already expecting his child...."

"It can't be," Ruchele said and began to cry.

"Ruchele," I said, "forgive me for hurting you like this. I only told you because I want you to understand how hopeless Mamme's situation is. I'll tell you something else. I'm afraid that once Itzhak sees you, he won't let you go. He could drag you into his gang in the same way he dragged in Mamme. Look, he even tried to get me to join his gang. We have to stay away from them. We have to forget about Mamme and go on with our own lives."

Ruchele walked like a blind person. I felt very sad for my sister. I knew well the pain she was feeling. I had lived with it for four years and now my sister would have to share it with me. We walked back to Ksiel and Lotte's house without another word between us.

At 30 Electoralna Street, I said good night to Ruchele and began to walk back to Twarda.

"Schloime," Ruchele called me suddenly. "Wait."

I turned around. "What is it?" I asked

"I want to see her," Ruchele said.

"Even after everything I told you?"

"I can save her."

69

"Are you crazy? Didn't you hear a word I said. Nobody can do anything for her. Not even you."

"Together," Ruchele said, "we can save her. I know that we can."

Ruchele's Hopes

RUCHELE'S FOOLISH HOPES that she could rescue our mother affected me strongly. I knew how painful the meeting with Mamme, into which my sister was rushing, would be. I had gone through two such useless meetings myself. And yet, as I lay on the folding bed in the dark workshop, I found Ruchele's hopes arousing my own. Who knew? Maybe Ruchele could bring Mamme back to her senses? Maybe Mamme would realize how much her daughter needed her? Or maybe seeing both of her children together, maybe that more than anything, would remind Mamme of what she had lost and make her come back to us? Could it be, after all, that Ruchele had been flown to Twarda Street on the wings of an angel?

These thoughts kept me up late into the night.

I woke up as light from the street seeped through the thick green curtain into the back of the store. Fine specks of dust floated in the air. I remembered that soon I would have to go back to 46 Stafke Street and confront Itzhak Copperstein and his gang. Worst of all, I would have to see my mother among them. I was tired, but I couldn't go back to sleep.

I folded the bed and pushed it back against the wall. After breakfast, I put on my best clothes. As I was preparing to leave, I recalled the darkness on the stairs leading to the Copperstein's cellar and I made sure I had a small box of matches. Finally I locked the store and began my long walk. Stafke was a short street in the northern end of the Jewish Quarter, only a block away from Muranovska, where Frau Liebe lived.

It was a warm morning in May. There had been a short rainfall at dawn. As the sun dried the puddles and a breeze stirred the air, the sweet smell of the blooming trees spread across the city.

Out of habit I walked along Zamenhoff, the street I used every Sabbath on my way to visit Frau Liebe. I was already on Mila, just a block away from Muranovska when I realized that I couldn't risk being seen by anyone who knew me. I quickly turned left and walked to Smotcha, a street parallel to Zamenhoff. I was soon on the corner of Stafke. When I saw the building with the black front gates where the Copperstein's lived, my heart began to hammer. Before fear could stop me, I crossed the street and walked into the courtyard of No. 46. The three story building, made of mournful gray stone, was old but not quite the slum I remembered. I went in. In the lobby the slats of the wooden floor, which I had expected to be rotted, were only worn. The walls, which I thought were scarred with deep cracks, had merely lost their brown paint in spots.

I pulled out the box of matches and opened the door leading down to the cellar. The stairs, however, were not dark; daylight seemed to be flooding in from somewhere below. As I walked down the wooden staircase, voices of men drifted up. *Itzhak's gang of thieves* was my first thought. But a surprise awaited me at the bottom of the steps. To the right, spilling out of an open apartment, I saw a group of men smoking and chatting; a sign over the door said, "Shoemaker's Guild." I looked at the hands of the men; their blackened, cut fingers were proof that these were indeed shoemakers. To the left of where I stood, I saw an air-shaft, through which sunlight and fresh air poured into a corner of the basement. Someone had strung a rope under the light and had hung clothes up to dry. I took a few steps and I was at the Coppersteins' door. My hand shook as I knocked. I drew courage from the presence of the shoemakers. If I screamed for help those men would come to my rescue.

"It's open," a man's voice said from inside the apartment.

I braced myself for the repulsive sight that awaited me and turned the door handle. To my astonishment, all I saw was an elderly couple in a poor but neat room, sitting at a table, drinking tea.

The man, in his seventies, wearing a trimmed white beard, put his glass of tea down. "What do you want?" he asked. I recognized at once Itzhak Copperstein's features on the old man, the long, hard face, the deep set eyes under the heavy brow, the hollow cheeks.

"Moishe, do you know who this is?" the wife asked, squinting her eyes as she examined me. She was in her sixties, a woman with long, iron-gray hair and a lined, leathery face. "That's Roise's son."

"I'm looking for my mother," I said.

"She may come later," the old man said. "We can tell her that you're looking for her. Where can she find you?"

Even though the Coppersteins didn't look as menacing as I had expected, I still didn't trust them. "I'll find her myself," I said as I began to back out of the room.

"How are you going to find her?" the man asked. "Do you know where she lives?"

"No," I said.

"Falinitsa," he said. "What's the address?" he asked his wife.

"Luma Street, No. 16."

I repeated the address to myself so I wouldn't forget it and left. Thankfully, no one followed me this time as I ran up the stairs and out of the building into the street.

Although I had never heard of Falinitsa, I guessed that it couldn't be far from Warsaw. I decided to go into Praga to the train station and find out how much a ticket to Falinitsa would cost.

A fire-bright red trolley came clanging along as I walked across the Kerbedia Bridge. It reminded me of one of my first sights of Warsaw, which I had had from the arriving boat, floating up the Vistula River. It had been the first trolley I ever saw and it was crossing one of Warsaw's bridges, spraying sparks into the air like fireworks.

On the other side of the Bridge, walking in a crowd of rosy Christian faces, I felt like a stranger. I looked for a Jew. I saw a man in black gabardine, with a thick beard and sidelocks and I asked him for directions to the train station. I rarely crossed into the Praga suburb. Here all the stores were open on the Sabbath and business went on as usual. I was soon inside the gigantic, dark bubble of the station. Every train that rolled in or out filled the air with a thunderous rumble. I felt the noise in my whole body.

"How much is a ticket to Falinitsa?" I asked the clerk at the ticket window. My less-than-perfect Polish wasn't helped by the noise of the station.

"Falinitsa?" the clerk repeated.

I nodded.

Immediately, the clerk shoved a ticket at me through the little window. "One zloty," he said.

"Where is the train?" I asked as I paid him.

He pointed to the gates at the other end of the station and spoke quickly. The only word I understood was, "Hurry!"

I ran to the gates, showed my ticket to the guard, and a few minutes

73

later I was sitting on a train that was rolling loudly out of Praga.

As I stared out the window, I wondered about the sharp difference between my memories of the Coppersteins and what I had just seen. Could they have changed so drastically in the year-and-a-half since I had been there? It was obvious that the Coppersteins weren't well off, but they didn't seem to be the horrible beggars and thieves I imagined them to be. Even the building at 46 Stafke Street, which I remembered as a run-down slum, was no different from the building in which Frau Liebe lived. Was it possible that I had made the same mistakes in judging Mamme's situation? Was Ruchele right? Had I given up too easily?

The ride across farm fields, through small villages, lasted less than half an hour. I got off at a small train station in a suburban village. Among the few people who also got off, I noticed a middle-aged man carrying a Yiddish book. I approached him and asked if he knew where Luma Street was. He told me to follow him.

We walked to the front of the train station, onto a dirt road. After a short distance, the man pointed me straight ahead and said, "Keep walking until you get to a hill. You'll see a field and some scattered houses. That's Luma."

The street on which I began to walk, with its low cottages and gardens, reminded me of Otwock. And just as in Otwock, when I came to the end of the street, I suddenly found myself facing a familiar poverty—a small hill, beyond it a torn up field, and a handful of old, two-story brick houses. From a distance they seemed deserted. I turned off the paved road. The walk on the muddy earth was difficult. If Itzhak Copperstein started to chase me here, I would never be able to escape him. I read the crudely painted numbers on the doors. I crossed a ditch, walked up a small hill, and finally, isolated from the other houses, I found number 16.

The windows on the first floor were boarded up. I looked up. There were no boards covering the windows on the second floor. Suddenly I heard the cry of a baby coming from the house. I listened carefully. I heard the voice of another child. Could Itzhak be away? Could Mamme be alone inside? I walked up to the gray door on which the paint was blistering and peeling off. I pushed it lightly and it creaked open. I entered a small hall. The door to the ground apartment was padlocked. A narrow stairway leading to the second floor stretched in front of me.

I decided to go up. The creaking of the stairs under my feet sounded like the muffled cries of children. As I reached the top, I saw that the door was open.

"Come back here!" a girl suddenly yelled at a small boy. She grabbed him and her dress went flying up as she swung the boy around the room. He laughed and screeched with glee. A baby in the apartment let out a wail.

I took a step through the door.

"Who are you!" the startled girl screamed when she saw me. "Get away from me!" Clutching the boy to herself, she flung open the drawer on the kitchen table and pulled out a sharp knife. "I'll stab you!" she said pointing the knife at my chest.

"I'm just looking for my mother," I said, backing away.

"Who are you? What do you want here?" She was about sixteen years old, a sturdy girl, with massive calves above men's boots. Her features were coarse—thick lips, pug nose, small eyes; her stringy black hair fell across her face.

"I'm Schloime. I'm looking for my mother."

"Who's your mother?" she asked, still suspicious of me.

"Roise," I said.

The girl suddenly let out a shrill laugh and threw the knife on the table. "I thought you were going to rape me," she said, putting the small boy back down on the floor. "Come in. I hope I didn't scare you too much. Do you know who this is?" she asked, pointing to the boy who now was clinging to her legs. "Your little brother Hershele." She bent down to pick up the boy again. "Come here, Hershele, and give your brother a kiss."

The little boy squirmed out of her hands. "No!" he shouted, ran off to the other room, and slammed the door shut. The noise frightened the whimpering baby and set it to a full-throated shrieking.

"Look what you did now!" the girl screamed as she banged open the door and ran into the other room. She came out a moment later holding a smaller boy, who clung to her neck.

"Do you know who this is?" she asked, showing me the sleepy, cranky child. "It's your other brother, Moishele."

A year and a half earlier, I had seen my mother with a small baby wrapped in rags at the Coppersteins. It had been this boy.

The girl pointed to another boy who had come out and was clinging to her leg and said, "And this is my own brother, Shmuelke."

Another boy, about seven years old, stuck his head out into the kitchen. "And that's Beirel. Khanka's boy," the girl said.

"And who are you?" I asked her.

"I'm Itzhak's daughter, Mattel."

"Where is my mother?" I asked.

"You missed them. They went to Warsaw about a half hour ago. Do you know your way around Warsaw?"

"I live there."

"They're at my grandparents, on Stafke Street, No. 46."

"I just came from there."

She looked at me and gave a scornful laugh. "Then you know about them?" Mattel asked.

I nodded.

I saw a look of disdain and sadness on the girl's face. She put the boy who had been clinging to her on the floor next to some painted wooden blocks. "Don't bother me now, Moishele," she said.

"My mother is in jail again," Mattel said. "If not for Malke and your mother the children would have starved to death long ago."

"Who's Malke?" I asked.

"She's the only one without children," Mattel said. "She must be the stupidest of them all to keep hanging on to my father. She could at least escape. She doesn't have any children of her own to worry about. But she worries about the boys. She used to take care of me too. But now I can take care of myself...I only come back sometimes to visit my brother. I don't have a job right now that's why I'm here."

Listening to Mattel speak I realized that all the incredible things her father had told me a year and a half earlier were true. He did have four wives, and the wives, except for my mother, were thieves, constantly getting caught by the police and being thrown in jail.

"I have to go," I said to Mattel.

Anger began to boil in my blood again as I remembered how that loathsome man had deceived my poor mother. I was appalled at myself. How could I have given up on trying to save Mamme? Ruchele was right, we had to try again. Together we had to do all in our power to drag Mamme out of this cesspool.

"Wait," Mattel said. "I'll walk with you to the train station. Beirel!" she screamed. "Come here."

The oldest of the boys came out of the other room again followed by Hershele, my half-brother.

"Look after the children. I have to go out. Don't do any mischief or I'll beat you to death."

"Do you really live in Warsaw?" Mattel asked me as we walked across the hill towards the road. "What kind of work do you do?"

"I'm a tailor," I said.

"A tailor?"

"Yes," I said. "Why do you ask?"

"Just so...I'll tell you later, at the train station."

I didn't know what to make of her strange remark. "What about you?" I asked. "Where did you work?"

"I used to work in a restaurant," she said, "for one of my father's friends, Mayer. He used to be a thief, until he gave it up and opened the restaurant. Most of his customers were his old friends, other thieves. They boozed all night long, carrying on like idiots, fighting with knives. They wouldn't leave me alone. Any time I passed them carrying a loaded tray, their dirty hands crept under my skirt and grabbed at my flesh. If it hadn't been for the boss, they would have raped me long ago. I had to quit that hellhole."

We walked in silence. Near the train station, Mattel said, "I'm just waiting for my mother to get out of the slammer. I won't let her go back to pulling jobs again. I'm taking her and my brother and we're getting out. We'll go anywhere my eyes lead me. Let that drunkard hang himself together with all of his wives. I don't mean your mother," Mattel said at once. "I feel sorry for her too. But I hate my father. He's a bastard."

At the train station, Mattel asked me if I had to buy a ticket. I showed her my round trip stub. We sat down on a bench to wait along with a few other people.

"What were you going to tell me?" I asked.

"I'll tell you when the train comes," Mattel said. She got up from the bench, looked down the track, came back, and sat down next to me without saying anything.

"Can you leave the children alone for so long?" I asked her.

"Don't worry about them," she said. "They're used to it."

Suddenly we heard the train whistle.

"So, what did want to tell me?" I asked.

"Wait until the train gets here," Mattel said, watching the train as it stopped with a roar.

A few people got off and the few who had been waiting got on.

"I have to go. What were you going to tell me?"

"Get on the steps of the train," Mattel said.

I walked up a step and turned around. "Well?"

"I like you," Mattel said taking a step back. "If you want, you can come and see me again." Then she quickly turned around and began to run away.

I walked into the car and sat down at a window. Mattel, who had stopped near the entrance to the small station, was waving to me. I waved back until the train started to move.

As I watched the farm fields and the scattered villages move in the distance, I felt sad for Mattel. I was flattered that she liked me, but I didn't want to see her again. I knew that she and her mother would never escape from her father. Mattel's mother was Itzhak's first wife and Itzhak himself told me how she had refused to leave him even after she came out of jail and found him living with another woman. Even when he was living with three other women, Mattel's mother still continued to love that thief and drunkard.

It was already midday when I returned to Praga. The sun beat down on me as I quickly dodged through the thick crowds filling the streets. Overheated and sweating in my suit, I crossed the Kerbedia Bridge back into the Jewish Quarter. My determination to save Mamme grew with my every step.

On Stafke Street, I went immediately into the courtyard at No. 46, and without hesitation I ran down the stairs to the Coppersteins' basement apartment.

This time I heard voices inside. I pushed the door open. The conversation stopped as everyone in the apartment looked at me. I saw the same ugly group of people sitting there that I had seen the first time. But now, perhaps because I wasn't as afraid of them, they didn't seem nearly so menacing. The palest face in the crowd belonged to my mother. She was sitting between Itzhak Copperstein and the plump woman, one of the four wives.

For once, my mother looked at me and didn't cry. The grief which I had seen on her face the other two times had by now hardened itself on her features. I didn't think she was capable of ever smiling again. She looked at me with her pale green eyes, drained of any spark of life, and the sight of my mother, so devastated, began immediately to tear at my heart.

"Have you been looking for me?" my mother asked in a hollow voice.

"Ruchele is in Warsaw and she wants to see you," I said.

"Ruchele?" Mamme asked, her voice choking, as if the word had been a red coal burning its way out of her throat. "Where is she?"

I noticed the silent men who were staring at me and I remembered that I had to protect Ruchele.

78

"Can you come out?" I asked my mother.

"What does she have to come out for?" Itzhak Copperstein said. "You come in and sit down for a while."

I looked at him closely now. I realized that he was just a middle-aged man with the washed-out, sagging face of a drunkard. For the first time, I wasn't afraid of him.

"Mamme, can you come out," I repeated.

"Why are you so stubborn?" Itzhak asked angrily.

"I can come out," my mother said, standing up.

"Sit down, Roise," Itzhak barked, reaching to pull my mother down by her arm.

But Mamme pulled her arm away. "Let go of me," she said.

Itzhak suddenly gritted his teeth and tensed his jaws so strongly to keep from shouting, I thought his face was going to fly apart.

Mamme pulled her shawl about her and we walked up the stairs together. She had finally stood up to Itzhak. In silence we walked out of the building, but as soon as we came out into the sunny courtyard, my mother buried her face in her shawl, slumped back against the door, and began to cry. "What am I doing? My daughter can't see me like this."

I quickly looked back into the building to make sure that Itzhak wasn't coming up the steps. "You can leave with me, now," I urged her. "Run away from them, Mamme."

I took hold of my mother's elbow, put my arm around her to keep her from falling, and I began to lead her away. She was so thin and frail, I felt as if I were holding a small bundle of dried twigs.

My mother allowed me to guide her across the courtyard. Each time I glanced back I expected to see Itzhak Copperstein running out after us. I was ready to fight him, now. This time, no matter what happened, I wouldn't let him stop us. When we came to the black gates leading out of the courtyard it was my mother who stopped.

"Where am I going?" she said in a daze. "I can't leave. I have to go back."

"You can't go back!" I said to her. "They're killing you. How can you live with these people?"

"They're all I deserve. Let me go."

She struggled with me, but I tried to hold on to my mother. "We need you, Mamme. Ruchele is in Warsaw and I don't know what to do with her. You have to help me."

"Look at me, Schloime. What can I do for her? You know what's become of me. Please, don't let her see me like this. I'll drag her into the same hell."

"She *wants* to see you. Don't you understand? She doesn't stop asking about you."

"No, no. Have pity on me and on her." My mother pulled herself out of my arms, turned around, and began to walk across the courtyard towards No. 46. "I have to go back," she repeated in her dazed tone. "Tell my daughter that her mother is dead."

Desperate now to keep my mother from returning to Itzhak Copperstein and his gang, I blurted out to her, "Babbe died."

My mother stopped. "When?" she asked, in a broken whisper.

"A month ago."

"May she rest in peace."

After a long silence, my mother asked, "Did I kill her? Did she find out about me?"

"No," I said. "I never told her. Nobody told her. She didn't know anything. She died from a bad cold."

"Then there is a merciful God, somewhere," she said. And with her back still turned to me, I heard Mamme whisper, "*Yiskadal V'yiskadash....*" for her dead mother. "*Yiskadal V'yiskadash....*" Mamme repeated the only two words of the Kaddish she knew. "*Yiskadal V'yiskadash...*"

When my mother was silent again, I said, "We're alone now, Ruchele and I. That's why we need you. "

"Why didn't Ruchele stay in Lublin with Simke and Yankel?" my mother asked.

"Yankel wanted to force Ruchele to marry Heniach."

"But she's just a child," my mother said. "How could he think of marrying her off?"

"Yankel is stupid and stubborn and after Babbe died he thought he could do whatever he wanted with Ruchele. She wrote to me that she couldn't stay in Lublin anymore and she asked me to help her. I spoke to Liebe and she helped us."

"God Bless, that Liebe," my mother said. "She's truly a guardian angel."

"Mamme, we can't depend on Liebe forever," I said. "We need you."

"What do you want me to do?"

"Come and live with us," I said.

"Where?" she asked.

"You can stay with me. I have a room in the back of the store where

I work."

"I have two small babies, Schloime," my mother said. "I can't leave them behind."

"Then take them with you."

"And how will I feed them?"

"We'll help you, Ruchele and I."

"I have cursed my life, and now do you want me to curse yours and Ruchele's also? I can't do that. Go away, Schloime. Tell Ruchele that you found out that I died. She'll cry and grieve for a while but she'll get over it and go on with her life. Now I have to go back."

I ran in front of my mother. "Don't go back to them!" I pleaded with her.

"I don't have a choice anymore," she said and began to walk back into the building.

"I'm going to get Ruchele," I said.

My mother stopped again. "No! I beg you Schloimele, no!"

"Don't go back into that cellar!" I said. "I'm coming back as soon as I can with Ruchele."

I turned around before my mother could stop me and started to run.

I flew over the streets of Warsaw. I didn't know what miracle I expected Ruchele to perform with our mother, but if my sister hadn't pushed me to find Mamme again, I wouldn't have found the tatter of hope that was like a sail sweeping me now towards Electoralna.

Ruchele was eating her lunch when I barged into Ksiel and Lotte's apartment. Luckily my sister was alone in the kitchen. I motioned for her to keep quiet and follow me out the door. She knew immediately that I had something important to tell her and without a question she got up and left with me.

On the street, I asked my sister, "Do you still want to see Mamme?"

"Yes! Where is she?"

"Not far. Come, let's walk fast. See if you can convince her to come away with us. I tried, but she won't listen to me."

"Let me talk to her," Ruchele said.

Ruchele recognized Muranovska Street as soon as we approached it. "Isn't this where Liebe lives?"

"Yes, watch out that someone doesn't see us."

"Are we still far?"

"It's around the corner from Liebe's apartment."

On Stafke Street, I pointed to the large gates black gates of No. 46.

"There's the building."

"Is that where the drunk's parents live?" Ruchele asked. "The cellar with all the thieves and murderers?"

"Yes," I said.

"I don't want to go down there," my sister said. "I'm afraid."

"Don't worry. I'll go down and call Mamme. You wait outside the gates."

We crossed the street. Ruchele stopped at the black gates. I was about to go in when I noticed our mother approaching along the street. I looked back at Ruchele. My sister looked at me. I was sure that she could see our mother past me, but Ruchele still didn't seem to understand why I didn't go into the building. By now our mother was next to us. The shock on my sister's face as she began to recognize the thin, worn out, gray woman in front of her suddenly made me realize that the last time my sister had seen her mother, five years earlier, Mamme had herself been a young, pretty woman with thick black hair that framed her face and made her green eyes sparkle. And when I turned to look at my mother, I saw in her face the shock of seeing instead of the ten year old girl she had left in Lublin a lost image of her own self as she had looked just a few years earlier. A moment later my mother and sister weeping bitterly embraced each other so strongly that ten men couldn't have torn them apart. I had always believed that I was the closest person in the world to my mother. But now, watching Mamme and Ruchele clasping each other, and kissing each others faces and tears, I felt jealous. *I* hadn't been embraced or kissed like that after I had risked my life to find Mamme in Otwock. When she saw me for the first time, in that God forsaken little shack on Reimanta Street, all Mamme could do was stumble away from me and sob with shame. With a torn heart, I patted and caressed my mother's and Ruchele's backs to help them calm down a little.

"Are you sick, Mamme?" Ruchele asked through her tears.

The question only made our mother cry harder.

"Come with us, Mamme," Ruchele said and began to lead our mother away.

Mamme followed briefly then tore herself out of Ruchele's arms and ran into the courtyard.

"Mamme!" Ruchele cried as she chased after her.

I ran after my sister as Mamme disappeared into the building. I caught up to my sister and took hold of her hand. I couldn't bear to look anymore at this tragedy. I began to pull Ruchele away from there.

On our way back, we didn't say a word to each other. When we were near the building where my sister was living I asked Ruchele to keep her courage up and to forget about our mother's bleak fate. And I walked away to be alone.

Shifra

RUCHELE AND I PAID DEARLY for the hopes my sister stirred up of saving our mother. On Sunday morning, I didn't even feel like getting up. I finally forced myself to get dressed only because I didn't want the Blumensteins to find me in bed and start to ask me questions.

That whole day, however, I couldn't eat anything. I bought myself a pack of Wandas in the morning and smoked one cigarette after another. Since it was Sunday and we couldn't keep the front door open, there wasn't any ventilation in the workshop. By the middle of the day, Mrs. Blumenstein complained that I was trying to choke her. I realized that the smoke in the back room was so thick we could hardly see each other. I put my cigarette out. My head hurt from all the smoking but my grief was still raging like a fire.

At night, after the Blumensteins left, I began to smoke again. I smoked cigarette after cigarette until I made myself sick. As I sat with my head on the table, I remembered the first time I had seen my mother in Warsaw. I had been so upset, I didn't care what happened to me, caught a bad cold, and almost died. For two weeks I had been a burden to Liebe, who had to nurse me back to life. And then, as if that weren't enough misery, I lost my job. I couldn't let that happen again.

On Monday I forced myself to eat. For the rest of that week I kept reminding myself of the advice I had given my sister; I had to try to forget about our mother.

I could well imagine what torture poor Ruchele was going through, but I didn't know how I could make her feel better. It wasn't until late Sabbath afternoon that I felt well enough myself to visit her.

I found Ksiel and Lotte and their three children in the kitchen when I opened the door of their apartment. I asked them if my sister was at home. Ksiel told me that Elke and Tsutel had come by and had taken her to Muranovska. As I was about to leave, Lotte said that Ruchele was not her usual self. She had been so quiet and withdrawn the whole week, they were afraid she might be sick.

I promised Lotte I would try to find out what was wrong with my sister and I left. But there was nothing to find out. I had tried to protect Ruchele for as long as I could. I had warned her. She wouldn't listen to me. Now, Ruchele had to struggle with the bitter truth, just like me.

When I walked into Liebe's, I saw my sister sitting with Frau Liebe, having a quiet conversation. Ruchele's face looked pale and sad. On the bed, which Elke and Tsutel shared, and which served as a sofa during the day, the two sisters were playing a game of checkers. Everyone else seemed to be out.

"Good *Shabbes*, Schloime," Liebe said. "Where have you been? We've been waiting for you the whole day. Aren't the boys with you?"

"No. Why should they be with me?"

"They went on a walk to Twarda Street to invite you over. We didn't see you last week and we got worried. What is the matter with you and Ruchele? You both look so unhappy? Did you two have a fight?"

"No, of course not. I've just been very busy at work."

I noticed that Tsutel and Elke had stopped playing their game and were watching me.

"Tell them already, Mother," Tsutel said. "If you don't, I will."

"I'm going, Tsutel," Liebe said as she got up from her chair. "Just give me a moment." She went into her small bedroom where her sick husband Hertzke lay resting.

"Do you know what's going on?" I asked my sister.

"It's some kind of surprise," Ruchele said. "We've been waiting for you."

Tsutel and Elke smiled but said nothing.

Liebe came back holding an envelope in her hand.

"We received a letter this week," Liebe said. "It's from Russia, and it's addressed to a certain Schloime Renglich."

"Tatte," Ruchele said. For a moment the sadness lifted from her face. "Read it."

I tore open the envelope and pulled out a coarse sheet of paper.

"Dear Children," I read aloud. "Forgive me for being out of touch for so long.

"My son, you want to know if I still remember you and your sister. How can you even ask such a question? I have never stopped thinking about you. You can't imagine how many times I wondered why I never received a letter from you.

"For many years now I have been writing to Khumale, sending her money to give to you. My sister assured me that she was providing everything you needed. In every one of my letters, I asked Khumale to send me your photographs. She kept promising in the next letter. Now I realize that my own sister was lying to me.

"As you can see I have not forgotten about you. What happened was not all my fault. It was our miserable fate that the war dragged me away from you. But you can believe me when I tell you that I've spent many nights awake thinking and worrying about you. Believe me, it's not with ink that I'm writing this letter to you, but with tears. I have a proposal to make to you, my children. I know that your lives have been difficult and that I am in part responsible for that. If you will allow me I want to make it up to you. How would you like to come and live with me? Nothing would make me happier than to embrace you again and to have you near me. I wait to hear from you. Your father, Baruch."

Ruchele, pressing her handkerchief to her lips, was crying. Liebe and her daughters said nothing while my sister and I recuperated from the shock of the letter.

At last, after all the years of hoping that our father would come back from the war and rescue us from our poverty, after we had given up all hope of ever seeing him again, here he was.

"A miracle..." Liebe said softly, "It's a miracle. I remember during the war, living on the Tchurtic, your poor mother and I waiting for them to come back from the war. My Mendel, may he rest in peace..." Liebe couldn't hold back her own tears remembering her dead husband, the father of Tsutel, Elke, and Leibel.

"Let's not be sad, Mamme," Elke said. "Not tonight."

"You're right," Liebe said, wiping her tears away with the palm of her hand. "I was praying that this would be a letter with good news. Thank God."

Nachme, Khiel, and Yoinne came back from their walk as Liebe, helped by Ruchele, served us tea and cookies. Yoinne said that Leibel had walked with them halfway to Twarda and then had gone off to see his girlfriend. When the boys heard that I had already opened the letter and that it had been in fact from our father, they asked me to read it aloud again. And when they heard of our father's invitation that we come and live with him, Nachme and Khiel were quite enthusiastic about life in Russia. Yoinne making moon eyes at Elke said that nothing could tear him away from Warsaw.

It wasn't until that evening, when I was walking Ruchele back to Electoralna Street, that I had a chance to speak to her alone. The first thing I asked her was, "Do you want to move to Russia?"

"Anywhere. I don't care anymore."

"I know how much it hurts you."

"How could Mamme let that happen to her?"

"I told you, Itzhak trapped her with his lies."

"I'm so ashamed. When Tsutel and Elke came over today I wished the ground would open under my feet and swallow me up. Instead I had to act as if nothing was wrong. Does everyone at Liebe's know what happened to Mamme?"

"No, I think only Liebe knows. I don't believe she told her children. It hurt her just as much as it hurts us. The only reason Liebe even told me anything was to warn me to stay away from Itzhak and his gang."

"If Liebe was such a good friend to Mamme why didn't she stop her from destroying her life?"

"If only Liebe had known. If only Mamme had told Liebe that she had met Itzhak Copperstein. But Mamme didn't say a word. And when she disappeared, no one knew why or where. By then, it was too late anyway. Mamme was already pregnant...."

We walked in silence while Ruchele absorbed my painful words.

"Don't let it eat you up," I said. "Be careful. I got so sick the last time I saw Mamme, I almost died."

"When are you going to write to Tatte?"

"Tonight."

"Good. Tell him I can't wait to see him."

That night, when I wrote our father, I told him that we had not received a grosch of the money he had sent for us over the years. We didn't even know he had written. But we were eager to see him and if he could help us, we would very much like to live with him. I also asked my father to write a few words to Frau Liebe and her family for all the help they had given us in Warsaw.

The letter from our father helped Ruchele and me recover somewhat from our meeting with our mother. The following Sabbath, when we saw each other at Liebe's, I told Ruchele that I had sent out my answer to Tatte. In the evening, when I walked Ruchele back to Electoralna Street, neither one of us mentioned Mamme.

It took a while but late in the summer on a Sabbath, Ruchele and I had another pleasant surprise waiting for us at Liebe's, a second letter from our father. Again, I read it aloud for everyone.

"Dear Children, I have been busy preparing to bring you over and I wanted to have some concrete news before I wrote. Now I can tell you that I have been to Moscow and have completed the necessary formalities. I am only waiting for the authorities to send me the permit for your entry to this country. As soon as I receive it, I will mail it to you. When you get the permit, go to your Emigration Bureau and ask them to allow you to leave Poland to join your father. It may take awhile before you get the Polish permit, but let me know as soon as you have it. I will wait for you at the Russian-Polish border.

"To the precious Frau Liebe and her family, I send my deepest thanks for all the help they have given to my children. I hope that someday I can meet this good family and thank them in person.

"I cannot wait to see you, my children. While your papers are being processed, I beg you, send me your photographs. I kiss you a thousand times and wait to see you soon. Your father, Baruch."

Ruchele gave me a pretty photograph of herself in one of Mamme's dresses. It had obviously been taken recently in Warsaw. I asked Ruchele how much it cost her. She told me that a friend of hers from the club, a photographer, had taken it and given it to her as a gift. I was disturbed at the way Ruchele was making friends with the men from this organization, but I knew that I would only start a fight if I said anything. I hoped that we would soon be out of Warsaw. In Russia, living with our father, my sister would have to behave herself.

On Monday evening after work, I dressed up in my suit and went to have my picture taken. When I wrote my next letter to our father I included our photographs. I told him again that we couldn't wait to be with him. There was much I wanted to talk to him about.

Three months passed before all the papers arrived from Russia. Following my father's instructions, I went to the Polish Emigration Bureau with these documents and asked for permission to leave Poland with my sister. The officials at the Bureau took my papers and said they would let me know through the mail when I should come back.

While Ruchele and I waited for the great change in our lives, our reunion with our father in Russia, we saw many changes in the lives of our friends.

The first was that Yoinne Schneidleider married Elke. Since they couldn't afford an apartment, the newlyweds continued to live at Liebe's. Yoinne had been able to manage on his low wages while he was a bachelor, but now with a wife, and children soon on the way, he had to earn a better living. Thanks to Elke's push and Frau Liebe's help, Yoinne went into business for himself. He quit his job at the factory, bought himself a sewing machine and set up a workshop in the living room of the basement apartment.

After the wedding, Elke also changed and made it clear that she wasn't happy to share the small apartment with so many people. I expected Frau Liebe to stand up to Elke, but she didn't. It soon became clear that Frau Liebe had given the living room over to her married daughter to do with it as she pleased. Khiel and Nachme quickly rented a room together and moved out. Leibel announced that he was getting married soon and that after his wedding he would move to Paris. There he could earn a far better living than in Warsaw. True to his word, in less than a month, Leibel was married and in Paris. Tsutel continued to live in the basement, but Elke made sure that her sister slept in a corner of the kitchen. Elke and Yoinne finally had the living room to themselves.

One thing, however, remained the same; every Sabbath we gathered at Liebe's.

A few months after Yoinne's marriage there was a very sad change for the three Schneidleider brothers. Their father, Burach Leib Schneidleider, died. Hertzke, Liebe's husband, was so sick at the time, he had to be spared the news of his son's death. Unable to get out of bed, Hertzke didn't know that in the next room, his three grandsons were sitting Shiva for their father.

When Burach Leib died, he left his sickly wife and fifteen-year-old daughter alone in Opalle, a small town east of Warsaw. Soon after their father's death, the three brothers received a letter from their sister, Shifra, asking for help. Ruchele and I heard that letter read at Liebe's late on a Sabbath afternoon. Shifra, who couldn't find work in Opalle, wanted to move to Warsaw.

Nachme and Khiel would have gladly taken their sister in, but the room they were sharing was too small for two men and a girl. Nachme and Khiel looked to Yoinne. After all, since they and Leibel had moved out there was certainly room for Shifra at Liebe's. Elke immediately answered for her husband. She didn't even want to hear about Shifra coming to live in the basement. Nachme and Khiel argued that it would be only for a short time, until Shifra found work.

"Is that so?" Elke asked. "What can kind of work can Shifra do?"

"The same as everybody else," Khiel answered.

"Everybody else has a profession," Elke said.

Nachme perked up. "What profession do I have? Running around all day like a horse, delivering heavy loads. I call that a plague not a profession."

"So, my brilliant brother-in-law," Elke asked, "are you planning on making Shifra Warsaw's first female porter?"

"Elke," Frau Liebe finally spoke up, "you're worrying too much. I'm sure Shifra will find something."

"Mamme, you don't know what you're saying." Elke spoke with a sharpness I'd never heard her use to her own mother. "Please don't help them to spoil my happiness."

"Elke, what nonsense you're babbling," Frau Liebe said. "Nobody wants to spoil your happiness. All we're saying is that we found work for Ruchele and I'm sure that we can think of something for Shifra."

Elke rolled her eyes to the ceiling. "How can you even compare Shifra with Ruchele. Ruchele worked for a seamstress in Lublin for years. Did Shifra ever work in her life? Shifra can't wipe her own nose yet."

"I have connections," Khiel said. "Tomorrow, I'll talk to some people. Shifra is pretty. We'll dress her up and she can become a salesgirl for women's clothes."

"Like I can become the Pope," Elke sneered.

"With Shifra's looks and the opportunities here in Warsaw, she'll be a married woman in less than a year," Nachme said.

"If you start introducing her to your friends," Elke said sarcastically, "she'll be pregnant in less than a month but I doubt that she'll be married in ten years."

"Enough, Elke!" Frau Liebe finally got angry. "What a shameful way to talk. You should apologize."

Elke wouldn't change her mind; and Yoinne said nothing.

The letters from Opalle asking for help started to come more often and grew more desperate, until Nachme and Khiel forced Yoinne to stand up to his wife. In the end, Elke grudgingly gave in and Shifra was invited into Liebe's basement apartment in the summer of 1931.

From the conversation at Liebe's I knew the day of the week and the hour when Shifra was expected: Wednesday, at two o'clock. Nachme and Khiel were going to meet her at the train station.

On Wednesday, as I was working, I suddenly thought of Shifra and asked Mr. Blumenstein what time it was. My boss pulled his pocket watch out by a small silver chain, snapped open the lid, and said, "Two o'clock, exactly."

On the Sabbath, I put on my suit and set out to Liebe's earlier than usual. My plan was to first visit my sister and then walk with Ruchele to Liebe's.

It was just before one o'clock when I opened the door to the basement apartment on Muranovska and surprised Frau Liebe and her family at the table eating lunch. I realized that I had forgotten about my sister. At the same moment I noticed a small girl, sitting between Nachme and Khiel. Her feet were dangling above the floor. I had the impression that one of the children who played in the building's courtyard had come down, but I knew it had to be Shifra. She was supposed to be almost fifteen years old, but looked no more than ten or eleven. She wore a simple pink dress. Her fine black hair was cut short, and she had a childlike nose and mouth, and round cheeks. As she stared at me, however, her black eyes lit her pale face with an adult intensity.

"Who is he?" Shifra asked with startling boldness.

"Schloime," Khiel said. "Ruchele's brother."

Shifra gave a nod with her head, fixed her black eyes on me for another moment, and then, as if suddenly shy, she looked away.

"Come, sit down with us," Liebe said. "I'll get you a plate."

"I'm not hungry." I was embarrassed by my absentminded blunder. "I'm going to see Ruchele and we'll come back later."

I turned around before anyone could stop me and ran up the stairs.

As I walked to Electoralna, I was deeply disappointed by how young Shifra looked. I had hoped to see a young woman not a little girl.

When I got to Ksiel and Lotte's apartment, Ruchele wasn't there.

"She went out for a walk with her friend," Lotte said.

"What friend?" I asked.

"Haven't you met him yet?" Lotte asked. "A very nice young gentleman. He already came to visit a few times. Have some tea and cake. They'll be back soon."

My head was suddenly swimming with troubling thoughts. I didn't want Lotte to see how upset I was. I thanked her and said that I would return in a half hour.

On the street, I wondered who this gentleman friend might be. Could Ruchele have found a boyfriend so soon? I was very afraid that someone would take advantage of her. Even though she was almost seventeen and looked like a young woman, she was just an innocent girl. I guessed that my sister had met this man at the club to which Khiel and Nachme dragged her.

I suddenly heard my name called. I looked around and saw Ruchele waving to me from across the street. Standing next to her was a tall man dressed in a brown suit, white shirt, hat and tie. He was holding my sister's hand.

Ruchele, her face flushed, black curls flying out from under the red felt hat, ran up to me, pulling the young man by the hand. My sister had on a new blue dress with a white jacket and was wearing high-heels.

"Schloime, I want you to meet my friend Zygmunt Treiberg," Ruchele said.

I shook hands with my sister's friend. He was so much taller than me I had to look up. He also had a grip of iron and squeezed my hand with such heartiness, I thought he was going to break my fingers. Zygmunt Treiberg, however, was not such a young man. He seemed well over thirty to me. The thick, round eyeglasses he wore made his dark eyes look like two small dots. He had a clean shaven face, a large, bony nose, full lips, and a round jaw.

"We met at a dance," Ruchele said. "Zygmunt is a tailor."

"Your sister," Zygmunt said in a deep, gleeful voice, and with a beaming smile, "is the only girl that can tire me out on the dance floor."

I didn't know what to say. I didn't share his joy in Ruchele's wonderful talent.

After an awkward silence Zygmunt said, "Look, Ruchele and I were just going to have a little snack. Why don't you join us?"

"Yes," Ruchele said, taking my hand, "come with us."

"There's a nice place just around the corner," Zygmunt said.

I couldn't understand what an older man like him was doing with my sister. And when I forced myself to consider possible reasons, I was not happy with my thoughts.

We sat down in a small tea house and Zygmunt ordered a pot of tea and a plate of cookies.

"Ruchel tells me you also work for a tailor," Zygmunt asked. "Who's your boss?"

"Arele Blumenstein, on Twarda Street."

"Blumenstein? I don't know him. Are you in the Union?"

"No."

"Aha! That's probably why I never heard of him," Zygmunt said, then quickly added, "Don't worry, I'm not a fanatic Union member. I say, Live and let live. I work in a factory on the Nalefky. Has the Union ever bothered your boss?" Zygmunt asked.

I was surprised at his question. "Why do you ask?"

"Just to warn you to be careful. A few weeks ago my boss hired a boy. Somehow the Union found out about it and sent down three men. My boss didn't even argue; he had to fire the boy."

"What gives the Union the right to dictate where people can work?" I asked.

"A good question," Zygmunt said. "But how else can workers ask for better wages if they don't have some organization, some power, to stand up to bosses?"

"That's also a good question," said Ruchele.

"Watch, Schloime, your sister will end up joining the union," Zygmunt said, throwing his arm around Ruchele's shoulder and pulling her towards him.

I thought he was going to pull Ruchele off her chair and onto his lap.

"The union wouldn't bother us at Lotte's," Ruchele said. "What tailor wants a job where he has to jump up and run in to change a baby's diapers?"

"If the tailor works in his own home and the child is his, why not?" Zygmunt said.

Ruchele blushed. Zygmunt laughed and slapped me on the back. Finally, Zygmunt said that he had an appointment to meet another friend. Outside the tea house, as we said goodbye, Zygmunt held Ruchele's hand in both of his.

"Are you going to keep your promise?" he asked her.

"Yes," Ruchele said, blushing again.

"Good," Zygmunt said. "And bring your brother along to the dance." He grabbed my hand before I could pull it away and gave it another finger-breaking squeeze.

I was glad to watch him run off finally. I was furious with Ruchele. "Why is he so familiar with you?" I asked.

"He is not familiar with me," Ruchele bristled. "He's my friend."

"He's an old man."

"He's only twenty-seven years old."

"He's twenty-seven like I'm your aunt."

"You can't tell me what to do," Ruchele snapped at me. "I like him!"

Talking to her was like talking to a brick wall. "I'm only trying to protect you. Didn't you see how he couldn't keep his hands off you? Who is going to look after you if I don't?"

"I don't need your protection. I can take care of myself. Leave me alone."

Rather than have a fight, I bit my tongue and swallowed my words. "Let's go to Liebe's," I said.

As we walked, I noticed that Ruchele was floating with delight from the time she had spent with Zygmunt.

"Wait till you see Shifra," Ruchele suddenly said.

"I saw her."

"I pity Elke. Shifra's going to be on Elke's hands for the next five years."

"Shifra's a poor girl. Her father just died. What is she supposed to do?"

"I have nothing against Shifra. But Khiel and Nachme should have some consideration for Elke. She's only been married a few months. Men don't understand these things."

When we walked into the basement apartment, everyone was in the living room having tea, except Shifra and Liebe.

Elke looked at Ruchele and threw up her hands. In a strained whisper, barely containing her anger, Elke said, "Ruchele, what am I going to do?"

Khiel laughed. "Elke, you should be on the stage. What do you want from Shifra's life? Give her a chance to catch her breath. She just got here."

Elke shot Khiel an angry look. "That child won't find work for years."

But Elke stopped talking the moment she saw Shifra coming back from the kitchen carrying a glass of tea on a saucer.

Shifra sat down, put her tea on the table, and looking firmly at Elke, she said, "Don't worry, I'll find work."

"Doing what?" Elke asked.

"If Shifra says that she's going to find work, she's going to find work," Khiel defended his sister.

Yoinne sat in quiet anguish, unable to look at his wife, his brothers, or at his sister. I saw that Ruchele, sitting across from me, was also uncomfortable with all this bickering. Just a few months earlier she had been the one who asked for help in coming to Warsaw. I felt very sorry for Shifra.

"Yoinne," Elke, almost in tears, turned to her husband, "why do you always sit there like a lump? Why do I always have to be the bad one?"

"You're right," Yoinne said, drawing himself up in his chair. "I'm taking charge. Enough talk. Elkele, as your husband, I order you to get ready to go to a cinema."

"That's my husband's answer to any problem, a cinema." Elke turned to Ruchele and said, "Why don't you have some tea? I'm going to get myself a fresh glass too."

"As a matter of fact," Ruchele said, "I've just been taken out to tea by a dear friend."

Tsutel and Elke's eyes lit up.

"Don't tell me," Elke said, excited. "You saw Zygmunt?"

Ruchele nodded, a pleased smile on her face.

"Better watch out, Ruchele," Tsutel said. "Zygmunt Treiberg likes to play around. He has left more than a few broken hearts."

"Don't worry, Ruchele," Elke said, "Tsutel is jealous because he wouldn't break her heart."

"He's not a bad catch," Tsutel agreed, "but as long as there are still a few more bachelors left in this world, I won't commit suicide."

Elke's and Tsutel's descriptions of my sister's new friend confirmed my worst suspicions; he was another Itzhak Copperstein. I was responsible for my sister and yet I had not power over her. My only hope was that our permit to leave Warsaw would arrive soon. Ruchele wouldn't listen to me but she would have to obey her father. I stole a glance at Shifra. I was struck again by how young she looked. Her face was pale, like that of a child who had been kept indoors all winter. She was only half listening to the chatter going on around her. Her black eyes burned with such intensity, I realized Shifra was really absorbed in her own problem of survival. Without understanding why, I felt a sudden closeness to her as I had never felt before towards a stranger.

The Parisian Restaurant

THE POLISH EMIGRATION BUREAU was in no hurry to send the papers that would allow Ruchele and me to join our father in Russia. When I went to ask the officials what was taking so long, I was told to be patient. I wrote to our father. He wrote back that until we had the papers his hands were tied. The three-month wait stretched into six and then twelve months. In the meantime, I was watching Ruchele fall into the same fire that had devoured our mother. My sister's boyfriend, Zygmunt Treiberg, was in my eyes a character no better than Itzhak Copperstein—a seducer of women, even if he wasn't a drunkard or a thief. My attempts to talk to my sister only made matters worse. Ruchele either laughed at my fears, or we fought bitterly. I desperately needed to rent some place where my sister could live with me and I could watch her closely. Unfortunately the security and the first month's rent on a room came to at least 40 zlotys. An overwhelming sum. No matter how hard I tried, I could never save more than a fraction of that money. After working for the Blumensteins for almost a year I was still earning only ten zlotys a week. I couldn't waste any time. I decided to ask for a raise. If I didn't get it, I made up my mind to look for another job.

I picked a Sunday morning when Arele and his wife were in a good mood. I guessed how they felt from the little tunes they were humming under their breaths as they worked. He would start a song, she would pick it up, and back and forth they serenaded each other.

As I stitched and pressed I kept rehearsing my speech to myself.

I chose to speak to my boss after lunch. Before we started to work again, I plucked up my courage and told Mr. and Mrs. Blumenstein that I had something important to discuss with them.

The little tune they were humming dropped out of their mouths note by note.

"I'm going to be eighteen years old soon," I began my speech nervously. "I have to think of a future for myself. I have a lot more experience now than when you hired me, and in over a year I never got a raise. I need to earn a little more now."

My boss and his wife turned to each other with blank stares.

"I'm not saying that you don't deserve it," Arele Blumenstein said to me. "But the truth is that we don't have any money."

I had my next point ready. "I'm not asking for much."

My boss seemed afraid to ask the next question. "How much?"

"Only five zlotys more a week."

My words struck Arele as if they were stones. "But that comes to fifteen zlotys a week," he murmured.

I delivered my strongest argument. "If you had to hire a regular tailor it would cost you two or three times as much as I'm getting."

"Look, you have a place to sleep here, right?" my boss asked. "And I'm not charging you any rent, am I? You have to count that in to your salary."

"But now," I said, "I want to save enough money so I can afford to rent a room."

"Aren't you happy here?" Mrs. Blumenstein asked. "Is it too cold? Is the bed too hard?"

"No, everything is fine. It's just too small. I would like to rent a large room so I can live together with my sister."

"My wife and I will have to talk about it tonight."

At last I was getting through to the tailor. I didn't hear another hum from either of them for the rest of the day. I became afraid that I might get fired. I decided to start looking for another job as soon as possible.

On Monday, I got up early, washed, dressed, and ran to the newsstand on Grzibowsky Square. As I had done before when I was looking for a job, for five groschen, I rented the page of The Express with the "Employment" section. In the pale dawn light, I stood against a wall and read through the advertisements.

When I returned to the store, I was surprised to see the Blumensteins already there.

"Where've you been?" Arele asked.

"To buy bread," I lied.

Both the husband and the wife looked at my hands as if to ask, Where is the bread?

"I ate it," I said quickly.

There was an embarrassed look between the sheepish tailor and his young wife.

"We have discussed your raise," Arele said. "I think you know that I can't afford to give you as much as you ask, but I am ready to give you three zlotys. With one condition. You say that you want to save money for a room, right?"

I nodded.

"Then let us hold the money for you until you've saved enough. Every week I'll pay you your usual salary, and the extra three zlotys I'll add to your savings account. That way you won't be tempted to spend the money."

Even though the raise wasn't as much as I'd hoped for, I had to accept the offer. I trusted the Blumensteins and their condition that I let them hold my savings until I had saved enough to rent a room appealed to me. I just asked that we keep a written account of the money I put away. I took a sheet of paper, wrote "Schloime's Savings" on the top, and under it I drew a line dividing the page in half, one side for dates and the other for money. On the following Friday afternoon, I was paid my ten zlotys in cash and I made the first entry into my savings account. I still kept hoping that the papers from the Emigration Bureau would arrive soon, but I had no idea how long it might take. Now, at least, within three to four months, I would have saved up enough to rent a room.

As Elke and Ruchele had predicted, and in spite of everyone's help, Shifra had trouble finding a job. Her biggest problem was her lack of experience. It didn't help, of course, that she looked like a child. For a while Yoinne even tried to teach his sister to sew. Shifra, however, was a total novice and Yoinne couldn't afford to take too much time away from earning his own living. Shifra's situation finally turned critical when Elke became pregnant. Elke, who never spared her sister-in-law's feelings, bluntly told Shifra that after the baby was born she would have to move out. Desperate for any job, Shifra went to work in a restaurant on Zamenhoff Street as kitchen help.

On my Sabbath visits to Frau Liebe's family I noticed that from week to week Shifra looked more miserable. I guessed that her job was making her unhappy. But Shifra bore her troubles in silence. When I tried to talk to her, to find out what was going on, she wouldn't answer me.

The more I saw Shifra, with her pretty child-like face and her fierce black eyes, the more I was taken with her, and the more I wished she weren't so young. Soon I found myself thinking about her the whole week long. One evening after work, as I sat alone in back of the store, I decided to take a walk to the restaurant where she worked.

It was a warm night in July. All the apartment windows were thrown wide open. Music from radios drifted out into the night. The Jewish Quarter of Warsaw seemed to have thrown itself a party. Young couples, old people, fathers and mothers with their children, every one was outside trying to cool off. As I strolled towards Zamenhoff Street, I debated with myself whether to actually enter the restaurant.

By the time I was walking along the Saxony Gardens, a few blocks from Zamenhoff, I found my heart racing so fast I was afraid that if I tried to speak to Shifra I would embarrass myself.

A puddle of yellow light lay in front of the Parisian Restaurant, as if someone had spilled a glass of stale beer out the door. Through the large black letters painted on the plate glass windows, I saw about fifteen tables. Half were taken. The clientele didn't impress me. The men were dressed like dandies, in dark suits and hats with sharp-edged crowns, and the women were dressed like streetwalkers, in gaudy dresses. One waiter, a thin, stooped man in a black suit and a stained white napkin draped across his forearm, shuffled from table to table with cups of coffee, glasses of tea, and plates of pastries. Suddenly the kitchen door opened and out came Shifra pushing a small wagon. Her hair was tied in a kerchief and her face was flushed from hard work. She moved quickly from table to table gathering the dirty dishes. At one of the tables a man waved to her and then patted his thigh, inviting her to sit on his lap. Shifra did her work without looking up and then disappeared back into the kitchen. I had seen more than I could stomach and I left at once. I understood Shifra's misery.

On the Sabbath, when I saw Shifra at Frau Liebe's, I tried again to talk to her about her job. I was hoping that if her brothers heard what a cesspool she was working in, they would make her stop. But Shifra refused to be drawn into a conversation about the Parisian Restaurant.

The next day, Sunday, as I was working, I wondered whether I shouldn't speak to Shifra's brothers on my own. I was sure that if Khiel and Nachme knew that customers in the restaurant were bothering their young sister, they would make her quit. The only thing that stopped me was my fear that Shifra would be angry with me if she found out what I had done. I thought so much about Shifra and her situation that by the middle of the week I wanted to see her again. On Wednesday night I tried to resist my urge for as long as I could, but around eight o'clock I gave in. I locked the store and left.

This time, as I looked in through the plate glass window of the Parisian Restaurant, I noticed that almost all the tables were taken. The customers were rowdy and the sad waiter was hopping as fast as he could from one table to the next to keep up with the orders. Shifra was nowhere in sight. When the door from the kitchen opened and the little wagon came rolling out, it was being pushed by a fat middle aged man who seemed to be one of the cooks. He quickly cleared away the dirty dishes and pushed the little wagon back into the kitchen. I waited awhile longer, began to feel self-conscious, and walked away.

I had just rounded the corner of Djelna and Zamenhoff, when I suddenly saw Shifra. In the distance, down the darkened street lit by tall lampposts, I saw her carrying a heavy bag, the weight pulling her body to one side. For a moment, I felt tempted to cross the street but my feelings of pity for Shifra were stronger than my embarrassment. "Shifra!" I called out and ran to help her.

Shifra, her head bent to the ground, was so absorbed in her struggle with the heavy bag that she didn't see or hear me. I called her name again. Finally, she looked up and put the bag down.

"What're you carrying?" I asked as I approached her.

"Groceries," Shifra said, rubbing the small palm of her red, swollen hand. "The cooks are running out of everything. They keep sending me to all the stores. It's my third trip already." She looked disheveled and tired.

"Let me carry the bag," I offered.

"I want to catch my breath first," Shifra said, straightening out her body. "What are *you* doing here?" she asked, as if the strangeness of my presence had just dawned on her .

"I was taking a walk," I said quickly. "When I've got nothing to do, I like to take a long walk and have a smoke."

"You're already finished working for the day?" Shifra asked with envy.

"Only because we're in the off season. During the season I work until ten or eleven sometimes. How late do you have to work?"

"Sometimes midnight."

"How do you get home?"

"One of the owners lives close to Liebe. He walks with me." Shifra spat on the ground. "May he burn in hell!"

"Why're you cursing him? Isn't he doing you a favor?"

"The Devil should pay him back for his favor," Shifra said and spat again. "I have to go back."

I picked up the heavy bag and we started to walk slowly towards the restaurant.

"I'll tell you something," Shifra suddenly said, "but you have to swear that you won't tell anyone else."

"I swear."

"On your life."

"On my life."

"This bastard," said Shifra, "this owner, who's supposed to be such a decent person, told me that I could earn a lot more money than I'm making. I just had to be willing."

Shifra was just a child. I was outraged.

"I told him that if he dared to repeat such a thing to me, my brothers would break his head open."

"Leave that place. It's not for you."

"Where can I go? If only Elke wasn't such a bitch, I would have quit that place long ago."

"Why don't you get another job?"

"I've been trying. But it seems useless and I'm getting very tired. If I can't find something soon, I may have to go back to Opalle."

"You're still so young," I said as we approached the restaurant. "Maybe if you learn to become a seamstress in Opalle and then come back to Warsaw it would be easier for you to find work."

Shifra led me through an alley to restaurant's kitchen entrance. In the darkness, she turned to take the groceries from my hand. I felt an urge to embrace her. Instead, I just looked into her pale face. For a moment I felt completely lost in her beauty. She thanked me for helping her with the bag of groceries. When she opened the door to the kitchen, a blast of heat escaped as if Shifra were stepping back into Hell.

I took a walk around the block, came back to the Parisian Restaurant and looked in again through the large glass windows. This time I saw Shifra, her head bent to avoid the leers from the men, pushing the wagon from table to table, picking up the dirty dishes.

Shifra's plight bothered me deeply. I felt more and more tempted to speak to her brothers about what she had to suffer at the restaurant. I couldn't tell them how the restaurant owner had propositioned their sister because I had sworn on my life that I wouldn't. But I could tell them how the customers were treating Shifra. I was only afraid of Shifra's reaction if she found out that I had meddled in her life. I put off speaking to Shifra's brothers for a few weeks. One Sabbath, when I came to visit Liebe's family, I found out that Shifra was no longer living there. She had returned to Opalle.

I was relieved that she had gotten out of that hellish restaurant. At the same time, I missed her.

The Garment Workers' Strike

ROSH HASHANAH came and went. A new year had begun and I still hadn't received an answer from the Emigration Bureau. According to the sheet of paper on which I kept track of my savings I now had forty-two zlotys. I began to look for a room. I needed to find one that was large enough to divide with a partition so that Ruchele would have her privacy and I mine. After searching for two weeks, I realized that for the amount of rent I could afford, such a room wouldn't be easy to find.

One afternoon in late October, as Mrs. Blumenstein and I were working in the back room, and my boss was in the store, I suddenly became aware of raised voices coming from the front.

"There's a table and a few chairs in the back," I heard Arele Blumenstein say. "I cook a bit of soup for myself there."

The next voice was high-pitched and almost singing with sarcasm. "So maybe you'll treat us to a plate of chicken broth and noodles."

"Let's just have a look," another man said.

"What do you have to see?" Arele asked. "My misery? It's a private room."

"Let us through already," the man with the high-pitched voice said. "We don't have all day."

"Please don't embarrass me like this." Arele pleaded. "My wife is back there. She helps me out a little."

As Mrs. Blumenstein jumped up from her chair and started to walk towards the front, the curtain was suddenly thrown aside and two men appeared. One was short, barrel-chested, around fifty years old, wearing a brown suit; the other was of average height, heavyset, in his thirties, and wearing a navy suit. They were followed by Arele, his face pale like a white-washed wall.

"And who is that?"The barrel chested man, who had the high-pitched voice, pointed at me. "Your son?"

"You're on strike," the younger man said to me. "With the rest of us."

"I am his son," I exclaimed wildly.

The tailor and his wife exchanged bewildered looks. The two intruders smirked.

"And is she your mother?" the barrel chested man asked, laughing as he gestured towards the young Mrs. Blumenstein.

"When did she have you?" asked the other. "When she was three years old?"

"Oh, dear God," Arele moaned.

"I'm his son from his first wife," I said. "She died giving birth to me."

This only made the two union men laugh harder.

"Is he telling the truth?" the short man, poking his partner's side with an elbow, asked my boss.

"Ah, these lies, Schloime, these lies," Arele moaned. "Heaven forbid. No wife of mine ever died. He's not my son."

"Let's go," said the younger man to me. "On strike!"

I stood my ground. "I'm not in the union. Why do I have to strike?"

"For the betterment of all garment workers," the short man squeaked.

"But I just bettered myself a few months ago. I just got a raise. I don't need to better myself anymore."

"It's not good enough that you got a raise," the younger union man said. "You have to think of your co-workers. You're not the only garment worker in Warsaw."

"When did they ever think about me?"

"We're not here for a debate." The high-pitched voice cut into me with its sarcasm.

"And what if I don't want to strike?"

The two men started to laugh again.

"Go ahead," the barrel-chested man challenged me, "ask your boss if he'll let you work."

"He's right, Schloime," Arele said. "You can't work until the strike is over."

"What am I going to do?"

"Everybody is meeting at the union headquarters," the younger man said. "Go over there. Remember, you're on strike!"

The two men left at once.

"Go and find out what's going on." Mr. Blumenstein made sure they were gone. "If I let you work while the strike is on, they'll start by breaking my windows and end by breaking my bones."

I pulled on my jacket and ran to the union. When I got there the crowd of men was so thick, I couldn't even get up to the offices. Listening to the talk around me, I found out that the workers didn't expect the strike to last more than a few hours.

"They'll see we mean business," one worker said to another, "and they'll give in. That's our advantage if we stick together. They can't run the shops without us. When everything stops at once it can't go on for too long. Remember my words, this strike will be over faster than you with your lame pressing could burn a hole in a pair of pants."

I waited outside the union headquarters most of the day. The strike didn't end. Towards evening, I walked back to Twarda Street.

"What did you hear?" my boss asked as I stepped into the store.

"They were hoping that it would end today but they're still on strike."

"Well, better take your things with you and come back when the strike is over."

I couldn't believe my ears. "What do you mean?"

"You're on strike. You're not working for me anymore."

"Where am I going to sleep?"

"Why don't you sleep at your aunt's place?"

By now Elke was due to give birth any day and her belly stuck out like a huge balloon. I was sure she wouldn't let me sleep in the basement.

"There's no room there," I said. "You have to let me sleep here."

"How can I?" my boss pleaded. "Don't you understand? You're on strike. I don't know what you could do to me."

"Me? Why should I do anything to you?"

"It's not just you. It's the union also. Those two officials who were here earlier could come back at any moment. If they find you here, they'll think, Heaven forbid, that you're working for me. They could wreck the whole place."

"I'll stay hidden. I won't let anyone in."

"Please understand, Schloime, this place is my livelihood. I can't take such a chance."

It was almost six o'clock already. In another hour, the Blumensteins would lock up the store and I would be left out on the street. I did have my savings, of course, but I didn't want to waste them all at once, especially now that I had no idea how long I could be out of work.

I ran back to the union headquarters. The mass of garment workers had thinned somewhat. I pushed my way into the crowded offices upstairs.

"I have to talk to someone," I said to a clerk behind a desk. "I have a big problem."

"So does everybody else," the clerk said. "You have to wait your turn."

I looked behind me at the long bench of waiting strikers. I figured that by the time I spoke to someone, the Blumensteins would have left the store.

"What's your problem?" The sudden question came from a striker, a short, thin man in his early thirties, poorly dressed, stubble on his face, a small mustache, and a friendly smile over rotting teeth.

"I live in the back of the tailor shop where I work. Now my boss won't let me sleep there."

"Tell me, are you registered with the police at that address?" the man asked.

"Of course."

"Then your boss can't kick you out. Go to the police. Tell them that you're being driven to sleep on the street because your boss threw you out. It happens to be illegal to sleep on the street. The police will force your boss to let you sleep in the back of the store."

I shook the hand of my fellow striker.

I ran to the police station. I was afraid that by the time I got back to the store, the Blumensteins would have already locked up and gone home.

It was growing dark when I entered the police station. I walked up to an officer in a gray uniform decorated with shiny brass buttons, sitting behind a large desk. He was a stocky young man with a reddish face, close-cropped, blond hair, and small blue eyes.

In my best Polish I explained my situation. He asked for my name and address and wrote them down. In the back of the police station there were large file cabinets. He began to open and close drawers until he found my registration form. After he had read through it, he said, "Let's go talk to this boss of yours."

The police station was only two blocks away from the store on Twarda Street. When we turned the corner, I saw the Blumensteins locking up. I called out and ran towards them.

"What's going on?" Arele asked when he saw me approaching.

"Please, Mr. Blumenstein, you have to let me sleep here," I said.

"I've already explained to you that I can't do that."

The policeman came up behind me.

"What's *he* doing here?" Arele asked.

"I had to get help," I said. "I have a right—"

"Hey, you two, stop this jabbering in Yiddish," the policeman said. "I can't understand a damned word you're saying."

"What does he want?" Arele asked.

"He wants us to speak in Polish," I said.

A small crowd of curious onlookers began to form around us.

"What a misfortune!" Arele moaned.

"Did you hear what I said?" the policeman bellowed, beating his night stick against the building, "Quit your Yiddish jabbering! You," the policeman said, pointing a finger at Arele. "Why can't he sleep here tonight?"

"Why is he pointing a finger at me?" my boss asked me.

"He wants to know why you won't let me sleep here."

"Tell him that my miserable piece of bread is sunk into that hole. If the strikers think that I'm hiding a worker, they'll come back and destroy my store."

"I already told you that I'll stay hidden," I said.

"The union has spies everywhere," Arele said looking at the crowd surrounding us.

"What the hell are you two going on about?" the policeman screamed.

A Jew who spoke good Polish stepped out of the crowd and translated our conversation for the policeman.

The policeman delivered a mouthful to the translator, who turned to Arele and said, "This officer says since the boy is registered at this address, this is where he has to sleep. If they catch him sleeping on the street, they'll arrest and fine you."

Arele turned to the translator. "I'd gladly let him sleep here, but there's a strike on. Tell this good officer that I'm afraid of my store being vandalized."

Our translator spoke to officer and then translated the officer's words for us. "The officer says if the boy or the union harms anything, the police knows where to find them."

"Arele, don't argue," Mrs. Blumenstein said. "Let him in."

Defeated, Mr. Blumenstein pulled out his keys and unlocked the door. "Go in, Schloime. Believe me, I know that you're a decent boy, but those union hooligans, you have no idea what they can do. Go in and let me lock the door."

"What do you mean lock the door?" I asked. "What if there's a fire?"

"A fire, God forbid, what are you talking about a fire for? I have to lock the door. I can't give you the keys."

"What are they jabbering now?" the policeman asked.

Our translator explained.

"Give him the damned key!" the officer bellowed. Arele listened with a bewildered expression as the officer continued to yell at him in Polish.

"The policeman says that you have to leave the key in the store," the translator said. "It's illegal to lock a man up unless he's in jail."

As he handed me the key, my boss said, "You're holding my life in your hands."

"Mr. Blumenstein, I don't want to do you any harm."

"Hold the key during the night, but in the morning make sure you give it back to me. Come, Natachale," Arele said to his wife.

The crowd dispersed. I locked the door and went into the back of the store. From all the running and fighting, I was exhausted. I sat down at the table and tried to gather my thoughts. I was angry at Arele for trying to keep me out, even though I understood his fears. I pulled out the money from my pockets. All I had left were two one-zloty bills and fifty-five groschen. Luckily I still had the money I had saved up with the Blumensteins. I took out the sheet where I kept track of my savings. I had forty-two zlotys. As long as the strike lasted, I would need that money to buy food.

In the morning, when the Blumensteins came to work, I was dressed and waiting for them. I handed Arele his key. He thanked me and assured me that I could have it again in the evening.

"It looks bad," Arele said to me. There was a gloomy look on his face. "I was talking to a friend, he says the strike could drag on for weeks."

"How is it possible?" I asked. "How is any work going to get done?"

"It's going to be hard on everyone," Arele said. "I hope my friend's wrong. This is going to be some day, I can tell already."

"I'm going to the union," I said. "Maybe they'll announce something."

On the way to the union building I stopped in a grocery and bought myself a roll and an apple. On the street, as I took a bite of the bread and a bite the apple, I decided that in the evening I would ask Arele for some of my money.

Outside the union headquarters, I found a crowd of strikers.

"To hell with the bosses and the union," one man said. "I have a wife and four brats. How am I going to feed them?"

"You can afford to take a day off," said another man. "Tomorrow we'll all go back and get a decent wage."

"This could last a month," a third man said. "And it will end in mayhem."

"Get out of here with your pessimism," the second man said.

"What do they care if my wife and children starve," said the first man. "They have money, those union leaders. Is this what we pay them to do? Get rid of the whole stinking lot. I needed a strike like I need a hole in my head."

Other strikers heard him say this and got angry.

"Hey, hold your tongue! If we don't stand together now, everything is lost!"

I was afraid of a fight. I moved into the doorway of the union building. This time I was able to walk up to the offices. Garment workers with anxious faces were sitting on benches while union officials, in good suits, white shirts and ties, ran back and forth with papers in their hands, shouting orders to each other.

From one office, a union worker came out carrying signs that read, "ON STRIKE FOR BETTER WAGES." He distributed them to waiting workers who left to picket.

In the late afternoon, I ran over to Ksiel and Lotte's apartment to check how Ruchele was doing.

The door to the apartment on Electoralna Street was locked. I knocked. After a while, I heard Lotte's voice. "Who is it?"

"Schloime."

"Come in," Lotte said, opening the door. She was holding her youngest girl. The small rack with work had been taken out of the kitchen. "You know why I have to keep the door locked, don't you?"

Ruchele came out of her room. "Did you have to go on strike?"

"I had no choice," I said. "Two union men came into the shop and told me I had to stop working."

"Where are you sleeping?" Ruchele asked.

"In the store. My boss can't throw me out because I'm registered there. Has anyone bothered you?"

"Only the suppliers," Lotte said. "They're running around like poisoned rats trying to collect everything that's owed them. They know if the strike goes on a few more days, no one will have a grosch left."

I left feeling relieved for Ruchele. It was only four in the afternoon, but I was getting hungry and I needed money to buy dinner. I decided to go back to the tailor shop get a few zlotys from my savings.

At 18 Twarda Street I found my boss and his wife sitting in the store instead of in the workshop. Three hours before closing time they were all packed and ready to go home.

"We were only waiting for you to come back. There isn't a stitch of work. We're going home," Mr. Blumenstein said wearily. "Here's is the key." He laid it down on the counter of the store. They gathered up their belongings, and opened the front door.

"Mr. Blumenstein," I said, stopping them at the threshold, "I need my money."

The tailor and his wife suddenly looked very disturbed. Shaking his head, Mr. Blumenstein turned to me and said, "Bear with me, Schloime. Every supplier has been here today. I've given away my last groschen."

"What does that have to do with my savings?"

"Schloime, I had to borrow your money. God forgive me."

I couldn't believe what I was hearing. "What do you mean? You couldn't give away my money. It wasn't yours."

"I was being threatened."

"But that was my money!" I shouted, trembling with anger. "Forty-two zlotys! You have to pay me back! I'm broke! I worked hard for that money!"

"Stop yelling," my boss begged me. The door to the store was partly open and a few people who had heard me stopped outside.

"I want my money now!" I shouted, not caring who knew. "You're a thief! You're stealing my money!"

The door opened all the way and a large man with a blood-smeared butcher's apron tied around his thick waist stepped in. "What's going on here?" he asked. "Why is the boy screaming?"

"He stole my money," I said.

"Is it true?" the butcher asked my boss.

"God in Heaven," Arele Blumenstein said. "I was holding his money but we're in a strike—"

"I don't even have money for food."

"Give him his money," said the butcher to my boss.

"You have to believe me," Arele implored, "I don't have a grosch left to my name."

"How much money does he owe you?" the butcher asked me.

"Forty-two zlotys." I pulled out the sheet with the account of my saved money. "I've written everything down."

He took the sheet from me and waved in my boss's face. "Is this right?"

Mr. Blumenstein looked blindly at the paper and said, "It must be."

"Then pay him part of the money."

Arele Blumenstein reached into his pockets and turned them inside out. "Take my empty pockets."

"I'll lend you ten zlotys right now," the butcher said, reaching into his own pocket. "You pay the boy, and at the end of the week, you pay me back."

"No," Arele said, "please. I can't afford anymore debts. I'm not making a grosch out of this hole of a store. How am I going to pay you back?"

"Go out," the man ordered me. "Go on!"

I stepped out into the crowd of people who had gathered at the windows. A moment later I heard Mrs. Blumenstein scream.

"Call a policeman!" someone in the crowd yelled as everyone started to run away.

The butcher came out of the store. Calmly, he took two zlotys out of his pocket and gave them to me.

"Come back tomorrow and he'll give you your money," the man said. "If he doesn't, let me know. I'm around the corner in the butcher shop on Sliska."

I approached the store cautiously. Through the window, I saw Arele Blumenstein sitting on a chair, his head tilted back, while his wife pressed a towel to his face. At once, I noticed an angry red stain growing on the towel. Suddenly Arele Blumenstein began to slide off the chair and fell sprawling to the floor. Natacha Blumenstein sank to her knees and leaned over her husband. Frantically she called his name and slapped his face, trying to revive him. He didn't move. She put her ear to his heart. All at once, Mrs. Blumenstein gave out a frightening shriek. "They've killed him! My God!" she cried. "They murdered my husband! Help! Help!"

Murdered!

"MURDERED!"

The thought exploded in my head and sent me racing across Twarda. In the dim twilight I ran blindly through the crowded streets, bumping into people on their way home from work. At any moment I expected a policeman to start chasing me. Arele's wife would surely blame me for starting the fight and even though I hadn't dealt the blow that killed her husband, I would be arrested and thrown in jail with the butcher.

I ran without stopping along the quiet gravel paths of the Saxony Gardens. Near the exit to Pilsudsky Square, gasping for air, I collapsed on a park bench. Sweat poured from me.

I was deathly afraid of going to jail. I had to escape from Warsaw, but where could I go with less than three zlotys in my pocket? Everything I owned, my small bag of clothes, my suit, was still in the back of the store on Twarda Street. The butcher, instead of helping me, had made my situation worse. If only he hadn't hit my boss so hard. Now I couldn't get my money back, I didn't have a roof over my head, or a bed to sleep in.

I stood up as soon as I had caught my breath and began to walk. I didn't know where to go or what to do. This time no one, not even Frau Liebe, could help me.

I crossed Theater Square. On Bielanski Street, as I passed a restaurant, I suddenly remembered Shifra. I envied her. She was better off back in Opalle, away from this miserable city which had ruined our lives—first my mother's, and now Ruchele's and mine. Further along, on the Poniatowsky Bridge, looking down at the dark waters of the Vistula River, I realized that I was being forced to abandon my sister. What would become of her now, alone in Warsaw?

I felt the night grip me like a cold fist. I was surprised that the police hadn't caught me yet. In the Praga suburb, the streets began to empty of people. Most of those going home from work had disappeared into warm houses. From every window lamplight glowed peacefully.

I thought of my mother and grandmother. I missed them terribly. I remembered how safe I had felt next to them. I even missed my father, whom I hardly knew. If only I had been able to get the emigration papers I could have been with him in Russia instead of running for my life. I knew that I would never get the papers now. Suddenly, a wild thought occurred to me. There were people who crossed the border into Russia illegally. If only I could reach my father, I would be safe. But where was the border? And how far away?

There was only one thing to do. I had to get in touch with the Communist Party. The communists had ways of smuggling people across the border into Russia. Of course, the Party was outlawed by the Polish Government and it was dangerous to get involved with it, but what did I have to lose? If I stayed in Poland, sooner or later I would be arrested. I decided that if I managed to hide out the night, in the morning I would ask Khiel if he knew someone I could contact for help.

As I drifted along Praga's dark streets, I came upon train tracks. I started to follow the tracks and ended up at the Vienna Station. Passengers were still milling around, getting on and off trains. I sat down on a bench to rest. Almost at once a policeman on patrol strolled into the station. My body shook with each pounding thud of my heart. I forced myself to sit still. Finally the policeman walked away. I rested for an hour. As the station emptied of people, I felt too conspicuous and had to leave.

In the chilly October night, the city was fast asleep. I was exhausted from my aimless wandering. I couldn't even sit down in a doorway and close my eyes for a few minutes. If I got arrested for sleeping on the street, it would be the end of me. As soon as the police had me in jail, they would find out that I was wanted for murder.

I was hopelessly lost. I roamed through streets I had never seen before. I drifted without any sense of where I was going until suddenly I noticed a pale yellow glow around me. I looked up at the sky. The clouds had blown away leaving behind a full moon. In front of me I saw the Kerbedia Bridge and across the street, I caught sight of a policeman watching me. In a rush, I started to cross the Bridge as if I had a home and I couldn't wait to get back to it.

Not until I was on the other side of the bridge did I look back. The policeman hadn't followed me. Now I began to roam through the Jewish Quarter. I was too frightened to cross back into Praga and risk being seen by the same policeman.

The clouds covered the moon again. In the Jewish Quarter, however, I knew my way. I walked along the better streets until slowly a pale gray light began to edge the blackness out of the sky. As I passed Krashinsky Garden, I noticed the gates were already opened. I stole into the empty park. Not even the birds were awake yet. I sat down on a bench and fell fast asleep.

The wail of a child woke me up. I opened my eyes. It was a cloudless morning. Old men with canes, women pushing baby carriages, children dragging toys were strolling past me. I had to get up and move on; but I was too tired. My eyes closed against my will and I fell asleep again.

The next time I woke up, it was midday. The sun's warmth had settled on my head and back. A pair of policemen were standing a short distance from me. I began to panic but I quickly realized that I would call far more attention to myself by running. By now, I was sure, Mrs. Blumenstein had given a detailed description of me to the authorities. I waited a few minutes. The two policemen, caught up in an animated conversation, didn't move. I was starving. I stood up as casually as I could and left the park. Again no one followed me. At the first bakery I passed, I bought myself two rolls. A few steps down the street, in a grocery, I bought a piece of cheese.

As I walked and ate, I thought over my plan to escape to Russia. The idea of going to the Communist Party for help didn't seem as good now as it had during the night in my despair. If I got caught at the Polish border trying cross illegally, the guards would either kill me or throw me in jail for life. Besides, now that I had slept and eaten, and was thinking more clearly, I had to admit that no one was chasing after me. Could it be that Arele Blumenstein wasn't be dead? It seemed impossible but I wasn't far from Twarda Street and the temptation to take a peek at the store from a distance was too strong to resist.

Watching cautiously for police, I approached the corner of Zlota and Twarda Streets. Droshkys and automobiles drove down the cobblestoned street as the usual crowds of Jews going about their business crossed that busy intersection. For a few minutes I stayed close to the corner building. Finally, as casually as I could, I stuck my head around the corner of Twarda. The tailor shop was across the street, halfway down the block. Not a single policeman stood in front of the store. A good sign. But was the store open or closed? Suddenly a woman, holding a boy by the hand, opened the door to Blumenstein's shop and walked in.

I leaned back against the building. *The store was open.* Forgetting all caution, I crossed the street, walked up to the store at No. 18, and looked in. Arele Blumenstein, his back towards the window, stood at the mirror measuring a boy for a suit while the mother looked at swatches of fabric.

He was alive!

I was so relieved I began to laugh. I was a free man again. I could go anywhere, do anything, no one would arrest me. My life had been handed back to me. Nothing else mattered, not even the money Blumenstein owed me. I felt richer than if I had won the lottery.

"What are you doing here?"

I whipped around and saw Mrs. Blumenstein, an accusing look on her face, standing behind me. She was carrying her husband's lunch in a cloth sack. "You should be ashamed of yourself. You almost had my husband killed."

"It wasn't my fault," I said. "I only wanted my money. I don't have a grosch to live on."

"Come in," Mrs. Blumenstein said severely. "My husband will make an arrangement to pay you back. But I don't want to see you here anymore. Take your things with you and leave us alone."

Arele Blumenstein winced when he saw me enter the tailor shop. He had a black and blue ring around his left eye which spilled across the hump of his nose. "Go in the back," he said. "I'm busy right now."

I followed his wife behind the curtain. On a chair I saw my suit folded over my small travel sack. They had already packed my things for me.

Mrs. Blumenstein busied herself preparing her husband's meal.

After the fitting, when the mother and the boy were about to leave the store, I heard her ask, "What happened to your eye, Mister Blumenstein?"

"Oh, nothing," he said. "I fell down a flight of stairs."

I couldn't help thinking, And if you don't pay me back my money, you're going to fall down another flight of stairs.

The tailor poked his head around the curtain. "Get your things," he said.

I picked up my belongings and walked into the store.

"Have you got everything?" Blumenstein asked.

I showed him the bundle.

"Here then is five zlotys," he said, reaching into his pocket. "Every week, I'll pay you the same amount. But if you make trouble for me again, I'll call the police and have you arrested."

I had never seen my boss so angry. I took the money from him. I pulled out the sheet on which I kept track of my savings, crossed out the total, 42, and wrote under it, 37. Then I folded the sheet, put it back into my pocket, and I left.

I headed straight to the Union headquarters to check on the strike. The five zlotys in my pocket wouldn't last very long, especially since I didn't have a free place to sleep. I regretted losing my job with Blumenstein. I had learned a lot from him and the salary he had been paying me was the best I had ever earned. But now at least I had some experience. I was sure I could find another job, just as soon as the Union leaders stopped their madness and let the workers go back to earning a living.

At the Union offices, I found out that the situation instead of getting better was getting worse. The contractors screamed that they had no money and that they would rather do the work themselves than pay higher wages to their workers. I left the Union and stopped at a newsstand to look at the job advertisements in *The Express*. There was nothing in the paper; besides, it was already too late in the day to go looking for a job. I returned to the Union, sat down on a bench where a few men were sleeping, and holding my bag and suit on my lap, I also fell asleep.

When I woke up, I was the only one on the bench. I looked up at the clock on the wall, almost seven o'clock. I had to find a place to spend the night. I got up and walked down to the street.

I quickly rejected the idea of asking my sister to let me sleep in her room. Her room was tiny, but the real problem was that if Ksiel and Lotte didn't like the idea of my sleeping there, they could let Ruchele go. That would be a disaster. I no longer felt comfortable going to Frau Liebe's. Elke had given birth to twins, two girls, and I knew how jealous Elke was of her privacy. Khiel and Nachme shared a bed in a small room which they rented. They didn't have enough room for their sister and I was sure they had no room for me there.

Carrying all my belongings under my arm, I roamed around the Jewish Quarter trying to figure out what to do. It started to get late; finally I felt that I had no choice and decided to ask Liebe for advice.

By the time I came to 34 Muranovska Street, the gates to the building were already closed. Luckily, the janitor's son, a boy of twelve, was still sitting inside, opening the gate for the late-comers.

The door to Liebe's basement apartment was also locked. I knocked gently in case someone was already sleeping. Liebe, dressed in her nightgown, looking distraught, opened the door.

"Schloimele?" Liebe said, surprised.

"Mamma, is it the doctor?" Elke asked from inside the apartment.

"No, it's Schloimele."

"Oh..." Elke said.

I could tell at once from her tone of voice that I was not welcome to spend the night there.

"We're waiting for Doctor Feinberg. Hertzke is worse than ever." Liebe spoke with such grief I knew her husband's life was threatened. "What brings you here at this hour?"

"I don't have a place to sleep," I said. "There's a strike on and I lost my job."

"So you got caught in it too?"

"I thought maybe you could give me some advice where I could find a bed."

"Wait here a minute," Liebe said and turned back into the apartment.

I overheard a hushed conversation between Liebe and Elke although I couldn't tell what they were saying. In a few minutes Liebe came back to the door. She had dressed to go out.

"Come with me, Schloimele," she said.

"What about Hertzke?" I felt guilty taking Frau Liebe away from her sick husband.

"Elke knows what to do if Doctor Feinberg comes," Liebe said. "We're not going far. I'll be right back."

As we climbed the stairs, Liebe said, "I'm taking you to a friend of mine, Rivke Baindl. She rents part of her room, but I don't think she has anyone right now."

On the street Liebe held my arm and walked slowly.

"I'm growing old, Schloime. I can't work the way I used to. The basket of little fish becomes heavier to carry every day. Hertzke is sick, I have to depend on the children now, and they want their lives. Elke has her hands full with her two babies. May the Lord bless them, and give them happy and healthy lives... If only Hertzke would get better...but this time, I'm afraid...God forgive me."

We stopped at the closed gates of a building on Niska Street, only a

117

block away from Muranovska. Liebe rang the bell for the janitor. A minute later we heard him muttering in Polish and jangling his ring of keys. The creaking gates were opened by a large man, with unruly gray hair and sagging folds of flesh under his eyes. We walked into the courtyard and the janitor locked the gates again.

Frau Liebe reached into her pocket to give him a tip. The janitor gently pushed her hand back. "Never mind the groschen, Misses Liebe. When you remember just bring me a mouthful of your little fried fish."

The janitor returned to the building on the right. Liebe and I went into the building on the left. By the dingy light from the hallway Frau Liebe and I walked down a flight of stairs. There were about eight apartments in the basement.

"Knock hard on the door," Liebe said. "Rivke, God bless her, is a little deaf."

The door was opened by an elderly, stooped woman, leaning on a cane. She was thin and frail, her face as wrinkled as a turtle's, and a coil of dry, braided gray hair rested on her head. From the door, I could see the whole apartment at a glance. Baindl lived in a narrow hovel with a stove, a bench for water, a small table with two chairs, and two narrow beds. There was no room to even turn around down there.

"Oh, my dear, dear Liebe, come in, come in," Baindl said. "Sit down."

"I can't stay, Baindl," Frau Liebe said. We stood at the door while Liebe explained my problem to Rivke.

I noticed someone stir under the covers of one of the beds. I realized immediately that I could not spend the night there. Baindl apologized profusely but she had a sleeper for the next month.

In a few minutes, Frau Liebe and I were out on the street again.

"Come, let's go to my cousin Tsirel," Liebe said. "She takes in two sleepers but usually she only can find one at a time."

We walked slowly to Karmelitzka, a small street with elegant houses.

"Here we are," Liebe said when we came to a four-story white brick building. We climbed up all four flights of stairs. Liebe walked painfully and stopped at each landing to catch her breath. On the top floor, we climbed one more set of stairs and finally we walked out on the roof.

Clothes lines were strung up everywhere. White linen sheets flapped in the breeze, billowing out like sails as if the roof were the deck of a ship floating under a starry sky. I followed Frau Liebe through the maze of drying laundry until we came to an attic door.

Liebe knocked. Tsirel's apartment was no more than a hut on top of the fancy building. The door was opened by a short, slim man in his thirties, with close-set eyes, a hooked nose under which sprouted a thick mustache which covered his lips. A lit pipe stuck out from the mustache and a cloud of sweet tobacco smoke hovered above his friendly face.

"Teivel," Liebe said, "is your mother home?"

"Cousin Liebe!" Teivel exclaimed, pulling the pipe out of his mouth and throwing an arm around Liebe. "Mamma, look who's here!"

I followed them into the attic. A short woman, who looked like Teivel, except thirty years older and without the thick mustache, embraced Frau Liebe and kissed her on both cheeks. Tsirel, like Liebe, wore a *shaitl* of light brown hair.

"What's the matter, Liebe?" Tsirel asked with deep concern. "May our enemies know of grief, but you look sick."

"It's Hertzke again...." Liebe sighed. "What can I tell you, Tsirel. First it was the heart. Now it's the kidneys, and who knows what else. I can't stay long."

I was sure that there wouldn't be a place for me there. Besides Tsirel and Teivel, I saw a young woman and two men. The young woman, I could tell from her looks, was Tsirel's daughter. She was about twenty, a plain-looking, shy girl. And the two men, I guessed, were Tsirel's lodgers. Besides the living room the apartment also had a small kitchen. It had just enough space for a small stove, a cupboard, and a table with four chairs. Everyone slept in the living room, where I noticed only three beds.

After Liebe had told the bitter news about Hertzke, she explained my situation.

Tsirel, without hesitation, said, "If Schloimele doesn't mind, he can sleep on the floor next to my Teivel."

Relieved and thankful, I accepted the offer. Teivel gave me a hanger, opened the closet door and made room for me to hang up my suit. Frau Liebe embraced Tsirel and left at once to go back to her husband.

I soon found out that Teivel was a bachelor and a shoemaker. There was no strike in his trade and I envied him that he could work. Teivel, for his part, understood what I was going through and was sympathetic to my troubles. Tsirel's daughter's name was Gittel. I had guessed correctly about the two men; they were lodgers. One was a young man, in his twenties, who couldn't take his eyes off Gittel; and the

other, a hefty man in his fifties, was a widower who worked as a porter. Tsirel, herself, was a widow.

It was late already. We prepared to go to sleep. Each of the lodgers
laid himself down like a king in his own small bed. Tsirel and Gittel
shared the third bed. And in the last free corner of the room, Teivel
helped me to soften a piece of the wooden floor with rags, right next
to his spot. I used my own small sack of clothes as a pillow, and Teivel
and I slept back to back.

I was happy to be indoors rather than out on the street, although I
realized that I wouldn't be able to stay there more than a few nights.
Even on the floor there was hardly any room.

The next evening when I stopped at Liebe's basement to thank her
for helping me, I found the Schneidleider family sitting Shiva for
Hertzke. Frau Liebe's husband had died in his sleep in the middle of
the night. I sat with them until it was time for me to go back to Tsirel's
to sleep.

In spite of the cramped quarters, I was still sleeping at Tsirel's seven
weeks later.

The strike was reaching a critical stage. The contractors were finally
beginning to feel the strain. The ready-made garment trade depended
on two seasons which lasted no more than seven months out of the
year. The summer season ran from March to May, and the winter
season from September to January. It was already the second week in
November and the start of the winter season couldn't be delayed any
longer. Another week or two and the winter garments wouldn't make
it to the racks in the clothing stores in time to be sold. The financial
losses were about to become as disastrous for the contractors as for
the workers. In spite of this threat it seemed the bosses still didn't
want to give in to the raise demanded by the Union.

The odd jobs outside of the garment trade I had been able to find
through the newspapers never lasted more than a day or two. I barely
had enough to eat and I certainly couldn't afford to rent a bed for a
night. I was ashamed to be staying at Tsirel's for so long, they were
poor people themselves, but my only other choice was to spend my
nights on the street. I tried to impose on them as little as possible. In
the morning I left the attic at dawn. At night, I came back just in time
to go to sleep.

As the weeks wore on, the money which Blumenstein owed me,
and on which I was surviving, began to run out. On the first morning
of the eighth week of the strike, I left Tsirel's attic at dawn and ran to

a newsstand to check through the advertisements for work. The best notice I could find was from a restaurant looking for a dishwasher. I quickly wrote down the address and returned the page of *The Express*.

The restaurant, in the southern end of the Jewish Quarter, wasn't far from Blumenstein's store. I hurried. When I got to it, however, I found a sign saying that the restaurant wouldn't open until midday. I was hungry. I found a cafeteria and for my last seventy-five groschen I bought myself a bowl of oatmeal and a glass of tea with milk. As I ate I took out the sheet on which I kept count of what Blumenstein still owed me. I saw what I already knew; only four zlotys remained of that money. At most, I figured, I would have enough money to buy food for another four or five days. I finished eating and headed to 18 Twarda Street.

As I approached the store, Blumenstein, seeing me through the window, began to motion wildly for me to come in. I stopped. I was suspicious that my old boss should be so eager to see me.

"Come here!" Blumenstein called to me from the door of his shop. "Nuh? What're you standing out there like that?"

Was this a trap? Had my old boss hired a few thugs to give me a good beating to pay me back for the punch in the eye he had gotten because of me?

"Come on! Nuh?" Blumenstein, impatient, called me again. "I have something important for you. A letter came yesterday! It's from the government."

All at once it hit me. Our papers to leave for Russia had finally arrived. I ran up to the store.

"Where is it?" I asked him.

"It's on the table in the back. Wait here, I'll get it."

Blumenstein disappeared behind the curtain and came out holding the envelope with both hands away from himself as if it were a bomb.

"I'm glad you came around. I don't want to hold any government papers here. What kind of trouble did get yourself into now?"

"Trouble?" I laughed. "This could be my permit to leave for Russia and join my father."

"What father?" Blumenstein asked. "When I hired you, you told us that your father was dead."

I had forgotten that lie.

"That was my stepfather who had died," I said, making something up on the spot. "This is from my real father."

I could tell that Arele Blumenstein no longer believed a word I said.

121

I tore open the envelope and found a single sheet with Polish writing. "I have to find out what this says." I ran out, leaving Arele Blumenstein with a bewildered look on his face.

At the Union headquarters I walked up to one of the office clerks, a well dressed young man sitting behind a typewriter, and asked him whether he could read Polish.

"Of course," he said.

"Could you do me a favor then and read this for me?" I asked, handing him the letter.

"Let's see it. You're being called to the Emigration Bureau. Your permit to travel to Russia has been processed. You have to pick it up in person."

"Amen!" I shouted

"Who's screaming?" asked a striker dozing on the bench who woke up with a start. "What's going on?"

"Go back to sleep," I said. "And to all of you, good luck with your strike, goodbye, and good riddance!"

The men looked at me as if I were crazy. I grabbed the letter out of the clerk's hands and ran out the door.

"Excuse me!" I heard someone say behind me as I skipped down the steps.

I looked back. A thin, short man in his thirties was coming down the stairs towards me. He seemed familiar. "Forgive me for stopping you," he said, "but did I just hear that you got a permit to travel?"

I recognized him the moment he opened his mouth. He was missing teeth everywhere, and the few stubs he did have were broken and blackened. This was the same man who eight weeks earlier had advised me to go to the police to force my boss to sleep in the store.

"Yes," I said. "I'm going to pick it up right now."

We walked down the stairs together. He had a friendly face, large brown eyes, a bony nose, and a neat little mustache.

"I know you," he said recognizing me too. "Did your boss let you sleep in the store?"

"Only for one night," I confessed. "I ran into some other problem with him and I had to move. But I don't care anymore. I'm leaving as soon as I can."

"Did I hear right?" he asked on the street. "Are you going to Russia?"

"Yes," I said happily.

The poor worker stuck out his hand, I gave him mine.

"My deepest congratulations," he said. "My name is Eisen Broder.

122

Who do I have the pleasure of addressing?"

"Schloime Schmer," I said.

"I can hardly tell you how happy I am for you, Schloime," he said. "I wish the same for myself, my wife, and our children someday soon. I don't want to hold you up. If you don't mind, I'll walk a little way with you."

"I don't mind," I said. "Not at all."

"I wonder if I can ask you something," he said slowly, "I mean if I am not being too nosy..."

"Go ahead. Ask me whatever you want."

"How did you manage to get a permit for Russia?"

"My father lives there," I said. "He's been there since the War."

"Your father?" Eisen exclaimed as if I had just told him how to make gold out of thin air. "What a lucky man. You see our situation here? This would never happen under Marxism. There the worker has value. I couldn't earn enough before the strike and I'm sure I'm going to earn just as little after the strike. My views don't suit the Union leadership. They think I don't know the games they play. I have a wife and three children and they give me the worst jobs they can find...Anyway, who knows how long we're going to be on strike now. Well, good luck, Schloime Schmer," Eisen said. "I want to remember your name. Someday, I'll get to Russia with my family. I'll look for you and we'll celebrate together over there."

I thanked him for his kind words as we shook hands warmly. Eisen turned back to the Union headquarters and I rushed off to get Ruchele. I wanted her to join me at the Emigration Bureau.

I felt as if an angel was watching over me. I could hardly believe my own good luck. At the last moment, just as my money was about to run out, here was the letter I had been waiting for so long.

When I opened the door at Ksiel's apartment, I found Ruchele alone in kitchen, at the sewing machine. I guessed Lotte was busy with her children in the back of the apartment.

My sister was surprised to see me. "Schloime, what are you doing here? What are you grinning about?"

"Ruchele, I have good news."

"I've never seen you so happy since I came to Warsaw."

"Our papers have come! We can leave for Russia. We can finally go and live with Tatte."

Ruchele, far from sharing my joy, looked away.

"What's wrong?" I asked her. "Don't you know what this means?"

"I don't want to leave Warsaw," Ruchele said.

I couldn't believe her words. "What's wrong with you? How can you say that?"

"I know what I'm saying. I'm not a child anymore. I have a right to chose where I want to live."

"But what's holding you here?"

"I'm happy here," Ruchele said. "I'm in love."

"In love? What're you talking about?"

"I'm talking about Zygmunt Treiberg. You've met him."

"Forget about him. You're falling into a trap. He'll ruin your life."

"Don't talk to me like that!" Ruchele said, fuming. "Zygmunt and I are in love. We're going to get married—"

"Married?" I couldn't help laughing bitterly.

"Leave me alone! You go ahead and leave for Russia if you want," Ruchele said. "I'm not going anywhere without Zygmunt."

I knew that nothing I could say would change Ruchele's mind. "I'll talk to you again later," I said.

As I hurried to the Emigration Bureau I thought that I would have to ask Frau Liebe's help. Maybe she could talk some sense into my stubborn sister.

The Government buildings, clustered in the square, looked like small palaces. From my previous visits, I knew exactly into which one I had to go to. I entered a large wood paneled room, with a bright chandelier hanging from the high ceiling. There were six desks in the room, three on each side, at which the government officials sat. In the back of the room there were large wooden file cabinets. I waited at the front of the room until one of the officials, a man in his forties, elegantly dressed, hair perfectly combed, motioned for me to approach his desk.

"What can we do for you?" he asked in a soft voice not to disturb his co-workers.

"I received a letter," I said, unfolding the sheet of paper and putting it down on his desk. "My sister and I are waiting for a permit to join our father in Russia."

"Let's see," he said, taking my letter. "Wait here."

He disappeared into another office. After a few minutes he returned to his desk carrying a folder.

"I have your papers right here," he said, sitting down. He opened the folder and began to read through the legal papers.

"This," he said, lifting a document from the folder, "is your sister's permit." He took a stamp out of his drawer, stamped the paper, signed it, and pushed it across the table to me. "All she has to do is present it to the guards when she crosses the border. Tell her not to lose it."

I took Ruchele's permit, folded it carefully, and put it in the breast pocket of my jacket. The official meanwhile continued to read through the papers in the folder.

"As for you," he finally said, "your permit has been postponed."

"Postponed?" I repeated not understanding what he meant.

"Just for a few years," he said, "until you have performed your patriotic duty to Poland and served in the military."

"Excuse me, Sir," I said with great hesitation, "but I have a limp. It's from an accident when I was a small child."

"Don't worry about that," the official reassured me. "After you complete your military service you will also be given a permit to join your father and sister in Russia." And having said that he snapped the folder shut and got up to return the file to its proper place.

Good News

WALKING DOWN THE STEPS of the Emigration Bureau to the street, I felt as if I were stepping into a grave. My life was a bitter joke. Ruchele, who wouldn't even hear of leaving Warsaw, had been granted an exit permit, while I, who desperately wanted to join our father in Russia, was refused. What could I look forward to? Sleeping on the floor in Tsirel's cramped attic? My four zlotys running out in a few days?

I stepped distractedly into the street. "Watch out!" a droshky driver suddenly screamed as his horse charged towards me. I jumped back to the sidewalk and slipped. "Damned Jew!" the driver shouted as the carriage sped away. I picked myself up. My left hand was scraped. I spat into my handkerchief and wiped the wound.

As I began to walk back towards the Jewish Quarter, I felt completely defeated. Maybe I *was* damned, I thought. I reached for a cigarette. The pack of Wandas was empty and crushed in my pocket. On Masrshalkovska Avenue I stopped at a tobacconist and bought a fresh pack. I knew that I was wasting precious money which I desperately needed for food. The same cigarettes in a grocery store in the Jewish Quarter would have cost me half as much.

Dangling a Wanda from my lips, I walked through the downtown streets oblivious of the world, overwhelmed by the absurdity of my situation. At the corner of Marshalkovska and Jerosolymska, however, the sudden loud clang of the trolleys crisscrossing the busy avenues jarred me as if an alarm had gone off. I looked up. Sparks flew like fireworks as the trolley poles bumped the electrical cable grid above. Automobiles, horse drawn wagons and droshkys raced in all four directions. Neon advertisements sat like crowns on top of the tall office buildings. At night the letters and images in these advertisements glowed like jewels. The scene affected me, as it always did, with awe.

My problems, I realized, mattered little to the world and feeling pity for myself was useless. Now I regretted not having waited to buy the cigarettes in the Jewish Quarter. I decided to go back to Blumenstein and get the last of my money.

"I'm glad you came back," the tailor said as I opened the door to the tailor shop. "I thought you had left for Russia already. I have your last four zlotys."

"I'm not going anywhere," I said.

"I would have given you the money before," Blumenstein said, reaching into his pocket, "but you ran out so fast."

I tore up the sheet of paper on which I had kept my accounting.

"If you're staying in Warsaw awhile longer," Blumenstein said, "I have good news for you."

"What good news could you have for me?"

"The strike is over."

"Are you sure?" I had gotten so used to being on strike, I couldn't believe it would ever end.

"Some union organizer already came by to ask me how many workers I needed. I told him that thanks to his strike, I don't even have enough work to feed my own family."

The end of the strike, if Blumenstein was right, was great news. On the way to the union headquarters, I began to think that if I could just start earning a decent salary again, I would first of all rent a room. Then maybe I could still convince Ruchele to move in with me. I felt my hope slowly returning. I decided to write to our father. I would let him know that Ruchele had her permit to leave Poland. Maybe he could convince her to join him in Russia. Maybe he could even do something to help me.

As I approached the union headquarters I saw garment workers milling around excitedly. I joined the end of a long line of men waiting to go up to the offices. Many more men joined the line after me.

It was late in the afternoon when I finally made my way into the room of an official. Behind a large desk strewn with papers and open ledgers sat a white haired man wearing a gray pin-striped suit. The name plate on the desk read Shimme Tantzer.

"You look very young. Who are you?" he asked, squinting at me through his thick eyeglasses.

"I'm Schloime Schmer. I worked for Arele Blumenstein on 18 Twarda Street."

"Blumenstein...?" He pawed through the papers on his desk, flipped through ledgers, finally he gave up and asked, "Why don't you go back to this Blumenstein?"

"I've been there already. He doesn't have work."

"Are you a union member?" the puzzled official asked. "I don't seem to remember you."

"I'm not a member yet."

"Well, then," said the official, squinting past me out the door, "why don't you come back after I take care of the members?"

"What do you mean? It didn't matter that I wasn't member when you threw me out of my job! Why does it matter all of a sudden now?"

"Look," he said, leaning forward on his desk, "there are men out there who have little children to feed."

"I have to feed myself too."

"Let me take care of the members first."

"Then make me a member," I said.

"How can I make you a member just like that? What are your credentials? This is not the time. Come back after this commotion is over and I'll see what I can do for you."

I continued to argue with him but it was useless. He gave me a hundred excuses but not a single lead on a job. I left the union offices disgusted and strolled around the streets until almost ten o'clock before I went up to Tsirel's to sleep.

On the roof, as I made my way past the laundered sheets flapping in the darkness, I ran into Teivel. He was leaning against the ledge, smoking a pipe. He offered me a cigarette and asked how my day had gone. I knew Teivel was wondering how much longer his family would have to put up with me now that the strike was over. I didn't blame him. His family was poor and the last thing they needed was one more body in that crowded attic. When I told him that I expected my turn for a job to come up tomorrow, he seemed relieved and wished me luck.

The next day, however, after waiting again for hours to see Shimme Tantzer, I got the same story from him. "There are still men with half dozen children waiting to find work," he said.

"What does that have to do with me, Mister Tantzer? Do I have to wait until every man with six children is working before you give me a job?" I asked. "It would be quicker to have six children of my own."

The union official couldn't help smiling as he shrugged his shoulders.

"I'll starve before you do anything for me," I said and left his office. I had been an idiot to waste my time with the union. I decided to give up on the garment trade.

Early next morning I saw an advertisement in *The Express* for a kitchen helper needed at a restaurant on Pawia Street; bed and board were included with the job.

Golden's was a large cafeteria with over thirty tables. At one end of a long counter, three cooks prepared food. At the other end, the owner, a stained apron over his bulging stomach, sat behind the cash register. His lips and fingers were greasy from nibbling on the smoked meats piled up on a plate next to him. His chin sank into the folds of flesh around his neck.

"You're not exactly the type of boy I had in mind," the owner said when I told him that I was there for work.

"I may be short, but I'm strong and quick," I assured him.

He didn't seem convinced.

"Just try me for a week and you'll see."

"Do you need the room and board?" he asked. "The salary is only five zlotys a week."

Awful as that salary was, I accepted at once.

"Let's see how you do," he said, picking up a slice of salami with two fingers and placing it in his mouth.

I rushed back to Tsirel's attic. I caught her family about to leave for work. I told them that I had found a job and a place to sleep, and I thanked them all for their help. They were relieved to see me move my bag of clothes somewhere else.

Leon Golden, the fat owner of the cafeteria, showed me the tiny room in back where I would sleep. There was barely enough space for the folding cot. I put my bag down and started on my chores.

In the morning, as waves of customers came in for breakfast, I cleared dishes and wiped tables. After the breakfast rush, I ran errands for the cooks for lunch preparations. Before lunch I washed the breakfast dishes and during lunch, I again cleared and wiped tables. I didn't stop working even after the cafeteria was closed. At night I still had to wash the dinner dishes, scrub pots and pans, and mop the floors. The worst of it, however, I found out that night. Leon Golden wouldn't trust me with a key to the cafeteria. He insisted that if I wanted to sleep there I would have to be locked in. I felt like a prisoner but I was too afraid of losing my livelihood to complain.

On the Sabbath, the one day of the week when Golden's cafeteria was closed, my boss came strolling by in the morning and unlocked the door. "Be back at eight o'clock tonight," he said, "or you won't get back in."

During my hard times I had stayed away from Liebe and her family. They had enough troubles of their own. Now that I was working again, however, I felt better and I decided to visit my old friends. The reception I got was beyond anything I had expected.

"*Mazeltov!*" Yoinne said pumping my hand. Liebe smiled. Elke embraced me. Tsutel bent down and kissed me on the cheek.

I was a little surprised. Was my job really worth such a fuss?

"Thank you," I said. "But how did you find out so fast? From Tsirel?"

"Tsirel?" Elke said with a disdainful laugh. "Ruchele herself told us."

How could my sister know, I wondered. I hadn't spoken to her in weeks. It suddenly dawned on me that Ruchele, who didn't know that I had been rejected at the Emigration Bureau, had probably told Liebe and her family that I was leaving for Russia.

"Oh, no," I said. "I don't deserve any *mazeltovs*. It didn't work out."

"Good heavens!" Tsutel exclaimed. "Why not?"

Everyone suddenly seemed very concerned.

"I have to serve in the Army first."

"Heaven forbid such a calamity," Frau Liebe said. "Are you being drafted?"

"No," I said. "I was just told that I would have serve in the Army first."

"Why should Ruchele wait for you to serve in the Army?" Elke asked.

"Who says that she has to wait?" I said. "She's the one who doesn't want to go."

"She doesn't want to go?" Elke asked. "She just told us she can't wait."

"Now she wants to go to Russia?" I asked, surprised.

"What Russia?" asked Tsutel. "Ruchele told us that she's getting married."

"Married?" I was shocked. "To whom?"

"Zygmunt Treiberg!" Elke said. "Don't you know?"

I felt aghast at this news and embarrassed to admit to Liebe and her family that I didn't know my own sister was getting married. "I've been so busy trying to find work," I said. "I haven't had a chance to visit Ruchele."

"Well, don't go anywhere," Yoinne said, "because the happy couple is dropping by later."

"Your little sister caught herself quite a big fish," Nachme said.

"What do you think of him?" I asked Frau Liebe.

130

"I like him," she said with an affectionate smile. "He's a decent, hard-working boy."

I was relieved to see that everyone at Liebe's thought highly of Zygmunt. I was invited to stay for lunch. Soon they were asking me what had happened with my plans to travel to Russia, where was I living now, and what kind of work had I finally found.

After the meal, as we were settling down in the living room with glasses of tea and plates of cookies, Ruchele and Zygmunt walked in.

I had never seen my sister look happier or more beautiful. She was wearing a woolen red coat. Above the fur trimmed collar her face shone. Zygmunt, tall, square-shouldered, and handsome in spite of his thick eyeglasses, was also beaming with happiness. The moment Ruchele saw me, however, a troubled look crushed her smile. She was afraid that I would disapprove of Zygmunt. At once I walked up to my sister, embraced her, and wished her *mazeltov*. I felt her squeeze me with joy as she whispered, "Thank you," into my ear.

Forgetting the power of Zygmunt's grip, I gave him my hand and immediately regretted it. The prospect of being my brother-in-law was so delightful to him, he forgot himself and ground my fingers in his iron grip. As if that wasn't enough, he threw his other arm around me in a brotherly hug that knocked the breath out of me. I staggered away and didn't recover my bearings until long after all had drunk a hearty *L'chaim* to Ruchele's and Zygmunt's happiness.

At the wedding, which took place two weeks later in the home of a rabbi on Leszno Street, I was close to my sister as she stood under the wedding canopy with Zygmunt. Liebe, Tsutel, Elke, Yoinne, Khiel and Nachme were also there. As Zygmunt stepped on the glass goblet and shattered it, everyone shouted their *mazeltovs!*

I drank so many *L'chaims* to my sister's happiness that I couldn't walk straight. Khiel and Nachme, each holding me by one arm, had to lead me back to Liebe's basement where she and her daughters had prepared a splendid wedding feast.

Rent for apartments was so expensive, most young couples had to settle for a room with another family. And so it was with Ruchele and Zygmunt. They rented a small room at No. 6 Sherakovsky Street from Hersh Feigelbaum, a cobbler who had a wife and three small children. Hersh's workshop had been in his kitchen and after he rented the room to Ruchele and Zygmunt, the kitchen also became his family's living room and bedroom.

Hersh worked at his trade with great flourish. His long, unruly hair flew every which way as he hammered away at the shoes that lay in piles next to his work bench. On my first visit to my sister and her husband, I noticed that the cobbler had a lot of work. It surprised me that in spite of being quick, Hersh couldn't produce enough to afford his own rent. I had worked for shoemakers in Lublin, and it occurred to me that this might be my chance to quit the cafeteria.

"Why don't you hire a helper?" I asked Hersh as I watched him hammer.

"On what they pay me?" he asked. "How can I afford to give someone else a decent wage."

"Pay what you can afford," I said. "I bet you could find someone."

"Of course I could find someone to work for almost nothing," Hersh said, putting down his hammer, "but why take advantage of a man just because he's worse off than me. It's bad enough I get exploited."

"Hersh," his wife, a shapely woman in her thirties, turned from the stove and said, "don't start making a speech. Do your work."

"The leaders of this country have sold us all out," Hersh Feigelbaum said, paying no attention to his wife. "They've given away the country to the capitalists who get richer every day while the working class struggles in constant poverty."

Hersh's wife laughed at him. "You're more interested in other worker's rights than in earning your own living."

"I am concerned," said Hersh, "because a man without principles is an empty bag of bones."

"A man without money is an even emptier bag," his wife shot back. "Your children are starving while you stuff your head with nonsense at those Party meetings."

"Starving? Let the children speak for themselves. Is any of you starving?" the cobbler asked the little girl and the two small boys, who were playing on the floor.

"No!" they shouted in one voice, laughing.

Hersh was a fiery communist and I realized that if I worked for him I would be in even worst shape than I already was.

After her marriage, Ruchele quit her job with Ksiel and Lotte and started to work in the same coat factory as Zygmunt. Their plan was to earn enough money to rent an apartment of their own and start a family.

When Ruchele and Zygmunt asked me how I was doing, I told them that my situation at the restaurant was unbearable. Not only did I earn very little, but the work was exhausting; from dawn until late at night,

I never stopped for a moment. Worst of all was that my boss insisted on locking me in every night. I was always afraid of being trapped there in a fire.

Ruchele and Zygmunt asked if I wanted to come and live with them until I found a better job.

"We could put up a small partition," Zygmunt said. "You could have a corner of the room."

"And you could look for tailoring work," Ruchele said.

I was touched by their generosity, but I didn't want to impose on them. One morning, a few weeks later, however, without any warning, the fat owner of the cafeteria asked me to leave. A distant cousin had arrived from the provinces and was taking my place. There was no use arguing.

I didn't have much hope that the union would suddenly find me work. Carrying all my belongings under my arm, I stopped at a newsstand and checked the "Employment" section in the paper. I found a laundry looking for someone to mend clothes. I hurried to the address.

The whole laundering operation was run by an older couple in their small apartment. The wash was done by hand in a large tub in the kitchen. By luck, the job hadn't been taken yet. The wife showed me a pile of sheets, pillow cases, shirts, underwear, socks, all with tears and holes. She asked if I could fix them. I assured her that I could. She gave me a sewing case and I went to work. In the afternoon, I was fed lunch. At night, after I had finished sewing up the pile of laundry, the husband paid me three zlotys and thanked me.

"What about tomorrow?" I asked.

"Don't bother," he said. "My wife does the sewing. This week we fell a little behind. Our best customer's moving and she had to have all her linen washed in a rush."

It was dark when I left the launderers. The night was a cold one and I needed a place to sleep. I remembered Rivke Baindl and hurried to the basement where she lived.

When she answered the door, I reminded her that I was Frau Liebe's friend and asked whether the bed which she rented was available.

"Of course. Come in, come in." Her welcome was so warm, I guessed that she must have been starving and was overjoyed to earn a zloty.

I spent a decent night at Rivke's. I went back to sleep there the next two nights while my money lasted. Unfortunately I wasn't lucky in finding a job and on the fourth night, I didn't have the zloty to pay

Rivke. I was forced to visit Ruchele and Zygmunt.

If I still had any question about what kind of a man Zygmunt was, I had none at all after I knocked on their door and told them I had no place to sleep. They welcomed me at once. Since there wasn't an extra bed, my sister and her husband made sure that I had a soft place to sleep on the floor. While Zygmunt swept, Ruchele gathered up all the bed spreads and covers and laid them down for me.

By the following night, Zygmunt had put up a small partition and behind it, I found a comfortable folding bed. We were cramped, but we had some privacy and I felt lucky to have found that corner to sleep in.

I wasn't nearly as lucky in finding a job. At most, I had a day of work every week. And towards the end of winter my luck ran out altogether. One night, when I came in to sleep, I noticed that Ruchele had argued with her husband. As soon as I walked in, Zygmunt grabbed his coat and ran out.

When I asked my sister what had happened, she told me that Zygmunt had received a letter from his sister, Raisel, who lived in the provinces. She had lost her job and was desperate to move to Warsaw. I understood immediately. "Don't worry," I told Ruchele, "I'll figure something out."

Ruchele and Zygmunt were both apologetic. For the next few days, I doubled my efforts to find work. In the midst of this desperate struggle, I came back to sleep one night and found that Raisel had arrived. There simply wasn't any room for me to stay. Ruchele and Zygmunt gave me as much money as they could afford but it came to no more than a few zlotys. I saw how ashamed my sister and brother-in-law were. I assured them that I had a place to sleep. I asked Ruchele and Zygmunt if I could just leave my bundle of clothing for a day or two.

When I left their apartment, instead of walking down the stairs, I went up to the top floor of the building. Just before the door to the roof there was a small landing which was hidden from view. That's where I settled down for the night. The stone floor was cold and hard, and I slept very badly. At dawn I slipped down the stairs before most tenants were up.

I was the first one at the union headquarters. After the usual arguments with the officials and their standard excuses, I sat down on a bench, leaned back, and fell asleep. The union office, at least, was warm.

"Schloime?...Schloime?"

I felt someone shaking me. Groggy, I looked at the man sitting next to me. The thin moustache, the mouth with the few blackened teeth seemed familiar.

"What are you doing here?" he asked with an astonished expression. "I thought you had left for Russia to join your father?"

Slowly I recognized Eisen Broder.

"I couldn't go," I said.

"Why not?"

"I didn't get the permit to leave Poland."

"Why not? Didn't you have a letter from the Emigration Bureau saying they were giving you a permit?"

"They gave me a permit. For my sister. She could have left if she had wanted to."

"Didn't she want to?"

"No."

"What a pity!" Eisen exclaimed in misery. "To have such an opportunity and not be able to take advantage of it. She probably didn't want to leave you behind."

"She didn't want to leave because she had decided to get married."

"Oh, I see. Then, *mazeltov*," Eisen said, shaking my hand. "But what about you? Why couldn't you leave?"

"I have to serve in the military."

"Military?..." Eisen said. "Forgive me for saying this, Schloime, but you have a limp. They don't take men with limps."

"Sometimes they do," another union member chimed in.

"What're you talking about?" said a third worker sitting on the bench. "When did you ever see them take someone with a limp?"

"And if I told you that they took Mendl Geist would you know who I was talking about? He's a cook, and he had a limp. So he limped to the kitchen everyday. It didn't break the general's heart."

"Please, fellows," Eisen said. "What's the difference? This young man was all set to join his father in Russia, a father he hasn't seen since the War. What will you do now?" Eisen asked me.

"I don't know," I said. "I can't find work. I don't have any money. I don't even have a place to sleep."

"Didn't they give you a job after the strike?" Eisen asked.

"Not even for a day," I said. "They keep telling me they have to find work for all the men with wives and children, meanwhile I'm starving."

135

"Sometimes I wonder what good this union does us," Eisen said. "I just lost my own job."

One of the workers stood up from the bench, walked over to a union clerk, and demanded, "What's happening here? How much longer do I have to wait to see somebody?"

"Don't get overheated," the clerk said. "It's bad for your health. You're next in line. Let him finish in there."

"Listen to this," Eisen said.

"He's lucky," I said. "Sooner or later they'll give him job. Those bastards won't lift a finger to help me."

Eisen thought awhile and said, "I might be able to help you. Come with me. Let me show you something."

"Eisen, are you giving up already?" one of the workers asked.

"Maybe I'll come back later."

As we walked down the stairs, Eisen turned to me and said, "If nothing else, at least you'll meet my family."

Eisen lived on Krochmalna Street in a slum. The street was thick with dangerous men and loose women. The courtyard he took me into was swarming with dirty, squealing children.

"Tatte!" a little boy screamed, breaking away from his little friends, and leaping into Eisen's arms. Eisen lifted the boy up and carried him up a flight of stairs to the second floor.

A little girl of three and a boy who was still wobbly on his legs rushed out of the apartment to greet their father. Eisen managed to scoop them all up into his arms and carried them in.

The apartment we entered, a tiny hovel, was as run-down as Eisen's mouth. Everything in that place was broken and patched. The kitchen table had three legs. It managed to stand because one side leaned on a piece of wood that had been banged into the wall. The chairs had broken legs. Eisen and his family could sit on those chairs only because they were all so light. His wife, a small woman with a friendly smile stood over a basin washing diapers.

"Mirele," Eisen sang out his wife's name, "this is Schloime Schmer. We met at the union headquarters."

"Forgive me for not shaking your hand," Mirele said. "So, Eisen, did you find something yet?"

"Nah," he said. "They're going to keep me waiting a few more days at least. Mirele, give me the key to the cellar. I want to show it to Schloime."

"I can't touch anything now. Come here and take it out of my apron's pocket. Don't forget to take a candle if you're going down."

As Eisen took the key out of Mirele's pocket, he gave her a kiss on the cheek. His little children immediately began to imitate their father, puckering, smacking their lips, laughing hysterically.

"Is the fool egging you all on?" Mirele scolded her brood.

Eisen took a candle stub from the drawer of the kitchen table and told me to follow him. We walked out into the courtyard, down three crude stone steps. A murky light seeped into the dank cellar of the building. At the back we came to a row of stalls with wooden-slat doors. He lit the candle and while I held it for him, he opened the padlock of a stall. Cobwebs hung from the walls of the dusty hole. It was cluttered with old valises, a wooden trunk, a baby carriage with missing wheels, a broken chair, and pieces of wood.

"I'm embarrassed to even offer it to you," Eisen said as he moved into the little storage room with the candle. "It's not fit for a dog. But it's all I have and if it can help you, please use it."

He held out the key to me. I took it at once.

"It's a hundred times better than spending the night on the street," I said.

"Well, then," Eisen said, "let's clear this mess and make room for you."

We pushed the trunk into a corner, piled the suitcases on it, and put the broken baby carriage on top of the suitcases. The bits of wood, which Eisen was saving to burn in winter, we gathered up next to the trunk. Eisen found me a broom and while I swept up my new home, he ran upstairs and brought down an old blanket and some rags for my bed.

When I returned to my sister's room to pick up my clothes, Ruchele and Zygmunt were out showing Raisel Warsaw at night. The cobbler, who knew that I had been forced to leave the apartment, allowed me to pick up my things. As I was walking out he stopped me and asked, "Where are you staying?"

I described my new lodgings to him.

"What a find," Feigelbaum said sarcastically. "You've got a whole apartment to yourself."

"It's more like a whole grave to myself," I said. "Please don't tell my sister. Just say that I'm staying at a friend's house."

On my way back to cellar, my bundle under my arm, I stopped off in a grocery and bought myself a hard boiled egg, a few slices of rye bread, an onion, and a candle.

Krochmalna Street seemed busier at night than during the day. I held on to my few possessions and bag of food. Among the penniless workers, many of whom clung to their decency in spite of dire poverty, there were drunks, thieves, even murderers. Women, perfumed and painted, decked out in cheap jewelry, wearing gaudy dresses, came and went on high heels followed by customers. Dirty children seemed to sprout from the sidewalks.

In the courtyard to Eisen's building I tried to steal down the stairs to the cellar as inconspicuously as I could. I didn't need to bother. No one cared where I was going. As I lit the candle in the dark cellar, I saw darting shadows. Rats.

After I ate, I lit a cigarette. Suddenly I remembered a time when I had slept in an even smaller shed in Lublin. Our mother had already left us by then. Uncle Yankel had found out that I was smoking on the Sabbath and threw me out of the house. Now, I missed my crazy uncle, my poor aunt and the tiny kitchen where Mamme, Babbe, Ruchele and I had once slept. We had barely been able to fit our bed into that kitchen. On our first night there we were overrun by bedbugs. I never thought I would long for those days, but now I knew that those had been happy days for us.

The Stolen Ring

AFTER SLEEPING A FEW NIGHTS in Eisen's cellar I caught a cold. Even though I felt worse from day to day, I couldn't stop looking for work. Soon I was walking around with a fever, shivering one minute, sweating the next, and coughing. I went to the infirmary at the Jewish Hospital on Leszno Street. The waiting room was crowded with old men, women, and mothers with children. A nurse filled a chart out for me and sent me back to the waiting room. It was a few hours before I heard my name called. When I walked into the doctor's office, I recognized Frau Liebe's neighbor, Doctor Feinberg.

"Is this is your first visit?" the doctor asked as he glanced at my empty chart. "I seem to remember you."

"You treated me once. Frau Liebe Schneidleider took me to see you."

"Oh, yes, I do remember. She brought you to my apartment." The doctor placed the ear-tips of his stethoscope into his ears. "And what's wrong now?"

"I have a fever again."

"Lift your shirt and breathe deeply."

I took a breath and immediately had a coughing fit.

At the end of my examination, Doctor Feinberg gave me an injection. He also handed me a bottle of syrup and told me to take it three times a day.

"I don't like the sound of your left lung," the doctor said. He thought a few moments and continued, "I want you to come back and see me in two weeks."

The injection and the syrup brought the fever down in a few days.

Every morning I ran like a madman from the Union offices, where they never had any work for me, to the newsstand to pore over the advertisements. Most jobs were filled by the time I got to them. Eisen tried to help me. Whenever he heard of an opening for which he wasn't qualified he gave me the address. Since Eisen's work, shoulders and sleeves on men's suits, was highly specialized, I had quite a few leads from him. Thanks to my friend, I soon found work as a presser in a shop on Gensha Street.

My new boss, who knew I hadn't been sent by the Union, offered to pay me forty-five groschen for each suit, a third of the legal rate. I had to be happy with that much. But even that didn't last long. On my second day of work, a barrel-chested man walked into the shop and told my boss to get rid of me. I recognized the Union official as soon as I heard his high-pitched voice. He was the same man who had forced me to leave my job with Arele Blumenstein at the start of the strike.

Eisen was enraged when I told him what had happened. "Do you know who got you fired? Maisel Flanc, the biggest parasite in the Union. He does nothing except spy. He's only happy when we're on strike."

But there was little else Eisen could do to help me. His own situation was quickly growing as desperate as mine. Luckily, the Union soon found him a job.

The few times I visited my sister and brother-in-law, I saw the alarm on their faces as they looked at me. Unfortunately Zygmunt's sister still hadn't found work either. When Ruchele asked where I was living, I told her that a fellow worker from the Union was allowing me to stay at his flat. Before I left their house, my sister and brother-in-law made sure I ate a good meal, gave me as much money as they could afford, and insisted I come back soon.

And yet, the worse my situation grew, the more reluctant I felt to look for help. I was embarrassed by my torn clothes and sickly appearance. I didn't even go back to the clinic to see Dr. Feinberg. The medication had driven away the fever and I was coughing less.

One night, as I was returning to sleep in the cellar, I saw Eisen running towards me. "Good news!" he said with excitement. "I may have found you a job."

"Where?" I asked, as excited as if he had told me that I won the lottery.

"On Novanyarska Street. A friend of mine needs a presser. Come, let's go over and I'll introduce you."

As we walked, Eisen explained, "Nachem just started his own business a few months ago. Most of the time he doesn't have work, but when he gets some, it's usually from other contractors and they tear his head off with the rush."

We ran down Orla Street, across Krashinsky Place, and finally stopped at No. 12 Novanyarska. On the second floor of the three story building, I heard the sound of a sewing machine coming from an apartment. Eisen opened the door and we entered a kitchen where two men were working, one at a sewing machine, the other at a press table.

"Nachem!" Eisen called out over the noise.

The tall young man who had been pressing put down the iron and came to shake Eisen's hand.

"This is Schloime," Eisen said, "my friend who's looking for work."

Without wasting a moment, Nachem pointed to the press iron and asked, "Can you handle one of these?"

"Step aside," I told him at once. I walked to the table and felt the iron. It was hot. "Let me finish this jacket, then you tell me if I can handle an iron."

While Nachem and Eisen talked, I pressed as if my life depended on it. Not only did I get rid of every crease, I used the iron to get rid of mistakes the tailor had made. Even though the lapels hadn't been sewn to meet where they should, after I was done they were perfectly in place. I even got the length of the sleeves to match. When I was sure that I couldn't do anything more with the jacket I called Nachem over.

He took one look at the jacket and said, "Did we make this? When did that left-handed needle-jabber learn to sew like this? Yashke, look at this," Nachem showed the jacket to the tailor sitting at the sewing machine who agreed that I had done a good job.

Nachem shook my hand. "Can you start working now?" he asked.

"Where are the pants to the suit?" I asked.

Nachem immediately brought over the work which the tailor had finished and laid it down on the chair next to the press table.

"I've already started," I said, as I picked up the pair of pants and felt to see if the iron was still hot.

Eisen ran back home to his wife and children. I worked another four hours at Nachem's apartment and managed to press two suits. The tailor had already left when I finished pressing the last pair of pants. In the next room, I could see Nachem's elderly parents preparing for bed.

"Could you pay me now?" I asked Nachem. "It's not that I don't trust you, but I'm broke."

"I can't pay the union rate," Nachem said. "I wish I could, but I'm just starting out. I can pay fifty groschen a suit. If you think it's too little, I won't blame you..."

I had no doubt that Nachem was telling the truth.

"I believe you," I said.

Nachem paid me the zloty I had earned for my four hours of back-breaking work.

I thanked him and started to leave, "Wait," he called me back. He dug into his pocket and pulled out another two zlotys. "Can you use an advance?" he asked, extending the money to me.

I left Nachem's apartment with three zlotys in my pocket. I debated with myself whether to go back to the cellar or try to rent a bed for the night from Baindl. I wouldn't have worried so much if I had been sure of my job, but who knew how long it would last. The zloty I spent for the bed tonight could be the zloty I would sorely miss in a few days when I was starving. On the other hand, the cold stone of the cellar floor was killing me. Even though I was coughing less, every time I did cough my chest hurt. I walked to Niska to Baindl's basement. Luckily the gate hadn't been locked yet. I hoped that I would be as lucky in finding Baindl's extra bed available.

I knocked on her door. I could tell from Baindl's greeting when she saw me that she was as happy to see me as I was to see her. I gave her the zloty and I slept like a king under the covers of the soft bed.

The next morning, I was the first one to arrive at Nachem's workshop. I went to work at once. By the end of the day I had pressed four suits and earned two zlotys. My luck held out. The work didn't stop; no one from the union came to force me to leave the job; and my health continued to improve. With a little more experience, I was able to press five suits a day. I decided that as long as I had the job I wouldn't sleep in the cellar. I also began to eat better and gain back some weight.

I returned the key to the cellar to Eisen. He was glad I no longer needed to live in that miserable hole. But just as he had warned me, within a month, I noticed Nachem's work beginning to dry up. One day, he had to let his tailor go. Nachem, himself, did whatever little work fell in. I knew that unless business picked up soon, I would be next to go. For a few days, I earned no more than a zloty.

"It's no use," Nachem said to me early one morning. "I don't know how long it'll be before I have work. Either they tear pieces of flesh out of me with their rush, or they let me starve. I'm sorry Schloime, but for now I can't keep you."

"But it's only January," I said. "The season's still going strong. Someone could could come in with work at any minute."

"Believe me, if I have work, I'll hire you at once."

I had been sleeping every night at Baindl's, eating a decent meal every day, and now all I had left in my pocket were fifty groschen. What I feared most had happened. I had lost the job and I had no savings to fall back on. I would have to go back to sleep in the cellar of Eisen's building.

I felt desperate enough to try the Union again. I got the same old story. Union members, men with families, were still out of work and had to be helped first. The newspapers also had nothing. By eleven, I had explored all my possibilities for work. I decided to go back to Nachem.

From the hallway the silence of the sewing machine told me the whole sad story.

"I'm glad to see you," Nachem said as I opened the door to his kitchen. "Did you find a job yet?"

"No. Did you get any business?" I asked.

"Not a stitch," Nachem said. "But I have an idea for you. This morning after you left I heard yelling upstairs. I put my head out the door. My neighbor Moishe Chaim Borenstein fired his presser. Borenstein has a little factory up there. Little? What am I saying, he's a rich man. It seems his presser, Yankel, stole a little ring from Moishe Chaim's daughter while she was sleeping. I immediately thought of you. I was hoping you would come by soon."

I didn't waste a moment. I thanked Nachem as I was running out the door. It wasn't until after I had climbed the stairs that I realized I didn't know which apartment was this Borenstein's workshop. I stood still. At first I heard only the thumping of my heart and then, like a friendly call, a sewing machine gave it's familiar little roar from an apartment. That was the door I opened.

Either I had gone into the wrong apartment or I was already too late. A young man, no more than eighteen, stood at a table pressing a pair of pants. From the awkwardness with which he handled the iron, I guessed he had just started to work there. This factory, like Nachem's, was in the kitchen, except that this kitchen was larger than Nachem's living room. Two men in their forties, obviously experienced workers, were operating the electrical sewing machines, while a woman, in her thirties, was sewing by hand. In the kitchen there was also a woman in her fifties, short and plump, cooking at the large white porcelain stove. Finally, through the kitchen door, I saw a small man in the living room. He was in his fifties, had white hair, a short white beard, and was wearing a hat. He had a hump in front, as if his enlarged heart

143

were pushing out through his chest, and a larger hump in back between his shoulder blades. He was standing on a small wooden platform at a long table, his shirt sleeves rolled up, cutting material with large shears. As soon as he saw me, he stepped down from his wooden platform and came into the kitchen.

"Are you looking for me?" he asked.

"Are you Mister Borenstein?"

"And what if I am?"

I looked at the young man with the iron in his hand and thought of just apologizing and leaving. At the last moment, however, I figured that I had nothing to lose by asking for work, any kind of work.

"I heard you were looking for a worker," I said.

Everyone in the shop turned around and stared at me. The young man at the ironing table stopped working. I thought that he was looking accusingly at me, as if I were trying to steal his job.

"I need an experienced presser for boy's suits," the short man said. "I don't need anyone else."

I wanted to say that I was a presser with experience in boy's suits but I was afraid the young man with the iron in his hand would throw it at me.

"Itche, watch those pants!" the short tailor screamed.

"I'm sorry, Papa," the young man whined as he lifted the iron.

"I'm a presser," I spoke up immediately.

"Look," the small tailor said, "my son's a presser too. But I need an experienced presser. I don't have time to teach anyone."

"I have experience," I said. "Nobody has to teach me a thing."

The tailor looked at his son. The young man appealed to his father with an encouraging nod. The father threw up his arms. "You can't be worse than my son. Let's see what you can do. Finish the suit my heir almost burned." He pointed to the chair next to the table where I saw a suit jacket and a pair of pants.

Itche turned the iron over to me with a smile. He sat down, happy to pick up needle and thread again. Everyone else went back to work as well.

I looked at the pants on the table. They were badly creased even though I could tell by the shine of the fabric that the tailor's son had been pressing them for some time. I felt the iron. It was cold.

Without even asking, I took the iron to the stove. The tailor's wife stepped aside. One of the burners was open and I found a second iron heating up. I shoved away some of the burning coals, put down the cold iron and released the handle. I hooked the handle into the hot iron and picked it up.

The bowl of water, I noticed, was nearly empty. I filled it at the sink.

First I decided to fix the pants that the tailor's son had nearly ruined. I threw a cloth over the pants, filled my mouth with water, sprayed a fine mist over the cloth and began.

I lost all sense of time. I stopped ironing only to exchange the irons when they got cold. It was a pleasure to work in that kitchen. It was well lit, the smell of cooked chicken filled the room, and the noise of the sewing machines was like music.

"Let's see what you did," I heard the little tailor say suddenly.

I looked up as if awaking from a dream. I had ironed one pair of pants, the jacket, and was just finishing the second pair of pants. I pointed to the jacket which I had hung over the back of the chair and the pants folded neatly on the seat.

"Wait," the tailor said. He went into the living room, brought back a wooden hanger, and hung the pants up. He turned the hanger back and forth examining my work. He picked up the jacket, hung it up on the hanger, and studied it, back and front.

"Come here," he said to me. I followed him into the living room. He opened the door to a wooden closet.

"Hang up the finished the work in here," he said.

I was tempted to ask if I had the job, but I decided that it was best to just keep pressing.

I went back to the ironing table and again I was swallowed up by my work. When I looked up, everyone was preparing to leave for lunch. I had finished ironing another jacket and two pairs of pants. I went into the living room and got a hanger from the closet.

"Bring me the work and let me see," the tailor said from where he stood at the cutting table.

I hung up the jacket and pants and brought them to him. Again the tailor turned the suit this way and that and told me to hang it up.

"You can stop to eat now," he said.

I felt my empty pockets and asked him if he could pay me something for my work.

He handed me two zlotys. "We'll settle your salary later," he said.

On my way down the stairs, I heard Nachem's sewing machine through the open door. I walked in to thank him.

"I'm glad to see you have some work," I said.

"A drop fell in," he said. "So, did Borenstein hire you?"

"I've been working since I went up."

"How much is he paying you?" Nachem asked.

"We didn't discuss it yet. First, I hope he keeps me."

"If he let you work this long, he must like you. Don't tell him I said so, but he can afford the full price."

"Do you know if his tailors are Union members?" I asked Nachem.

"Are you afraid that they'll inform on you?"

"It's happened to me once before."

"Sruel and Mayer are decent people," Nachem said.

"What about the woman?"

"Esther?" Nachem asked. "That's Borenstein's niece. You don't have to worry about her."

Nachem wished me luck, and I wished him the same.

After lunch, I immersed myself again in my work. I stopped only to change irons and to hang up the pressed suits.

In the evening, as everyone was leaving, Borenstein asked me to stay behind.

"I can tell that you're not an experienced presser," Borenstein said as we stood in the kitchen. "How many suits did you press today? Four?"

"I didn't start work until almost eleven o'clock," I said. "Tomorrow, I'll start at seven and do a lot more."

"Tomorrow is too late. I have merchants coming to pick up work in the morning. Can you at least finish two more suits?"

I assured my new boss that I wouldn't leave until the two suits were done. I continued to work while Borenstein and his family ate dinner. I finished just as they were preparing for bed. Borenstein looked over the work I had done and asked, "How much do you want?"

"The regular rate," I said.

Borenstein laughed. "You're not worth it," he said with a dismissing wave of his hand. "Sixty five groschen a suit. That's what I can pay you."

"But that's half the rate."

"If you don't like my offer, I'll pay you the full rate for what you did, but don't bother coming back tomorrow."

I couldn't risk losing the job.

"I accept," I said. "But I hope you'll raise my price when I get more experienced."

"Get some experience, and then we'll talk." Borenstein advanced

146

me three zlotys and I left.

The following morning, as I was crossing the courtyard to Borenstein's building, I ran into Sruel and Mayer, the two experienced tailors.

"How did it go with the boss last night?" Sruel asked.

"Not bad," I said.

"Is he paying you the rate?" asked Mayer.

"No," I said.

"Didn't I tell you?" Sruel said to Mayer.

"That's illegal," Mayer said to me. "The Union won't allow lowering the rate."

"I can't do anything about it," I said. "I've been out of work for almost a year. Please don't make any trouble for me."

"Aren't you a member of the Union?" Mayer asked. "We saw you during the strike at the Headquarters."

"I want to become a member, but they say I don't have enough experience. And if I can't keep a job, how am I going to prove that I have experience?"

"Look nobody wants to make trouble for you," Sruel said, "but if we don't stick together, the contractors walk all over us. Borenstein is one of the worst. He's always trying to hire from outside of the Union."

"Don't worry," Sruel said. "We won't say anything. Get your experience and as soon as you can, join the Union."

I was relieved and promised them that I would join just as soon as I could. My luck had finally begun to change.

On my fifth day of work, however, the door to the shop opened, and a short, well dressed man walked in. I was in trouble. Maisel Flanc had found me again.

"You!" he said in his squeaky voice. "You're taking work from a Union member—"

"What's going on here?" Borenstein came running into the shop from the living room where he had been cutting cloth.

"Moishe Chaim, I don't want anymore trouble from you," Maisel said. "You know you can't hire a presser outside of the Union."

"For a year I've been begging the Union for work," I defended myself.

"And you can beg for another year," Maisel said. "Get out! You're finished here."

"You get out!" I said, lifting the press iron in a rage. "You're the one who's finished here! I'll break your head if you don't leave me alone!"

Maisel ran to the door as Sruel and Mayer jumped to their feet to stop me.

"I'm getting help!" Maisel shouted. "Don't be here when we come back, or you'll regret it!"

On Strike!

I STOOD TREMBLING, the iron still raised in my hand.

"Schloime!" Borenstein shouted. "Put that iron down!"

What had I done? To what stupid, rash action had my despair driven me? Maisel Flanc would come back with two thugs and break my arms and legs.

"Put the iron down!" Borenstein shouted again.

I did as he told me. I looked at Mayer and Sruel. One of them had betrayed me. My look must have been very clear because Sruel immediately turned to Mayer and asked, "What did you do?"

"What're you pointing a finger at me for?" said Mayer, stung by the accusation. "You talked!"

Sruel shook his head violently. The two bewildered tailors turned to me. "Schloime, we promised you we wouldn't say anything and we didn't," said Sruel.

Almost at once, the two tailors and I looked at Esther.

The timid girl gasped when our suspicions landed on her. "You don't think that I…?"

"Enough of this nonsense," Borenstein said, losing his patience. "Esther, close your mouth. What's the matter with all of you, accusing each other like children. Can't you figure it out? Yankel ran to the union after I fired him and when I didn't ask for a replacement, Maisel came sniffing around."

"What am I going to do?" I asked, my courage draining out of me. "They're going to kill me."

"Come here," Borenstein said, leading me into the living room. Quietly, so the others in the kitchen wouldn't overhear him, he said, "Keep working and don't worry. Nothing will happen to you. If anyone makes trouble, I'll take care of it."

149

I understood that a shrewd businessman like Borenstein probably had the union officials in his pocket, but I was still shaken as I went back to the kitchen to work. Every time the door opened and someone walked in, I jumped. I was so distracted I nearly burned a pair of pants. By some miracle, Maisel Flanc didn't show up again that afternoon.

The following day, a Friday, also passed without incident and two hours before sundown and the start of Sabbath, Borenstein called us one by one into the living room and paid us. I had ironed thirty suits and had earned twenty-two and a half zlotys—the most I had ever earned in my life for a week's work. Since I had already taken ten zlotys in advances, Borenstein paid me another twelve and a half.

Another week passed, no one from the union bothered me, and again I received twenty-two zlotys from Borenstein.

I desperately needed clothes. I went to the outdoors market on the corner of Stafke and Djika and browsed through the small mounds of garments that lay scattered on the ground. I paid two zlotys for two used shirts and two pairs of underpants; another two zlotys for a pair of gray pants; three zlotys for a second-hand brown jacket, still in good shape. And finally for three zlotys I bought a pair of black shoes. I had changed my wardrobe from head to foot for ten zlotys.

At work I kept pushing myself every day to increase my production. By the end of the third week I was pressing eight suits a day. I reminded Borenstein of his promise to raise my salary as I became more experienced.

"You're still too slow. You hold everybody up," Borenstein said. "I'll give you another ten groschen but that's it."

"That's still half a zloty under the price," I protested.

"Not a grosch more."

In spite of my protests, with my ten groschen raise and my third week's salary in my pocket, I left Borenstein's apartment light as a bird. I floated down the steps and flew through the courtyard into the street. Suddenly I was aware again of Warsaw's beauty, something which many months of hunger and poverty had made me forget. The houses and buildings, touched by the setting sun, shone as if they had been built with bricks of bronze. But what struck me with even deeper pleasure were the advertisements for the theaters on the announcement posts. *Hershele Ostropolier* was playing at the Nowasci and I decided to treat myself.

That night at the theater I laughed until my face was wet with tears and my sides ached. I finally had to close my eyes and cover my ears so I could stop laughing long enough to recover my breath.

After the play, on my walk back to Baindl's cellar through the warm spring night, my heart was full of memories and longings. I realized how alone I felt and how much I wanted someone to share my pleasure. My sister had already found her friend for life; Zygmunt had turned out to be a fine husband to Ruchele. When would I find the girl destined to be my companion?

By the time I got to Baindl's building the front gates were already locked and I had to ring for the janitor to let me in. The moment Baindl opened the door to her cellar apartment, I saw from her confused expression that she had rented out the bed for the night. The old, stooped woman began to apologize: it had gotten so late, she didn't think I would be coming back. I told her not to worry because I had money and would find a bed. I picked up my bundle of clothes and left.

I ran to Krochmalna Street and knocked on Eisen's door. He was surprised to see me but when I told him my problem, he let me have the key to his cellar stall at once.

I had become so used to the soft bed I rented at Baindl's, I could hardly sleep on my old bed of rags on the cold cellar floor. The time had finally come to rent a place for myself.

The following day, a Sabbath, I visited Frau Liebe's family. In the evening, on Liebe's advice, I went to see Zelig Lachman at No. 17 Lubetskiego Street. Liebe had been a good friend of Zelig's mother. The young man had lost both his parents within the same year and had inherited their apartment. He had two rooms. One was already rented to an older woman. The other room was his own. Zelig, however, earned so little from his work as a teacher that he had to rent half of it out. It was available just then and he invited me in to see it. The room was large, with two windows looking out on the courtyard. It had two beds and two chests of drawers, a table with chairs, a large wardrobe on one side and a smaller one on the opposite side, and one whole wall was taken up with bookcases.

I asked Zelig how much he wanted. He said twenty zlotys a month. I immediately stuck out my hand, and we shook on it. I gave Zelig ten zlotys and promised to give him another ten in a week. He went to his dresser, pulled out a set of keys, and gave them to me.

As I lay in my new bed that night, the fresh smell of the sheets reminded me of a field of flowers. I had returned to the world of the living.

At Borenstein's, I worked through the whole winter season at the rate of 75 groschen a suit. A number of times, I overheard the merchants who came to pick up their work ask my boss, "Who's your presser? The suits look wonderful."

Borenstein, thinking I couldn't hear him, would whisper, "He's a pisser not a presser."

I was furious. My speed was increasing all the time and towards the end of the winter season, I was keeping up with everyone in the shop. There were never more than one or two suits waiting to be pressed on the chair next to me during the day. The summer was always slow in our trade and it was necessary to save up as much as possible during the busy winter and spring seasons. In April of 1934, I decided to ask for a raise again. But before I said anything to Borenstein, I bought a large sponge cake in a good bakery and went to see my friend Eisen Broder on Krochmalna Street.

"Look at you," Eisen exclaimed when he saw me at his door. "A new man."

"Welcome," his wife called out from the kitchen. "Come in and sit down. I'll make some tea."

I handed her the bag with the cake. When she opened it, Eisen's children gave out a cheer and ran over to kiss me.

"You've become a millionaire?" Eisen joked as we sat down at the tottering kitchen table.

"Hardly," I began. As we drank tea and ate cake, I told Eisen how Borenstein was taking advantage of me. I was loosing half my salary because I wasn't a union member.

"Then why don't you join the union?" asked Eisen.

"I want to join but I'm afraid the union could refuse me again and then take my job away."

"Who can vouch that you've been Borenstein's presser for over a year?"

"His two tailors, Sruel and Mayer."

"Union members?"

"Both."

"Go to the union. If they refuse you this time, tell them that I, Eisen Broder, will make sure that everyone hears about it at the next membership meeting. My comrades in the union won't stand for this kind of business."

I considered Eisen's advice long into the night. The following morning, I went straight to the union. It was time to stand up for myself.

Once more I found myself sitting in front of Shimme Tantzer, the union official who had been unable to help me after the strike because I didn't have six children.

"I want to become a member," I said.

"And what's your experience?" Tantzer asked.

"I've been Moishe Chaim Borenstein's presser for over a year."

"Borenstein?" Tantzer said, surprised. "I seem to remember some incident with Maisel Flanc and Borenstein over a year ago... Hmmm, so that was you?"

"You can't say I don't have experience now," I said.

"And who can vouch that you've been his presser all this time?"

"Sruel Kalmen and Mayer Grish, Borenstein's tailors."

"I see," Tantzer laughed. "Well, I see you've come prepared this time. If that's so, I think you've made your case very well." Tantzer opened a ledger, picked up a pen and asked me to spell my name.

A half hour later I was the newest union member.

"Now," I said, "I have a dispute."

"Already a dispute?" the official asked. "The ink hasn't even dried on your membership card."

I explained my problem.

The official took off his glasses and began to clean them with a white handkerchief. "I know your boss," he said. "He's not a bad person. But he's more stubborn than a mule... Well, you're a union member now, and we can't let you work for less than the rate. We'll have to deal with Moishe Chaim. Go and tell him that Shimme Tantzer told you to ask for the full rate. Let's hope, for this once, he's reasonable. If we can't come to terms with him, we may have to strike."

I was shaken as I walked to work. I didn't want to cause a strike. On the other hand, I didn't like being taken advantage of. I wasn't a child anymore and I had to think of my survival.

I waited until the evening. After everyone had left, I approached my boss in the living room. "Mr. Borenstein," I said, "more than a year ago we agreed that when I had enough experience you would pay me the legal rate."

"I'm already paying you too much," Borenstein said looking me in the eyes.

"I'm the best presser you ever had. I hear what the businessmen say when they come to pick up the work." I pulled out my card. "I joined the union today. Shimme Tantzer said that you have to pay me the full rate now."

"Tantzer?" Borenstein laughed with contempt. "No raise. You don't like it? Leave."

"I'm not going to leave," I said.

"Good," Borenstein said smiling, "then go back to work and stop bothering me".

"I'm going to strike!"

"Is that so?" Borenstein laughed again.

"And I won't be the only one. The whole shop will strike."

"You think you're scaring me?" Borenstein asked. "Get back to work or get out!

I went back to work the next day. Borenstein wasn't afraid of my threats. He knew enough union leaders who would sooner side with him than with me. All the same, during my lunch hour I went to see Shimme Tantzer and told him of Borenstein's reaction to my request for a raise.

The next morning, while I was pressing and everyone else was sewing, the door to Borenstein's apartment opened and Shimme Tantzer walked in. He greeted the workers, who at once looked at me. Then the union official went directly to the living room and closed the door to the kitchen.

After ten minutes of negotiations, the door to the kitchen opened. The sewing machines stopped and Tantzer calmly announced, "My friends, this shop is on strike. Your boss has been underpaying his presser. Unfortunately, Moishe Chaim refuses to be sensible until we prove to him that we mean business. Let's put down our work and go to the Union."

Itche looked at his father in a panic. Borenstein's wife and Esther went pale. Borenstein, himself, however, had an amused expression on his face; he didn't believe that the strike would last long.

At the union headquarters Mayer and Sruel were immediately sent to work elsewhere.

"You, Schloime" Shimme Tantzer said to me, "you will be in charge of checking up on your boss to make sure that no one works there. If you see anyone working, just come back here and let us know. Understood?"

An hour later I returned to Novanyarska Street, No. 12. The door to Borenstein's apartment was closed, but not locked. I pushed it open and looked in. Only Esther, Borenstein's niece, was in the kitchen. She was at the stove, cooking.

"Schloime, what are you doing here?" she asked.

"I'm making sure that no one works during the strike," I said. "What about you?"

"My aunt asked me to help her out since I didn't have anything else to do."

"Remember, Esther, if I catch you working at a machine, your life won't be worth much."

"Schloime, I'm not touching a stitch of work, I promise you…"

Itche walked into the kitchen and was surprised when he saw me.

"What are you doing here?" he asked.

"I'm making sure that the strike is observed," I said. "Don't touch that machine, Itche."

"Schloime, what can I do by myself?" Itche said. "Don't worry, we can't do anything until this thing is settled. Papa is at the Union right now speaking to them."

"It won't do him any good," I said, "unless he's willing to be reasonable." I turned around and headed out the door.

I realized that important negotiations were going on at the Union and I ran back to our headquarters on Nalefky Street.

Mr. Tantzer's office door was closed. As I approached it I heard Borenstein's raised voice. "You're not going to push me!"

"Moishe Chaim," Tantzer's said sternly, "your tricks won't work with me."

"He's not a good presser!" Borenstein said angrily.

"Then why do you keep him?"

"That's my business."

"Then pay him the legal rate."

"Not a grosch more than what I'm paying now!"

"If you don't want to pay him, we'll take him out, and we'll give you an experienced presser."

"I don't want another presser," Borenstein said. "I've been training that ungrateful piss-pot. He's not a qualified presser yet!"

Tantzer had jabbed Borenstein's gall bladder by offering to send him another presser. He didn't want to let me go, just as I had suspected.

"I'll make you a deal," Tantzer asked. "I'll send over two expert pressers to watch Schloime work and evaluate him. If he is unqualified, we'll take him away; but if he does a good job, then you have to pay him the price."

"Never!" Borenstein screamed. "You're going to pay for this, Tantzer!"

The door to the office suddenly swung open and Borenstein charged past me in a huff.

I looked into Tantzer's office.

"From the way your boss acts," the union official said, "I can tell that you're a good presser. No matter what happens he doesn't want to give you up."

I couldn't help smiling.

"He's still going to try a few tricks," Tantzer said. "But I think that if we can keep him from reopening the shop, he'll give in. The season is picking up and if he doesn't get his garments out, the merchants are going to start taking their orders somewhere else. Borenstein is too smart to let that happen."

For the next two days, I walked up to Novanyarska Street at least three times a day to make sure no one was working at Borenstein's. On the morning of the third day, when I opened the door, I found Borenstein himself sitting in the kitchen.

"You!" he said to me, springing to his feet. "What are you doing to me? Is that how you repay me for giving you a chance to become a presser? Do you want to ruin me?"

"Mister Borenstein," I said, "the last thing I want to do is ruin you. I just want you to pay me a fair wage."

"I was paying you a fair wage—"

"You were underpaying me by fifty groschen."

"Schloime, we have to get back to work soon," Borenstein said. "We could lose the season."

"I'm ready to go back the minute you agree to pay me."

"Let's be reasonable. Sit down and let's negotiate for a price that will be fair to both of us."

"I'm not negotiating any other price than what the union has negotiated for all pressers."

"Traitor!" Borenstein shouted. "Get out of here!"

I left. But I kept coming back every few hours to check up that no one was working.

Early in the morning of the sixth day of the strike, when I walked into Borenstein's kitchen on my strike watch, I found my boss waiting for me.

"Schloime, enough is enough. I see that you're just as stubborn as I am. Let's settle and get back to work."

"You have to go to the union and sign some papers," I said.

"I told you already that I'm going to pay you the wage," Borenstein flared up. "What more do you want?"

"I want you to sign the union papers," I said. "I want to be sure that you're not going to change your mind at the end of the week when you have to pay me."

I expected Borenstein to scream at me again. Instead a respectful smile formed on his lips. He went into the living room. He came back wearing his coat.

"I was wrong," Borenstein said. "You're more stubborn than I am. Let's go to the union and sign a contract."

A *Man of Means*

AT FIRST I WAS AFRAID my boss would resent me for the trouble I had caused and would try to revenge himself. But nothing could have been further from his mind. I had won his respect. A day after Borenstein signed the contract at the union, Mayer and Sruel reappeared at the workshop and soon everyone was working as if nothing had happened. For me, however, something very important had happened. The contract that Borenstein had been forced to sign, guaranteeing that I would be paid the union rate for pressers, changed my life profoundly. After the first week at the new rate, my salary came to thirty-seven zlotys.

As I gained experience, my speed as a presser grew. The following season, with overtime, my salary jumped to fifty-five zlotys a week. At the busiest times, I earned sixty zlotys a week. This was the first time in my life that I earned a man's salary and I began to feel like a man—a man of means. I went to the good clothing stores on Nalefky Street and bought myself underwear, shirts, a suit, a pair of shoes, and a pair of boots, all new.

I was already twenty-one years old but so far my poverty made it impossible for me to think of marrying. Now the desire for someone to share my life became overwhelming. I was amazed by how many pretty young women there seemed to be everywhere I went. When I passed them on the street and caught their perfume, I was spellbound.

I had always loved the theater and now that I could finally afford it, I went often. As soon as the curtains flew apart, the world of the stage was more real to me than my own life. By the end of every play, I was in love with at least one pretty actress. Often I waited at the stage door with other admirers just for a glimpse of these beauties. But I didn't go to the theater alone for long. When Yoinne, Elke, and Tsutel found out where I was going Saturday nights, they decided to join me. After the theater we stopped at a coffee shop and as we ate dessert, we would go over the play, scene by scene.

I enjoyed feeling free again to visit Frau Liebe and her family. I spent almost every Sabbath afternoon with them. Elke, whose twin girls were already two years old, was pregnant again. Yoinne's business was doing well. Tsutel had lost her job and had gone to work for Lotte, doing Ruchele's old job. Frau Liebe still sold the little fried fish in the market and Elke helped her mother fry the fish at home.

Whenever I was invited to dinner at Liebe's, I always stayed behind in the kitchen after the meal to help clean up. While the others went into the living room to have their tea and smoke, Liebe and I talked. One Sabbath, as Liebe was washing dishes and I was drying, I caught her looking at me with a motherly smile.

"Do you remember when you first came from Lublin?" she asked. "The hard times? I always had faith in you. I'm so proud of you, Schloime. Goodness knows nothing was handed to you."

I was so moved by her kindness, I embraced her as if she were my mother and gave her a kiss.

"Schloime," Liebe said in a soft voice, "I don't have to tell you how much we think of you. Tsutel especially has been noticing how much you have changed. I think she admires you very much."

I thanked Frau Liebe for the compliment. She was letting me know that she wouldn't be against my marrying her older daughter. The truth was that I knew Tsutel liked me. At the theater, Tsutel always managed to sit next to me. Unfortunately, I wasn't attracted to Tsutel. She was so much taller than me, I had to look up to talk to her, and she was also a few years older.

"You know how it is with my trade," I said as tactfully as I could to Liebe. "I've just begun to establish myself. At most there's work eight months out of twelve. If I don't save to get through the rest of the year, I could be starving again. And I never know when there could be another strike. My plan is to save up a little more money. I want to feel I have something to offer someone else before I even start thinking about serious things."

Liebe understood.

In May of 1934 Elke gave birth to a little boy. During the winter season of that year Yoinne's pants factory began to bring in so much work that he couldn't handle it by himself. Elke tried to help her husband, but at the same time she had to care for her three small children, and also help her mother fry the little fish for market. I suspected it was only these circumstances that made Elke welcome Shifra back to Warsaw after Yoinne received a letter from his sister in the early spring asking for help. I had heard that Shifra had been working for a seamstress in Opalle and I assumed that it was the lack of work that drove Shifra back to Warsaw. I couldn't forget how badly Elke had treated Shifra a few years earlier. Now, Elke couldn't wait for her sister-in-law to arrive.

On a Sabbath evening, when I came to meet Yoinne, Elke and Tsutel for the theater, I opened the door to the basement on Muranovska Street and saw a pretty young woman with such piercing black eyes that for a moment I thought I had come to the wrong apartment. It was Shifra. She was plainly dressed, in a yellow blouse, a simple brown skirt, and worn brown shoes. Her silky black hair was cut in bangs and reached to her shoulders. Her face, without a trace of paint, was still as delicate as a child's, but her figure left no doubt that she was now a young woman. I was so overwhelmed by my feelings I suddenly became shy.

Yoinne looked at his watch and said, "What are we waiting for? We're going to be late."

As we walked up the steps of the basement I noticed that Shifra wasn't with us. "What about Shifra?" I asked.

"I only bought four tickets," Yoinne said.

"I'm sure we could still get another ticket at the theater," I said.

"She just got here." Elke said. "Let her rest. She's still tired from traveling."

I didn't want to argue with Elke, but I was sure that Shifra would have gladly come along with us.

At the theater, I couldn't concentrate on the play. For the first time none of the pretty actresses on stage caught my attention. My mind was full of Shifra's image.

The following evening, right after work, I took a walk to Liebe's. When I came in Yoinne and Shifra were still working. Elke was in Liebe's small bedroom putting the children to sleep. Shifra, meanwhile, was bent over the sewing machine in a struggle which the machine seemed to be winning. Each time Shifra pressed the heavy pedal with her foot, the machine gave out a shriek and with a savage appetite tore the heavy material out of her small hands. Shifra's fine black hair was disheveled and pasted to her sweating forehead. I felt sorry for her. I wanted to ask her out for a walk. I wanted to show her the sights of Warsaw and take her to a restaurant for tea and cake. Instead, I felt more nervous than the previous night and even more tongue-tied. An hour later, as I was leaving, Shifra and I had said very little to each other.

But no matter how awkward I felt, I couldn't stay away and I went to visit Liebe's family as often as I could. I always left feeling disturbed by what I saw. As I had suspected, the only reason Elke had welcomed Shifra back was to use her. Shifra wasn't given any freedom even on the Sabbath; whenever Yoinne and Elke took their children to the park, they made Shifra go along. They needed Shifra to watch the children.

One Sabbath evening in spring, when I got to Liebe's I found only Elke, Yoinne and Shifra in the living room. Frau Liebe was in the bedroom resting. Elke's little girls were already asleep, and Shifra was rocking the baby to sleep in her arms. I desperately wanted to take Shifra out and suddenly I had an idea.

"*The Rumanian Wedding* is playing at the Kaminska," I said quietly not to wake the baby.

Yoinne and Elke both perked up. Shifra also looked up at me with a hopeful smile.

"I'm inviting all of you to come as my guests," I said.

"And I'll take care of the treats after the show," Yoinne said.

"We won't get in," Elke said. "The show is too popular."

"We'll see," I said. "Get ready and I'll run over to the theater right now and get tickets."

I quickly dashed out the door and up the stairs. On the way to the Kaminska Theater I decided that if the show was sold out, I would run over to the Nowasci Theater and get tickets for whatever was playing there. The only thing that mattered was to finally take Shifra out.

From a block away I saw the line in front of the Kaminska Theater. It wasn't a good sign but at least the show hadn't sold out yet. I ran and joined the end of the line. "Do you think we'll get tickets," I asked a young man standing in front of me. "Why not?" he said. "They can always stuff some more chairs up in the balcony.

After fifteen agonizing minutes I finally reached the box office and bought my four tickets. I walked back to Muranovska Street feeling that I had tickets to heaven itself. I skipped down the stairs to the basement. As I was about to open the door, I heard Shifra crying.

"Yoinne," Shifra said, "give me at least fifty groschen."

"What?" Elke said in an angry hushed voice. "What do you need half a zloty for?"

I quickly opened the door. Yoinne and Elke were dressed for the theater, Shifra, however, still in her house robe and slippers, stood clutching a handkerchief to her lips.

"I have the tickets. Are you all ready to go?" I asked.

"Yes," Elke said. "Let's get out before she drives me mad."

"I'm not staying home tonight," said Shifra in tears.

"You better do what I tell you to do," Elke threatened her.

"I'm going out by myself to the movies," Shifra said.

"You ungrateful nobody!" Elke screamed as if scalding water had been poured on her head. "Is this how you repay me for pulling you out of that Oppalle sewer?"

"But I already bought the tickets," I said.

"Who's going to look after the children?" Elke snapped at me.

Shifra burst into angry sobs. The baby began to wail in it's crib in Liebe's small bedroom.

"Look what you've done now!" Elke yelled.

My heart began to beat with rage at the way Elke was insulting Shifra.

"What is going on here?" Liebe asked appearing at the door to her bedroom in her night robe. "Elke, what are you carrying on about? What have you done to Shifra? Come into my room at once." Liebe spoke with an anger that I rarely heard in her voice.

"Elkele, please," Yoinne pleaded with his wife as he followed her into Liebe's room. "Don't upset yourself."

I walked over to Shifra and I said quietly to her, "Don't cry."

She looked up at me, like a child in tears. I motioned with my head for her to follow me into the hallway. When we were out of the apartment, I turned to her and asked, "Do you want to go to the theater with me?"

Shifra was still so upset, she couldn't speak. Instead, she just gave a quick nod with her head.

"Let's go," I said.

"What about them?"

"After the way Elke behaved towards you, I don't want to go out with her or Yoinne ever again."

Shifra smiled and said, "Elke said that you had invited only them."

"That's a lie," I said. "Look, I bought four tickets." I pulled them out of my pocket and showed them to Shifra. "The main reason I asked everyone was so that you would be included also. Go and get your coat."

Shifra dashed back into the apartment.

A few minutes later, when she came running out again, I saw that

162

Shifra had not only gotten her coat, a old, green ,woolen garment, but she had also quickly changed her house robe and now wore the same yellow blouse and brown dress in which she had arrived to Warsaw. Her brown shoes were almost torn on the sides. She had thrown a red beret on her head and under it her fine black hair was in its usual disarray.

On Muranovska Street I glanced at Shifra and I realized that I had never seen her look happier. We walked side by side for a few blocks without saying anything. On Zamenhoff we passed a tea house. White curtains glowed in the lit windows, and when the door opened, the smell of freshly baked cake drifted out.

"We have time for a quick bite," I said to Shifra. "Let's go in."

The tea house was not large and every table seemed to be taken. I looked around and just as the waitress was approaching I spotted a couple getting up from a table near the window. We took that table and I immediately ordered tea for us and two slices of the cake that had just been baked.

We sat in silence a long time, drinking and eating.

"I've wanted to ask you out before," I finally said.

"Elke is going to be mad," Shifra said, lifting a spoonful of cake to her mouth.

"She got what she deserved," I said.

"Elke treats me like a maid, not her sister-in-law," Shifra said bitterly. "I work so hard for her and Yoinne, twelve to fourteen hours a day. When I finish at the sewing machine, Elke wants me to wash clothes, clean the house, and take care of her children. And with everything I do, Elke still walks around blown up like an enraged cow, insulting me with ugly names. Just look here," Shifra said, pointing down to her feet. "I can't even buy a decent pair of shoes."

"Why doesn't Yoinne stand up for you?"

"He's too stupid," Shifra said bluntly. "That's why."

I looked up at the clock. It was almost eight-thirty already. The play was starting at nine and we still had to find seats. I paid our check and we left.

When we were walking again, I felt less shy with Shifra. For the first time, I took her hand. It was small, soft, and cool. I gave her an affectionate squeeze. She squeezed my hand back and I felt in heaven.

"That's the Esther Ruchel Kaminska Theater," I said to Shifra, pointing down the block. "It was named after Ida Kaminska's mother. Look how thick the crowd is."

163

In the bright lights of the lobby of the theater we were surrounded by a mass of people. We moved slowly past the ticket-taker who directed us to the balcony.

It was bedlam up there. Everyone wanted a seat nearer the stage. People were practically crawling over each other's heads. Shrieks broke out. An elderly man who was skipping over the seats from one row to the next got a button from his coat caught up in a lady's blouse and nearly pulled her out of the seat. I was experienced in this situation and as my eyes quickly darted to the choice seats that were still available, I noticed an empty gallery box. I grabbed Shifra's hand, and with my eyes trained on the empty box I quickly wove our way to it. I pulled open the little curtain and we jumped into our seats laughing.

We were afloat high up on the side of the balcony with a clear view of the stage. Another couple joined us almost as soon as we had taken our seats.

"Look at all these fancy folks," Shifra said, pointing to the well-dressed below us taking their seats in the orchestra and in the loges. "Who are they?"

"Down there in the loges," I whispered to Shifra, "sits the cream of Jewish Warsaw. And in the orchestra is the milk of Jewish Warsaw. And up there," I said, pointing to the balcony, "is the sour milk of Warsaw. In fact," I continued, "it smells as if the sour milk is already turning into parmigiana cheese."

As Shifra laughed, her black eyes sparkling, the house lights began to dim and the curtain to rise.

Spring Nights

SHIFRA WAS AS DELIGHTED with the play as I was. We came out to a fresh spring night and began to stroll. We walked without direction and talked about the play until it became late and Shifra had to go back.

As we approached Muranovska Street I gathered my courage and said, "I could keep walking with you the whole night."

Shifra gave me a brief smile and then looked away.

Encouraged by her smile, I said, "I'd like to see you again tomorrow night."

"Elke and Yoinne don't want me to go out with you," Shifra said. "They don't even want me to talk to you. That's why they always drag me out of the house when they go somewhere on the Sabbath. Liebe likes you as if you were her son. But when Liebe is out, Elke and Yoinne talk against you."

I felt a cold shiver pass through me. "What do they say?" I asked.

"I don't understand it," Shifra said, "but there's something about your background they don't like."

I didn't know what to say. I didn't want to tell Shifra about my father and mother.

"Do you know what I told Yoinne and Elke?" Shifra suddenly said, as if guessing my thoughts. "I told them that I don't care. If Liebe likes who you are, then you must be a fine person."

The gate at No. 34 Muranovska was already locked and I had to ring the bell for the janitor. When he came with the keys and let us in, I tipped him fifty groschen. Shifra and I crossed the quiet courtyard and stopped at the steps leading down the basement.

Shifra thanked me for the theater and began to walk down the steps.

"Shifra," I called out in a whisper.

She turned around.

"You didn't answer me," I said, my heart beating wildly. "Can I see you again tomorrow night?"

"Why not?" Shifra said over her shoulder and walked into the apartment.

On the walk back to my room on Lubetskiego, I felt elated. This was the first time in my life that I had taken a girl out and she couldn't have been more beautiful.

At the apartment, Zelig was already asleep. I undressed quietly by the moonlight that filled the room and got into bed, but I was too restless to fall asleep. I lay in the dark and kept going over everything that had happened that night.

When I finally fell asleep, I dreamed that Shifra and I were together in Italy. We were staying at an old, luxurious hotel. In the daytime we visited the museums and saw famous works of art. At night, we glided along the canals of Venice in a gondola, our arms wrapped around each other. While the gondolier serenaded us, Shifra and I kissed passionately. We only stopped our kisses long enough to tell each other how strong our love was and that it would last to the end of our lives.

When I woke in the morning, the feelings of love which my dream had aroused were as strong as if the dream had been real. I whistled as I prepared to go to work.

"What happened last night?" Zelig asked as he too was getting dressed, "I've never seen you so happy."

"I've never been so happy," I said.

"Then it must be a girl," Zelig said. "And from the way you're whistling, I bet she's a beauty."

"All these books have taught you something after all," I said. "We went to the theater last night. It was the best time of my life."

At work I couldn't stop humming love songs. When I came into the living room to hang up a suit, Borenstein, who had been bent over the cutting table, put down his shears, and looked at me as if I were crazy. "What's gotten into you?" he asked. "Did you win the lottery?"

"What I've found is more precious than money."

"Listen to that fine talk!" Borenstein exclaimed. "Are we going to be toasting you soon with a *L'chaim*?"

"Everything is possible," I said.

"Aha!" Borenstein laughed. "Then, *mazeltov*! I wish you all the best."

At lunchtime I wasn't hungry and instead of eating, I took a long walk. As I strolled along the sunny streets, passing Christian people dressed in their fine Sunday clothes, I thought about my visit to Liebe's in the evening. I felt apprehensive about confronting Yoinne and Elke after I had stood them up the night before. I hoped they hadn't take their anger out on Shifra. Luckily, Frau Liebe didn't work on Sundays and she would have been at home to stop Elke from harassing Shifra. I was especially angry at Yoinne. How could he allow his wife to abuse his own sister so shamelessly?

After work I went back to my room, shined my shoes and changed into fresh clothes. I had decided to wait until eight-thirty before I went over to Liebe's. I wanted to give Shifra time to finish work. I lit a cigarette and suddenly realized that I still hadn't eaten since breakfast. With all my excited feelings, I was beginning to feel light-headed. I stopped off at a cafeteria and by the time I had eaten and paid my bill it was ten past eight. I forced myself to walk slowly to Muranovska Street. On the steps to the basement, I was glad to hear that the sewing machines were no longer running.

When I opened the door only Elke and Yoinne were in the living room. Elke who was rocking her little boy to sleep, looked angrily at me and lifting her nose high into the air walked into Liebe's small bedroom.

Yoinne, busy cleaning his machine, looked up. "So, how was *The Rumanian Wedding?*" he asked with a sarcastic smile. "Where are you inviting us tonight?"

"It was your own fault," I said. "I bought four tickets. Why do you let Elke treat Shifra that way? She's your own sister."

"What did Elke do to her?" Yoinne asked. But he knew I was right and I could see that he was embarrassed.

Shifra, who had been in the kitchen and must have overheard what I had said to her brother, suddenly appeared in the living room smiling. She seemed pleased that I had stood up for her. Liebe followed Shifra in from the kitchen.

"Schloime, you look like a millionaire," Liebe said. "Shifra was just telling me about the play you saw last night. How about some tea?"

"Don't bother yourself for me, Frau Liebe," I said. And then getting up my nerve I said, "Shifra, would you like to come out for a walk?"

"Yes," she said at once and went to get her coat from the closet.

"Shifra," Yoinne said, "remember what I told you. Next time, I'm—

"Stay out of my business!" Shifra shot back at her brother.

Yoinne was burning with anger even though he said nothing else. I was afraid that next Elke would come running out of Liebe's bedroom and start screaming at Shifra.

Shifra quickly pulled on her worn green coat and red beret.

"Don't come back late," Yoinne told his sister without looking up from the metal insides of the machine he was cleaning.

I said good night to Frau Liebe and we left.

As soon as were in the courtyard, Shifra said, "They think they can run my life just because they gave me the honor of being their slave."

"Are they angry at you for last night?"

"Elke is acting like a bitch."

We walked in silence awhile.

"I told Yoinne he's wasting his time," Shifra said. "I'm not afraid of his threats."

"If he fires you," I said, "I'll help you."

"He won't fire me. He needs me too much. He has so much work now he can't do it by himself. Especially now that he's looking to move."

"Can he afford it?"

"Elke is pushing him. She doesn't want to live in the basement. She says it's bad for the children. Yoinne started to look for an apartment for them..."

"A whole apartment?"

"A whole apartment, and a large one."

"I had no idea he was doing so well."

"He's doing much better since I started working for him. That's why I'm not afraid of him."

I admired the way Shifra fought back against her brother and sister-in-law. I realized that there was much about Shifra that I didn't understand.

"I thought a lot about you last night," I said. "I even had a dream about us."

"What kind of dream?"

"We were in Italy."

"Italy?" Shifra laughed. "What a strange imagination you have."

"We were staying in a hotel that was built like an old palace. During the day we visited all the museums, and at night we rode in a gondola through the canals of Venice. The gondolier sang for us. We were holding each other...and..."

"Well, why are you stopping all of a sudden."

"We were kissing."

I stopped walking and looked at her. Her smile was so enticing I couldn't resist her. Before I knew what I was doing, I said, "Like this," and I embraced Shifra, and pressed my lips against hers.

Suddenly, Shifra pushed me away. "I should give you a slap in the face for doing that!" she said, laughing nervously. "What do you think I am?"

"I think that you're the most beautiful girl in the world," I said. "I want to marry you."

"Don't play with my feelings like that," Shifra flared up angrily. "I know your type with the promises. I'm not—"

"I'm not playing with your feelings," I immediately reassured her. "Since I saw you, I've spent every second thinking about you."

I took Shifra's hands in mine and looked her in the eyes.

Shifra finally smiled. "Schloime," she said softly, "if you dreamed anything else last night, please don't show me." And we both started to laugh.

The Photograph

THE FOLLOWING EVENING I was so impatient, I couldn't wait for eight-thirty. When I walked into Frau Liebe's basement, Shifra was still bent over her work. She was concentrating so much on guiding the material for the pants legs through the sewing machine, she didn't notice me. Yoinne looked at me coldly and didn't return my greeting. When Shifra finally glanced up, I motioned with my head for her to come out. Yoinne let out a grunt and shot me another angry look. He was acting as if I were ruining his business. Shifra, without a word to her brother, shut her machine, got up, and began to prepare to go out. She took out fresh clothes from the closet and went into Liebe's bedroom to change. I waited for my girl in silence. I had nothing to say to Yoinne. And if he dared to say anything to me, I was ready to answer him.

As we were walking out of the building Shifra said, "Yoinne and Elke are ready to kill you."

"What am I doing to them?"

"You're interfering with their maid."

"I'll never let you be their maid."

"To Elke, that's all I am. If I listened to her, I'd never be able to do anything for myself."

Since neither one of us had eaten yet, I invited Shifra to have dinner with me. I picked a good restaurant on Leszno Street. After we were seated and had ordered our food, I asked Shifra if she had thought about my marriage proposal.

Shifra played with the edge of her napkin as she thought things over. Then she looked straight at me and asked, "When do you want to get married?"

Her boldness startled me. "As soon as possible. Are you saying yes?"

170

"It's not as easy as you think," Shifra said. "Nobody is going to give us anything. Can you afford to rent an apartment? Do you have furniture, dishes, silverware, linen? Men never think of these things. I have nothing. Look at me. I don't even have a decent pair of shoes."

"I've saved up some money. I'm a good presser and a union member. I can earn a good living for us. "

The waiter suddenly appeared at the table with a large tray and our food. As we ate, I thought about Shifra's words. She was right, I realized. Getting married wasn't such a simple matter.

"The first thing I want to do," I said, "is buy you new shoes and clothes."

Shifra looked at me without saying anything, but the sudden child-like happiness on her face told me all I wanted to know.

That night, when I took Shifra home, we stepped into the hallway leading to the basement, and in a small corner behind the staircase, I pulled Shifra to me and we kissed for a long time.

As I walked home, sure that Shifra loved me as much as I loved her, I was happier than I had ever been in my life. I wasn't alone anymore. I had found my love and friend for life.

From that night on, I went to see Shifra almost every evening after work and every Sabbath. She complained that since she had started going out with me, all three of her brothers were constantly pestering her. She was too young to get involved with anyone, they told her, and I wasn't a suitable choice for her. My background wasn't refined enough. Often, when I came to Liebe's basement to visit Shifra, I felt like asking Yoinne to tell me face to face what was wrong with my background. But I held myself back. Having a fight with Yoinne, who I hoped would soon be my brother-in-law, would not make him feel better about me; nor did I want to make Shifra's situation even more difficult.

Shifra and I had a very different reception from my sister and her husband. When I introduced Shifra to Ruchele and Zygmunt they took an immediate liking to her, and they were sincerely happy for us.

As I had promised Shifra I started to help her. I took her out to buy clothes. Her delight at finally having a new pair of gray shoes, a pretty purple dress, and a stylish brown coat, made me as happy as she was. From day to day, the love between Shifra and me grew stronger. We began to save money; and we began to talk more and more of getting married.

At the beginning of summer, when work slowed down, my trade

union organized a picnic in the woods right outside of Warsaw. I asked Shifra to go with me. She hadn't been out of the city since her return to Warsaw and she jumped at the opportunity.

The day of the picnic, a Sunday in July, was bright and hot. A crowd of people gathered on the dock near the Poniatovsky Bridge. A ferry boat soon picked us up. As we glided along the Vistula, a small band played on the deck. A buffet had been set up and a photographer went from couple to couple snapping pictures. While the river breeze cooled us, Shifra and I danced, ate, and enjoyed the sights moving past us.

The picnic area was set up in a grassy clearing surrounded by dense woods. The union officials who had planned the event organized many games: soccer, tennis, volleyball. Everyone participated for a while but soon many couples, tired of these activities, began to disappear into the woods. The photographer decided that following them would be more profitable than snapping pictures of the game players and he stole off after them to do some mischief with the camera. I was not a great sportsman and after we ate, I took Shifra by the hand and we went into the forest to enjoy the shade.

Sitting under a tree, looking at the new summer leaves glowing in the bright sun, I felt very moved. I took Shifra into my arms and began to kiss her. Suddenly, I heard a clicking sound. I looked up and there was the photographer laughing as he skipped off with our snapshot.

A week later I stopped off the Union headquarters after work to pick up our picture. The photographer had caught us at a passionate moment and the photograph showing our embrace in the woods left no doubt how much we loved each other. When I gave it to Shifra on our walk, she was embarrassed but also pleased.

The following Sabbath evening, when I went to visit Shifra, I walked into a strange sight at Liebe's. Everyone was there. I looked at Shifra, asking with my eyes, What's going on here? But before I could say anything, Yoinne reached behind his back and pulled out the photograph of Shifra and I kissing. "You don't take a bad picture," Yoinne said, "do you know that?"

"How did you get that?" I said, angrily trying to pull the picture out of his hands.

Yoinne jumped back. "Don't get so upset. Elke found it lying around."

"She found it in the bottom of a drawer," Shifra said.

"Does it really matter?" Yoinne asked. "Look, the important thing is that Khiel, Nachme and I have talked things over, and we agreed that since things have gone this far, they're not going to go backwards any-

172

more."

"If there's something that you want to talk to us about," Khiel said, "then let's have it now."

I was stunned. I couldn't believe what I was hearing. "I would have talked to you sooner but you were always so angry with me."

"We weren't sure of your intentions," Khiel said. "We didn't want anyone taking advantage of our little sister. But it's obvious how you two feel about each other and where you're headed."

All three of Shifra's brothers shook hands with me.

"Shifra and I have been ready for months already," I said, as Yoinne brought out the wine.

"We still have to talk to Uncle Ksiel and our mother," Yoinne said as he filled the glasses of wine, "but for now let's all drink a L'Chaim to Schloime and Shifra."

With that toast, Yoinne, Khiel, and Nachme became my friends again. Even Elke seemed to have grown a little friendlier towards Shifra.

"And now, Schloime," Nachme said, "since you're almost a member of the family, you're invited next Sabbath to Uncle Ksiel's birthday party at his house."

Sabbath afternoon, when I arrived at Ksiel's house I was surprised to see that not only had I been invited, but Ruchele and Zygmunt were there too.

The long table at which we sat was full of the best food and drink. We talked, we told jokes, and we sang songs. Having had a drink or two myself, I suddenly lifted my full glass of wine and proposed a toast, "To Uncle Ksiel," I said, "may you live to be a hundred and twenty."

A fit of laughter swept across the table but everyone shouted *L'chaim!* at once and we drank down the wine.

I couldn't understand why everyone was laughing at my toast.

Uncle Ksiel then stood up and said, "Now, I would like to propose a toast."

Ksiel himself poured the first glass of wine for Shifra and then one for me and finally one for himself. Yoinne and his brothers meanwhile had poured glasses of wine for everyone else. Ksiel stood up with his glass in his hand and said, "This toast I am making in my brother's place, may he rest in peace. I am proposing, Schloime and Shifra, that your wedding take place on the 30th of November, 1935, at six in the evening in the hall of Rabbi Mordkhe Finkelstein, on Zamenhoff St, No. 38. I am suggesting this date because that is the real date of my birthday and I want to have a double celebration on that day. Now, Schloime, do you agree?"

"I agree," I assured him at once.

"If so," Uncle Ksiel said, "let's all drink a *L'chaim* to Schloime and Shifra and wish them a hearty *mazeltov.*"

We tossed back the wine and I sat back in a happy daze holding Shifra's hand.

With the date of our wedding set for November, Shifra and I found ourselves quite busy with preparations. Our most difficult problem was finding an apartment. We were tired of living with other people and wanted a place of our own. Shifra and I asked everyone we knew for leads; and I constantly combed the listings in the newspapers. Any apartment that we liked, however, seemed to require more key-money than we had. Even though Shifra and I had put our savings together, and I gave all I could spare of my weekly pay to Shifra, we still didn't have enough.

Yoinne and Elke, on the other hand, were doing so well that in October they rented a large apartment and moved out, leaving Frau Liebe and Shifra in the basement. Yoinne also left his sewing machines in the basement at 34 Muranovska Street and came to work there every day. This move by Yoinne and Elke proved especially difficult for Frau Liebe. Elke had always been Liebe's assistant. Now that Liebe had to fry the little fish by herself, she had less time to sell them at the market, and her meager earnings dropped.

As the end of November approached, Shifra and I still hadn't found an apartment. Frau Liebe, seeing our plight, invited us to move into the basement. Shifra and I could have the living room to ourselves, Liebe said; the little bedroom was enough for her. I didn't want to live in a basement but the thirtieth of November was approaching quickly and we had no choice. We decided to move in with Frau Liebe after our wedding.

Our wedding day was one of the happiest days of our lives. As I stood next to Shifra under the *chupah* in Rabbi Finkelstein's home, with our close family surrounding us, I felt this was the end of my wandering days. I would never be alone again. Shifra's mother, a small, quiet woman, with a wrinkled face, stood close to Shifra and dabbed her eyes with a handkerchief. I thought of my own mother, my poor mother, who couldn't share this happy day with me. And I thought of my father, from whom I hadn't heard in years. But Ruchele and Zygmunt were there, and so were Frau Liebe, Uncle Ksiel and his wife, Shifra's brothers, and Elke and Tsutel. I let myself be swept away by my happiness and I forgot all the hard times I had lived through. I stomped down hard with my shoe and shattered the glass which had been wrapped in paper. After cake and wine at the Rabbi's house, the family went to Uncle Ksiel's house to celebrate our wedding and Ksiel's birthday. He had the wonderful birthday he had wished for, but the person happiest for Shifra and me was Frau Liebe. For me, she took the place of my mother.

Shifra and I settled into our new home, the living room of the basement at Muranovska Street. I could hardly wait for the end of each work day so that I could go back and be with Shifra.

A few months after our wedding Yoinne decided to move the sewing machines out of the basement and into his own apartment. He had a lot of room there and wanted to hire more people to work for him. Yoinne suggested that if Shifra had a sewing machine of her own he could keep her busy with work. Shifra and I bought a machine from Yoinne and she began to work at home, sewing pants for her brother. Living with Frau Liebe was very pleasant as well, and we were all happy.

In the fall of 1936, Shifra gave birth to a little girl. We named her Liebe after Shifra's grandmother. Little Liebele brought such warmth and sunshine into our home, that I walked around singing all the time. I had never imagined the powerful feelings that a small baby could call out in me. I couldn't stop hugging and caressing my wife and child. Shifra too was happier than she had ever been in her life. She seemed to blossom like a flower and became more beautiful from day to day.

Yoinne's business was going so well that he stopped manufacturing pants altogether. Early in 1937, Yoinne opened a clothing store. At the same time, Yoinne must have grown ashamed that his elderly mother-in-law still sold fish in the market and he invited her to retire and live in his large apartment.

When Yoinne had married Elke, Frau Liebe had signed the lease to the cellar over to her son-in-law. So that it was Yoinne who paid the rent. When Frau Liebe moved out, Shifra and I wanted to have the lease transferred to our names. Yoinne, however, urged us to leave the lease as it was; otherwise, he said, we could run the risk of losing the apartment. Yoinne told me to bring the rent to him and that he himself would pay the landlord.

Now that we had the whole basement to ourselves, Shifra asked me whether I minded if her mother, who was ageing and lonely, came to live with us. I told Shifra that it was totally up to her. The only thing I feared was a strike in my trade. If that ever happened, our situation could grow more desperate. But if her mother wanted to come and live with us she was welcome.

Shifra wrote to Opelle and within a few weeks her mother arrived in Warsaw. Sara Leah was a quiet woman, easy to get along with. She helped Shifra with our child and Shifra enjoyed her mother's company during the day.

Our happiness, while it lasted, was complete.

The Eviction Notice

ONE EVENING in the summer of 1937, in the midst of our happiness, I came home from work and found Shifra standing in a daze in the living room. Her face was tear-streaked. I stopped at the door taken aback by this miserable sight.

"Schloime!" Shifra cried out. "We're finished!" She reached into her apron pocket and pulled out an envelope. "Look at this!"

I took the letter from her trembling hands. "What is it?" I asked looking at the official Polish document. "Did someone read it?"

"We're being evicted!" Shifra wailed. "The landlord is throwing us out into the street!"

Liebele, who had been sleeping in her crib, woke up shrieking.

"What's going on?" I asked.

"Yoinne hasn't paid rent for two months!"

"Impossible! I gave him the money myself."

"We have to be out of here in two weeks!"

"Two weeks?"

"Or they'll throw us into the street!"

My mother-in-law, Sarah Leah, came out of the small bedroom, wearing her house robe and slippers. Shaking her head sadly, she went to soothe the baby. "Poor little soul," she said as she bent down and picked Liebele up.

"This has be to be a mistake," I said to Shifra. "I'm going to see Yoinne."

"We're lost," Shifra said as I left.

It was a warm evening in June. I ran without stopping through the crowded streets. Sweaty, my heart pounding, I bounded up the stairs to Yoinne's apartment.

"Open up!" I screamed, beating on the locked door with my fists. "Open up, you bastard!"

177

The door flew open. "What's gotten into you?" Yoinne asked. "Come inside. Everyone can hear you."

"I want them to hear me! What have you done to me? I'm getting chased out of my apartment!"

Yoinne took my arm and pulled me into his apartment. "Please, get in here."

I walked past him into his living room.

"Now, tell me what's the matter," Yoinne said following me in.

"Here, look at this!" I said, shoving the official document at him.

"What is it?" he asked, staring blankly at the paper.

"An eviction notice! Have you been paying my rent? What did you do with the money I gave you?"

"Calm down, Schloime. Please be calm," Yoinne said, growing nervous himself and starting to pace.

"Why am I being evicted? Is this a mistake?"

"What have I done," Yoinne began to mumble.

"You didn't pay the rent?" I asked with disbelief.

"Schloime…forgive me. My own sister, my own mother…how could I do this to them?"

"I'm sunk! Where's the money? What am I going to do now?"

"Schloime, I'm going to take care of it," Yoinne said. "I was having trouble in the store the last few months. I had to pay off the suppliers. They wanted to pull out the merchandise."

"Yoinne, you just sent Elke and the children and Liebe to the country for the summer! What kind of a bastard are you?"

"Schloime, I promise you," Yoinne said his voice shaking with remorse, "I will take care of this immediately. I'll go and see the landlord and straighten the whole thing out. I swear."

I had no choice but to believe him. I went home and reassured Shifra that her brother had promised to take care of our problem. Shifra didn't believe Yoinne. I tried to convince her that her own brother wouldn't let his sister and mother end up on the street. He had given me his sworn word. Sara Leah came out of her bedroom and said that she would walk over to her son's house the next day and also have a talk with him. My mother-in-law and I finally managed to calm Shifra down, but it was late at night before Shifra was able to fall asleep.

The next day at the shop, I found it hard to keep my mind on work. In the evening, when I came home, Sarah Leah told me that Yoinne had assured her that he was already taking care of the whole matter.

The following evening, after dinner, I went to see Yoinne myself.

"Come in," my brother-in-law said. "I was just about to sit down to eat."

I followed Yoinne into the large kitchen. On the table I saw a small feast: black bread, gefilte fish, soup with kreplach, boiled meat and kasha varnishkes.

"Have you taken care of it yet?" I asked him.

"Look." Yoinne reached into his pocket and pulled out a small roll of bills. "I have fifty zlotys right here. I just need to pull together another thirty and I'll take it right over to the landlord. I told you not to worry."

"When will you have the rest of the money?"

"In two days."

I found it hard to believe that anyone who lived in such a large apartment and could send his family to the country, would need to take days to pull together thirty zlotys.

"You can't believe that I don't have the rest of the money?" Yoinne asked, reading my thoughts. "You don't know what it's like having creditors on your back. But nobody gets paid until I take care of your rent."

I returned home and told Shifra that Yoinne had fifty zlotys of our rent money, and that he promised to have the rest of our rent in a few days.

"Don't trust him," Shifra said. "In two days go to his house and make sure that he paid the landlord."

In spite of what she said, I could see that Shifra felt better. For the first time since we had received the letter she didn't look distressed. When Shifra picked up Liebele from the crib and kissed her little face, the baby gurgled happily at her mother and I also felt happy again.

Two days later I went back to see Yoinne. As soon as he saw me at the door, Yoinne pulled out a slip of paper.

"Here," he said, smiling as he handed it to me "for you. Take that to my worried sister."

I looked at the receipt for eighty zlotys, rent for the months of May, and June.

"Every zloty has been paid back," Yoinne said.

I was so relieved, even though he had put us through a lot of unnecessary grief, I shook Yoinne's hand and thanked him. I rushed home to show the receipt to Shifra and my mother-in-law.

"From now on," Shifra said, "make Yoinne give you the receipt every month."

A few weeks later, when the whole business was almost out of our minds, as Shifra and I sat at the table drinking tea, the door to our apartment was pushed open. We looked up and saw three burly men with stony faces staring down at us.

"What do you want?" I asked, jumping to my feet, looking for something to defend ourselves with.

"We have an eviction notice against you," the man in front said in Polish, pulling out an official document.

I took it from his hand.

"But we paid the rent," I said. "Shifra, where's the receipt?"

Shifra ran to the chest of drawers and brought the receipt to me.

"Look at this," I said to the men in my best Polish. "Every zloty of the back rent was paid."

They looked at the paper. "So what?" one of the men said, shrugging his shoulders. "You're being evicted, that's all I know. This is a legal order." He motioned with his hand and the other two men walked into the apartment. Shifra cried out in terror. Liebele woke up in her crib and let out a wail.

One man picked up two chairs, another picked up a trunk with linen and clothes, and the third picked up Sarah Leah's valises.

"What're you doing!" I screamed at them.

Sarah Leah walked in from her bedroom. Seeing the men in our apartment, she cried out in terror, "Pogrom! Save us, Dear God!"

The Polish man, understanding the word pogrom, said, "Keep calm, lady. Nobody is going to hurt you."

Shifra, tears running down her face, holding Liebele in her arms, ran to her mother.

The men began to carry out our belongings.

"Give me a chance," I implored the man with whom I had been speaking. "I have a baby and an old woman here. Let me just speak to the landlord. I'm sure this is a mistake. I can straighten it out."

Shifra, clutching Liebele to her breast, huddled with her mother in a corner of the basement. All three were crying bitterly.

"Ladies, stop this crying," the leader of the men said. "Go ahead and try," he said to me. "Maybe you can work something out with the landlord. I'll tell my helpers to wait. But make it fast, we don't have all night."

I thanked him as I ran off.

I only knew Mr. Lerman, the landlord, by sight. He lived on Muranovska, across the street from us. He dressed in expensive suits and had little to do with the tenants. The few times I had seen him in our building, he had struck me as an unfriendly person. I prayed now that despite his appearance, he would turn out to be a decent man.

I ran into a luxurious apartment building, up a flight of stairs to Mr. Lerman's door and knocked on it. I waited. Finally, the peephole cover opened and I saw an eye looking at me.

"Mr. Lerman," I said to the eye staring out from the brown door, "there's been a mistake. I live in the basement at No. 34. Three men are trying to evict us. They say you sent them. My rent is paid up. I have the receipt." I shoved the piece of paper against the peephole.

I heard the peephole slam shut. I took my receipt away and waited for the door to open. But I soon realized that the landlord was not opening the door. I knocked again, this time harder, with my fist.

"I must speak to you, Mr. Lerman!" I shouted. "I have a wife and a baby and an elderly mother-in-law! You must help me!"

I waited for an answer and then I began to knock on the door again. There was a scurry of footsteps within the apartment, but still my knocks went unanswered.

"Mr. Lerman," I called through the shut door, "please have mercy. Please don't throw my wife and my child into the street!"

Suddenly I heard footsteps on the stairway behind me. I looked around and saw two policemen running up the steps. One had drawn his revolver and was pointing it at me; the other held a black rubber club in his hand.

"Put your hands up and don't move!" the policeman with the revolver shouted at me.

I immediately threw my hands in the air. I was so frightened that my blood drained out of my head and I felt faint.

The other policeman searched me for a weapon.

"What have I done?" I asked.

"Come with us," the policeman with the revolver said.

"But I haven't done anything!"

The policeman with the club raised it and said, "If you don't go quietly, you'll go with broken bones."

"I have to speak to my landlord," I pleaded with the two men. "This is a terrible misunderstanding. I'm being thrown out of my apartment for no reason. I have a wife and a baby and an old mother-in-law—"

The policeman with the black rubber club pulled out a pair of handcuffs and slapped them on my wrists.

"Enough talk!" the policeman said, dragging me by the handcuffs.

181

I walked down the steps, my arms held by a policeman on each side.

"Let me at least talk to my wife," I asked the officers when we were out on the street.

"Keep walking," one of them answered.

Across the street, outside of 34 Muranovska, I saw the leader of the moving men looking for me. "Wait!" he shouted as he ran across the street.

"Who is that?" the policeman with the gun asked me.

"One of the landlord's men," I said.

The mover approached us cautiously. "What's going on?"

"What do you want?" the policemen with the gun asked.

"Nothing. I was just waiting for him to talk to the landlord. Why is he being arrested?"

"None of your business," the policeman answered.

"Let's go," the other policeman said to me. "You," he said pointing his nightstick at the moving man, "stay out of this." And I was dragged off.

At the police station, just a block away from where we lived, I was ordered to sit on a bench. While one of the policemen watched me, the other filled out papers and talked to the commander, a tall man with a bushy moustache and white hair.

"Please let me talk to your chief," I asked the policeman who was watching me.

"You will talk to him as soon as he's ready to talk to you," he told me.

I was jumping out of my skin with nervousness and worry about Shifra and our baby but there was nothing I could do. It was a half-hour before the commander ordered that I be taken into an office. One of the policemen led me into a small room where there was a desk and a chair. The policeman told me to sit and remained standing guard over me. In a few minutes the commander walked into the room with a sheaf of papers in his hands.

"Take his handcuffs off," he said to the policeman behind me.

The policeman immediately unlocked the cuffs.

"Sir," I said, "I am not a criminal. Please let me explain."

"Just answer my questions," the commander said. He asked me where did I work, how long had I worked there, where did I come from, had I ever been arrested before, and did I belong to any political parties.

After I had answered his questions the commander said, "You don't have a criminal record, and you're probably not a criminal, but you have broken the law just the same."

"How did I break the law?" I asked.

"You threatened the life of your landlord."

"But I didn't say a threatening word."

"Didn't my men find you trying to break down his door?"

"I just wanted to speak to him. He is evicting my family. We have a small baby, my wife's mother lives with us and she is over seventy years old. He has no reason to throw us out. I was trying to explain to him that my rent is all paid up. I have a receipt for the back rent. My brother-in-law—"

"Do you have a lease for that apartment?" the commander interrupted me.

"No," I had to admit. "My brother-in-law advised me not to change the lease over into my name."

"That's why you're being evicted. You're living in that apartment illegally. Didn't you receive a notice two weeks ago?"

"Yes, but that was for the back rent—"

"It was also for living illegally without a lease."

Now I really had nothing left to hold on to.

"We're not going to arrest you," the commander said. "But we are going to take your finger prints for our records and you have to sign a statement that you will report here every Saturday for the next year. If you stay out of trouble for a year, we'll forget about the whole matter."

He shoved the paper in front of me. I had no choice but to sign it. The policeman who had been guarding me took me to another room where my fingers were inked and my prints taken, and I was let go.

As soon as I was out of the police station, I ran back to 34 Muranovska. When I entered the courtyard of our building, I saw my wife, the baby in her arms, and my mother-in-law sitting in the middle of a pile that looked like garbage but which was really all of our belongings. The kitchen table lay overturned, two legs broken off. Our clothing was strewn all over the courtyard. Some plates had broken and pieces littered the ground. When she saw me Shifra burst into the most heart-rending cries. I held her and tried to comfort her.

"They told me you were arrested," Shifra said as she sobbed bitterly against my chest.

"The landlord called the police," I said. "But they let me go."

"Why did he call the police?" my mother-in-law asked.

"Because he's a bastard," I said. "He evicted us for not having a lease.

We have to do something," I said to Shifra.

"What can you do?" my mother-in-law asked.

"I have to see Yoinne," I said. "I'll be back in a few minutes."

I left them in the courtyard and ran to Yoinne's house. When I realized that he wasn't home yet, I ran immediately to his store on Wolynska Street.

Yoinne, who was wrapping a customer's purchase when I walked in, saw at once from my expression that something terrible had happened.

"Sit down and take it easy," Yoinne said to me as he handed the package to his customer.

I kept standing, shaking with rage. The moment the customer left the store, I turned all my anger on Yoinne. "We've been evicted from our apartment because of you. If my wife and child have to spend one night on the street, I'm going to tear you apart!"

"Don't scream. I swear I paid the rent. Didn't I give you the receipt?"

"We don't have a lease!" I shouted at him. "Didn't you advise me to leave the apartment in your name? Shifra and the baby are sitting in the street now. Yoinne, if anything happens to them, I swear that I will kill you—"

"Stop talking like that. Here are the keys to my apartment. Take them all over there. I'm closing up the store and I'll get a man to help move your things to my apartment."

I rushed back to Shifra. I gave her the keys and told her to take our child and her mother to Yoinne's apartment and stay there. They left and I waited with our belongings.

Yoinne arrived a short time later. He had hired a man with a wagon. We loaded everything up on the wagon and we drove to Yoinne's apartment.

We brought our bed, the chest of drawers, and the sewing machine into Yoinne's living room. The rest of our furniture, the broken table, the chairs, the closet, sofa, beds, we moved into Yoinne's large storage space in the cellar.

On Friday afternoon, as he did every weekend during the summer, Yoinne traveled to the country to be with his wife and children. When he returned on Sunday night Yoinne assured me that he had explained everything to Elke and that he had prepared her for finding us in her house. At the end of the summer, however, when Elke finally came back with her children and mother, and saw us installed with our belongings in her living room, Elke stared at us with a shocked expression. Then she ran into her bedroom and slammed the door. Frau Liebe, ashamed of her daughter's behavior, apologized for her. In spite of his assurances to Shifra and me, Yoinne hadn't said a word to Elke about what happened to us.

From the day we had been forced to move in with Yoinne, I had been looking for a new apartment, but finding something we could afford was not easy. As the weeks passed Elke's patience wore out. The moment Yoinne and I left the house for work, she began to pick fights with Shifra. Nothing my wife did was right. Frau Liebe and Sara Leah tried to stand up for Shifra, but it was useless. Almost every evening when I came home from work I found my wife in tears. Shifra complained to me that Elke didn't let her live. It drove me half mad. Finally I told Elke that if she didn't leave Shifra alone, I would stop looking for an apartment altogether and she would have us on her head forever.

My threat was effective. Elke realized that being vicious would get her nowhere.

Even though Shifra was no longer crying from fights with Elke, I wanted to get away from my sister-in-law as soon as possible. During my searches, I had seen a large room to share with a Jewish woman and her two children. She was a widow. I didn't want to rent that room for a few reasons. The first was that the widow's husband had died of tuberculosis. I took that as a bad omen. The second reason was that I still didn't want to share an apartment. And the third, was the address of the building, No. 18 Stafke Street. I couldn't walk on Stafke without remembering my mother. Just a block away, at No. 46 Stafke, was the basement where Itzhak Copperstein's parents lived.

I kept looking for another week. Elke's venom began to rise again and I realized that as much as I wanted an apartment to ourselves, we simply couldn't afford it. In the early fall of 1938, I moved my family to the third floor at No. 18 Stafke Street.

A Small Fortune

THE WIDOW GOLDE KARP, a spindly woman in her mid-thirties, was a nervous type. The least noise startled her and made her jump. Her complexion, a chaffed, reddish color complemented her character. Golde earned her living by taking in laundry which she washed in a large tub in her kitchen. Even though she was a hard-working, driven woman, she still couldn't make enough money to support herself and her two teen-aged sons. Why else would she rent out half of her one room flat? As for Golde's sons, we almost never saw them. Our landlady insisted that her children become scholars and the two pale boys spent all their time at the Yeshiva. They only came home to eat and sleep.

The half of the room that Golde rented to us was furnished. It had a small closet, a chest of drawers, and a bed; all we had to bring with us were Liebele's crib and Sara Leah's folding bed. We also brought along the sewing machine. Golde didn't object to Shifra working as long as we promised to be quiet at night. The rest of our furniture we had to leave in Yoinne's cellar.

The building at 18 Stafke Street was old and the toilets, shared by all tenants, were three flights down near the entrance to the courtyard. Within a few days it became obvious that the climb was too much for Shifra's elderly mother and Sara Leah went back to live with Yoinne. Shifra lost her mother's help and now that Shifra had to take care of Liebele by herself, she had far less time to work.

When we moved in, Golde put up a divider, a little Spanish Wall. Shifra and I had the back of the room, where the windows were located; while Golde and her boys had the front, where there was a kitchen, a small corridor, and the door to the apartment. It was hardly an ideal situation that any time Shifra or I wanted to enter or leave the apartment we had to pass through Golde's area. Still, as long as we were healthy, life was bearable. One night, however, a few months after we had moved in, Shifra and I both suffered an attack of diarrhea. Every time our stomachs cramped up we had no choice but to run through Golde's part of the room and down three flights of stairs to the toilet. While Golde was still up, it wasn't a problem. In the middle of the night, however, as Shifra raced to get out the door in a hurry, Golde, who had been asleep, jumped up from her bed as if an earthquake had hit Warsaw.

"What happened?" I heard Golde's dazed voice ask in the darkness as her two boys snored peacefully.

When Shifra came back, Golde was again startled. "Mrs. Schmer, have pity. It's the middle of the night," Golde complained. "You're not letting me catch a wink of sleep."

"I have a bad stomach," Shifra whispered angrily. "What do you want from me?"

Of course, no sooner was Shifra back in bed than I felt my insides twist up in a knot. Respectful of our landlady, I danced to the front door on the tips of my toes. I had almost made it out of the apartment when a board creaked. Golde let out a startled scream as if I had attacked her. "Are you trying to kill me?" she cried out in the darkness. I didn't even have time to answer her.

When I returned from the toilet, feeling only slightly relieved, I found Golde waiting up for me. "I'm shaking like a leaf," she said, clutching her robe around her thin body. "You have to stop this running at once."

"Mrs. Karp, we're not running out every five minutes for a stroll and a breath of fresh air," I tried to reason with her.

"Can't you control yourselves a little?"

"Control ourselves? We have loose bowels. Do you want us to go in our beds?"

"Well you must do something!"

"Believe me, Mrs. Karp, if this weren't the third floor, we would gladly jump out through the window in order not to disturb you. Look, why don't you switch places with us. You sleep in the back and we'll sleep here in the front. That way we won't disturb you. And as far as I'm concerned, if you or the boys get the runs, you can go through at any time, day or night, as many times as you need."

"We can't do that," Golde said. "The windows are in the back. We catch colds so easily we would always be sick."

"Well, then," I told her, "you can't have it both ways. There's an old saying, You can't comb a fancy hairdoo on a head full of lice. "

Golde Karp must have understood what I meant, because she went back to sleep and a while later, when Shifra and I both had to run through her room at the same time, Golde nearly jumped out of her skin, but we didn't hear a word of complaint.

As soon as winter started, it became clear to us why Mrs. Karp didn't want to sleep in the back. The cold night air blew in as if the windows had no glass. We tried covering them with curtains, a bed-spread, and finally a blanket. Nothing helped.

Liebele was the first one to get sick. She caught a bad cold and developed a fever. Shifra, already six months months pregnant, was beside herself with worry as she watched our little daughter struggle to breathe. The third night of Liebele's illness, her fever rose so high, I had to run out and look for help. Since we were only a block away from Muranovska Street, I ran first to Dr. Feinberg, the same doctor who had treated me for my severe colds. Luckily I found him at home and he agreed to come back with me.

Shifra stood back and wrung her hands as the doctor listened to Liebele's chest. "Not good," the doctor said. The concerned tone of his voice frightened us. He immediately gave Liebele an injection. Then, he pulled a bottle of alcohol out of his bag, poured it over a thick wad of cotton, and began to rub Liebele's small body. "Do this every two hours," the doctor said to us. He also wrote out a prescription and ordered that it be filled as soon as the pharmacy opened.

By the time Liebele recovered, a few weeks later, I had caught a cold. I felt weak, coughed, and soon I had a low fever. But no matter how I felt, I couldn't afford to stop working. I hoped I would recover soon. To Shifra's questions as to how I was feeling, I lied and said that I was getting better. Whenever she urged me to go to a doctor, I said I would and put it off. A month later I was still sick. At work, even my boss noticed that I was slowing down and asked me what was wrong. I lied to him as I did to Shifra. A slight cold, I said, I'm getting better. In truth, I felt worse from day to day. I managed somehow to struggle through the winter. In the spring, when I hoped to start feeling better, I actually began to feel worse; until, one morning in late May I couldn't get out of bed.

Shifra called Borenstein on the telephone and told him that I would be in tomorrow. When I couldn't get out of bed for the second day, Shifra asked our landlady to watch Liebele and took me to see Doctor

Feinberg on Muranovska Street.

"How long have you been sick?" the doctor asked after he had listened to my lungs.

"A short while," I said.

"Liar," Shifra said angrily. "Doctor, he's been sick for months. I begged him to go see you but he wouldn't listen to me."

"You should have listened to your wife," Doctor Feinberg said as he sat down at this desk. "Mrs. Schmer, do not allow your husband to go to work until his fever is gone." The doctor thought for a moment and then added, "I also want you to go to the clinic on Leszno Street and take an X-ray of your lungs. Go now and give them this slip of paper."

Shifra forced me to get into bed as soon as we came back from the clinic. Again she called Borenstein for me and told him that I was sick and would be out a few more days.

For a whole week Shifra nursed me. She brought me food in bed and every four hours, according to the doctor's prescription, she gave me medicine. I had never experienced such exhaustion. I felt as if all my blood had been drained out of me. At end of the week, although I felt only a little better, I told Shifra that I was ready to go back to work.

"You look like a corpse," my wife said.

"I feel stronger than I look," I lied. "I'm going crazy lying here all day. I need some air. I need to do something."

"I don't want to be left a widow with a baby on the way. I needed another child now like the plague. Promise me at least that you'll go back to the doctor," Shifra said.

I promised. That same evening, after work, I went to see Dr. Feinberg.

He listened to my lungs again.

"What kind of work do you do?" he asked as he looked at the X-ray of my chest.

"I'm a presser."

"Throw away that work at once," the doctor said. "You need fresh air. You have to spend a few months in the country."

A feeling of dread gripped me. "What's wrong with me?"

"There's a small spot on your left lung."

His words struck me like a death sentence.

"Don't panic," the doctor tried to reassure me. "If you do as I say, you can heal yourself in a few months. But you must stop working, you must stop smoking, and you must go to a sanatorium."

"Stop working? Go to a sanatorium? And who will feed my wife and daughter?"

"Borrow the money. If you can't afford a sanatorium in Otwock, move to Miedzeschien for a few months. I have to be honest with you," the doctor said as he scrubbed his hands at the white porcelain sink in his consultation room. "If you don't do what I tell you, you'll die."

I walked out of the doctor's office in a bleak daze. Shifra was a few months away from giving birth. She was already angry at being pregnant again and frightened by our worsening situation. The bit of happiness we had shared was slowly being destroyed by my illness. I simply couldn't stop working and I decided not to say a thing to Shifra. I also decided to look for another job. I wouldn't earn as much, but I hoped that if I gave up the pressing I wouldn't have to go to a sanatorium.

When I returned to our apartment, our landlady was out delivering a bundle of laundry and her boys were still at the Yeshiva. Shifra was sitting at the edge of the bed. Next to her, Liebele was playing with a rag doll. My little daughter greeted me with a smile.

"What did the doctor say?" Shifra asked at once. The heavy roundness of her belly made it difficult for her to get up from the bed.

"He said that I'm getting better."

Shifra didn't seem to believed me. She looked at me coldly and without a word, went to the kitchen to prepare our dinner.

"Tata," Liebele called out to me, extending her little arms to be picked up. I didn't have the strength to lift my own child. I sat down next to her on the bed. At once Liebele crawled over to sit in my lap. As I held my daughter, I heard a crash in the kitchen and Shifra began to cry. I immediately put Liebele down and went to the kitchen. A pot of soup had fallen to the floor. Shifra stood leaning against the kitchen table, crying.

"What's the matter with you?" Shifra screamed at me through her sobs. "I'm going crazy from all this worry! What are you hiding from me? Tell me or I'm going to ask the doctor myself!"

"I told you. Nothing's wrong—"

"Liar! I'm not blind! I'm not an idiot!"

I couldn't keep the truth from her anymore.

"The doctor found a small spot on one of my left lung."

"I'm finished!" Shifra cried wildly, tearing at her own her face. "What am I going to do now? I'm finished!"

I ran to stop her from hurting herself. I pulled her hands away from her face and tried to put my arms around her to comfort her. Shifra shook me off with a violent shrug.

"Get away from me!" she sobbed. "Don't touch me! Don't come near me again! My brothers were right! I never should have married you!"

These words poured into me like poison. I wished they would kill me at once.

"Why didn't you leave me alone?" Shifra moaned through her sobs. "Why didn't you keep your hands off me! You lied to me! You said we would live like people! We're cursed! I'm too young for this life!"

Liebele, frightened by the noise, began to wail along with Shifra. It was more than I could bear. I slammed the door shut after me and ran down the steps.

On the street, I lit a cigarette. The smoke stabbed at my lungs but the pain I suffered from Shifra's words was still greater. I walked like a lost man. My own wife hated me. And what she said was true. I had made her life a hell. If it hadn't been for me, she wouldn't have been saddled with babies and a sick husband. What good was I to her? How much longer would I live, anyway? I decided to just keep going. Wherever I ended up, dead or alive, there I would stay. The hours passed. The streets emptied. I had a few zlotys in my pocket, and I started to walk to the train station. Standing at the ticket window, I remembered how my father had abandoned us in Lublin; how my mother, alone with two babies, had to struggle without him; and how, in the end that had destroyed her life. I couldn't do the same to Shifra and my Liebele. No matter how long I had to live, I would spend that time taking care of my wife and child. I turned around and began to head back home.

Our landlady and her boys had already gone to sleep when I walked into the apartment. Beyond the partition, in our side of the room, a small lamp was lit. Golde, of course, jumped awake as I crossed the room, but she simply lay down again and didn't say anything to me.

Shifra, leaning against the headboard of the bed, had fallen asleep in a sitting position and Liebele was sleeping with her head on her mother's lap. I sat down on the bed next to my wife and daughter and I began to cry. Suddenly I felt Shifra's arm around my shoulder.

"I'm not letting you go back to work," Shifra whispered. "You have to get your health back. I'm going to start working again. I shouldn't have stopped. Tomorrow, quit your job."

The following morning, I left for work an hour earlier than usual.

Borenstein was sitting at the kitchen table eating breakfast with his son and daughter when I opened the door. Mrs. Borenstein was already at the stove, cooking.

"What are you doing here so early?" Borenstein asked pulling out his watch from the vest pocket. "It's not even seven o'clock."

"I have to talk to you," I said. "In private, please."

Borenstein looked at his family then rose from his chair. I followed my boss into the living room. He closed the door to the kitchen and led me to the couch.

"Sit," he said. "You look like a ghost."

"I'm sick," I admitted. "The doctor told me that I have to stop pressing, and I have to go away to recuperate.

"So it is that serious? I suspected as much. How long will this recuperation take?"

"A few months."

Borenstein was silent for a few moments and then he said, "Your health must come first. Let's see. How much do I owe you?" My boss pulled out a small notebook from his shirtpocket on which he kept count of the suits I pressed. "I have twenty-three."

I nodded in agreement.

"That's about twenty-nine zlotys," Borenstein said taking out his wallet. He counted out my money and gave it to me. "I hope you have some savings."

"How can I have savings? We have a small baby, and my wife is seven months pregnant and can't work."

Borenstein took his wallet out again, and pulled out some more money. "Here's fifty zlotys," he said. "When you feel better come back and see me."

I thanked my boss and left. On the street, I was suddenly filled with a strange sense of freedom. I had just quit my job. I had no means to feed myself, my wife and child, and I was sick with a disease that could kill me. And yet, now that I was finally confronting my illness with the desperate measures it required, I found new strength and courage. It was still early in the morning of a sunny, warm day. With eighty zlotys in my pocket, I walked to the train station.

In the late afternoon, as the electric train sped back to Warsaw, the flat fields shimmered like lakes of copper.

"Schloime?" Shifra called out from our part of the room when I walked in. "Where have you been all day? I didn't know what to think."

"I took the train to Miedzeschien."

"What were you doing there?"

"Doctor Feinberg wants me to move there for a few months. It's a health resort. There are small buildings right in the middle of the woods and the rooms aren't too expensive. Shifra, I rented an apartment for the summer. It's not too small and it has a stove and some furniture. It's thirty zlotys a month. I put down a deposit of fifty zlotys."

"Where did you get the money?"

"Borenstein lent it to me."

"I still owe another ninety zlotys for the rest of the summer. The landlord wants all of the rent paid in advance."

"What are we going to live from? What kind of work will I find there?"

"Shifra, you're seven months pregnant. You can't go to work anymore than I can. We'll borrow the money. When I get better and start to work again, I'll pay it back."

"Who do you think is going to lend it to us?" Shifra asked with a gloomy face.

"Yoinne, Uncle Ksiel. They have money."

"I already went to see Yoinne today. Do you want to know what my brother says?"

"What?"

"He says that you're faking. He says you don't want to work."

"He should be faking like I am."

"Then I went to see Uncle Ksiel. Times are hard, he says to me. He doesn't have any money."

"We'll have to sell everything," I said, "the sewing machine and all the furniture we left in Yoinne's cellar."

"That garbage? You won't get ten zlotys for it."

"I'll get at least a hundred and fifty zlotys for the sewing machine. I can get another fifty zlotys for the furniture. And tomorrow I'm going to see Ruchele and Zygmunt, maybe they can help me."

"You're dreaming," Shifra said.

"Leave it to me."

"Come," Shifra said to Liebele who was playing with her rag doll on the bed. "Let's cook some food."

Liebele quickly rolled to the edge of the bed, carefully slid down to the floor and with wobbling footsteps followed her mother into the kitchen.

My biggest problem was to sell the sewing machine. I looked at my watch. It was just half past six. The Union hall was still open. Someone there had to be interested in buying a new sewing machine. The sewing machine which we had bought with the last of our savings and which we thought would be our salvation, was going to save us, but not in the way we had hoped.

My visit to Ruchele was a painful one. My sister was shocked to hear how sick I was. In spite of her desire to help me, however, she and Zygmunt didn't have much to spare. They gave me thirty zlotys and I promised that I would try to pay them back as soon as I was working again.

My intuition about the Union turned out to be right. Within two days I not only found a buyer for my sewing machine, I also found buyers for the six pieces of furniture we had in Yoinne's basement.

Slowly I was amassing the small fortune I needed to save my life.

The Enchanted Village

ON THE MORNING Shifra and I packed our bags to leave for Miedzeschien we had two hundred and twenty-five zlotys. From that money I still had to pay seventy zlotys to our new landlord, leaving us a hundred and fifty-five zlotys to live on for the summer. Somehow I had managed to scrape together enough to get us through the worst.

The train station on Djika Street was only a block from where we lived. The summer warmth was already settling over the city. I carried a suitcase in one hand, two bags in the other, and a sack slung across my back. Liebele trailed along on her short legs for as long as she could. When she got tired, she sat down in the middle of the sidewalk and stretched her little hands out towards her mother. Shifra, almost eight months pregnant, picked up our daughter and carried her. Resting her face on Shifra's shoulder, Liebele stared at me. My little daughter looked tired and puzzled. In Shifra's face I saw a dull bitterness.

The train station, dark, full of loud echoes, frightened Liebele. She clung to Shifra's neck. When our train rolled up to the platform, there was a look of panic on Liebele's face.

"Don't be afraid, Mammele," I reassured her. "We're going to a new house in the middle of a beautiful forest."

"No!" Liebele suddenly started to cry. "No! I want to go back!"

"Look what your talking did," Shifra said angrily to me. "Shah," she patted Liebele's head. "Mamme is going, too. Come, let's go."

We carried our belongings into the car. At ten thirty in the morning we had our choice of seats. We made ourselves comfortable next to a window. Liebele continued to whimper in Shifra's arms. I tried to take my daughter to let Shifra rest, but as soon as I reached for her, Liebele began to cry louder.

"Leave her with me," Shifra said.

Liebele was cranky until the train started to move, but as soon as we rolled out of the station, she became fascinated with the passing scenery outside the window. She squirmed out off her mother's lap, stood up on the seat, and pressed her nose against the glass. Liebele's pleasure helped to take our minds off our problems for a while. Shifra's face softened as Liebele laughed, pulled at her mother's chin and urged with delight, "Look, Mamme! Look!"

Just as she had cried getting on the train less than a half hour earlier, Liebele cried when it was time to get off.

The train pulled away and left us standing on a deserted station in a small clearing surrounded by woods. The sky was as blue as a summer lake. Miedzeschien looked like an enchanted village.

I picked up our suitcase and bags and began to walk. Shifra followed me and Liebele straggled behind. We were soon on a dirt road in the woods. Above our heads the trees were full of bird song. I breathed in deeply. The air was sharp, refreshing. I knew at once why Dr. Feinberg had sent me away from Warsaw. The air I had breathed every day at work, filled with the damp steam that rose from the suits I pressed, tasted like stale water. My hopes rose almost immediately as we walked. I slowed down to let Shifra and Liebele catch up to me.

"Everything will work out," I tried to reassure my wife.

"Just make sure that you get well soon," Shifra said.

Shifra's distant attitude melted when we approached the pink, three story building in the middle of the woods. I could see that she liked it.

"What is this?" she asked.

"Our new home. Wait until you see the apartment."

We walked up the three steps to the veranda. Behind us, Liebele, using her hands, climbed up from step to step.

"Where are we going to buy groceries?" Shifra asked. "I don't see a store around here."

"There's a small grocery nearby and a market comes twice a week."

The windows in the lobby were open and a cool wind blew as I opened the door. Through the widows of the lobby we saw trees. This was by far the prettiest building Shifra and I had ever lived in.

Our apartment was on the first floor in the back. I pushed open the door and stepped aside. My wife and little daughter looked in with awe. The bright room had two large windows with white lace curtains. Through the windows we saw millions of shimmering leaves in the green woods. The walls were painted a bright yellow, as if washed in sunlight. The furniture was simple but comfortable: a large bed, a

196

small sofa chair, a stove, a kitchen table and three chairs, and a closet made of dark wood.

While Shifra and Liebele stood speechless and looked around, I brought in our suitcase and bags and closed the door.

"Well?" I asked Shifra. "What do you think?"

"How long can we afford this?" Shifra asked.

"Until the end of September. We'll have enough," I reassured her. "We'll spend the summer here. I'll get better. And then we'll go back to Warsaw."

Liebele, like a shy kitten, began to explore her new home. She walked slowly over to the bed, touched the mattress and looked back at us.

"Where is she going to sleep?" Shifra asked me.

"The sofa chair opens into a bed." I went to show her.

"Don't bother now," Shifra said. "Just open the suitcase and the bags on the bed so I can put everything away. I want you to rest."

Shifra's kind words brought on such tenderness in me, I couldn't stop myself from hugging her. Liebele ran over and joined us, embracing our legs.

"Enough," Shifra said, shaking herself free. "I have to put everything away now."

I pulled the suitcase and bags on the bed and untied them. Then I opened the windows wide. At once a fresh breeze rushed in, pushing the curtains aside, filling the room with the smell of the forest. I sat down on the sofa, next to the window. Shifra moved slowly back and forth folding our linen away into the drawers. My little daughter sat on the bed playing with her doll. I looked out at the shady woods, breathed deeply, and filled my lungs with the healing air.

In the afternoon, Aleck, the manager of the building, knocked on our door. He was a Pole in his early thirties, a short, stocky man, with a sullen face. He wore a cap on his head, a sports jacket over his overalls, and a belt of tools hung from his hips as if he were an American cowboy decked out with holsters and guns. He greeted us at the door, respectfully tipping his cap. I knew that he had come by for the rest of the rent and I immediately handed it to him. Aleck counted the seventy zlotys and wished us a happy stay.

Within a few days, we had become completely acquainted with the small town and were comfortably settled in. Every morning, Shifra prepared a healthy breakfast for me; one day it was kasha with milk, mixed with a large pat of butter, sprinkled with sugar and cinnamon; another day, omelettes filled with sweet cottage cheese. And with every dairy or parve meal, I drank a large glass of buttermilk.

After breakfast Shifra took Liebele on a walk down a pebbled path along the woods to the grocery store and bought food. I wanted to help my wife, but Shifra refused to let me do anything. I spent my days resting in the woods, taking slow walks, and napping by the open window.

At the end of July, as the time drew near for Shifra to give birth, I took the train into Warsaw and arranged for her stay at the same hospital where Liebele had been born.

One afternoon, a few days after I had made the arrangements, Shifra told me that she was feeling contractions. We threw a few items for Shifra into the suitcase, dressed Liebele, and the three of us took the electric train to Warsaw.

Liebele cried when she had to leave her mother at the hospital.

"Don't you want a little brother or sister?" I asked Liebele as I carried her to the train.

My daughter stopped crying long enough to think over this offer. Then she answered with a forceful No and started to cry again. My little daughter didn't calm down until she was standing at the window of the moving train.

The next morning, when Liebele and I arrived in Warsaw to visit Shifra, we were stopped at the entrance. The hospital did not allow men to visit their wives. Liebele greeted this news with such a squall, the nurses took pity on her and made an exception for us.

Shifra had gone through a painful delivery and she looked weak. I held Liebele as she hugged and kissed her mother. A few minutes later a nurse brought our family's newest member to Shifra. My new baby daughter was a dark, reddish color, with a little mop of black hair, and powerful lungs to let us know that she was hungry. Liebele had been named after Shifra's grandmother and now I suggested that we name our second girl after my Babbe Zlate.

A week later Liebele and I again travelled to Warsaw and brought Shifra and little Zlatele back with us to Miedzeschien.

For the first week, I helped Shifra. I cooked, cleaned, and shopped for food. Soon Shifra took back charge of the house and only asked me to go to the grocery for her every morning. Again I was sent out every day to breathe the fresh air and rest.

Everything returned to normal, except for our expenses. With Zlatele's birth we were spending more than anticipated and by the middle of August we were running out of money. I had to think of going back to work. After recuperating for two months, I was feeling much better. I rarely coughed, my chest no longer hurt me when I breathed deeply, and I no longer felt tired all the time. I still wasn't ready to go back to my old job, but I was sure that I could handle working half a day, as I continued to live and recuperate in the country.

I talked our situation over with Shifra. She agreed with my plans and the next morning I took the electric train into the city. As soon as I arrived in Warsaw, I went to the Union headquarters and let them know that I was looking for part-time tailoring work, anything except pressing. I was told to come back and check the next day. As I was about to leave the Union offices, I noticed a few men standing around a table with a pot of coffee and cookies. I walked over and asked them if anyone knew where I could find part-time work. One of the men mentioned he had a friend who made spring raincoats; this friend didn't have much work but sometimes he needed a presser. I hesitated but I took down the name and address of the raincoat factory, and thanked my fellow Union member. On the street, I debated with myself whether or not to go over to this raincoat factory. I would have preferred going to my old boss Moishe Chaim Borenstein, but I already owed him fifty zlotys and from part-time work I certainly wouldn't be able to start paying him back. Still, I had to earn some money and I decided that a day or two of pressing, until the Union came up with a better job, couldn't hurt me.

The whole raincoat factory was run by a young man with a sewing machine in his mother's kitchen on the second floor of an old building. He needed a presser, but only for a few hours a day and not every day. That schedule suited me. I took off my jacket and started to work at once.

At three o'clock I put my jacket back on and before four o'clock I was out in the woods of Miedzeschien again, sitting on the roots of a large tree. I didn't want to worry Shifra. I told her that I was working as a tailor. The next morning I checked at the Union headquarters, but they still had nothing for me. As it turned out, I stayed at the raincoat factory for the rest of the summer. I never worked for more than four hours a day and never more than four days a week. The work nevertheless was tiring. After less than a month at my new job, I began to feel ill again. One morning, as summer was coming to an end, I woke up with a cold.

Shifra said nothing as she got out of bed to prepare breakfast, but I could tell from the distant looks she gave me that she was as frightened as I. Our savings were almost all gone and we depended on what little money I earned from my job.

I felt dizzy, chilled, and I suspected that I had a fever. I was afraid to let Shifra know just how sick I was. I took the train as if going to work, but I knew that I had to stop working again. The day was bright and warm, when I walked out of the station in Warsaw. I went to see Yoinne at once. He was my brother-in-law, after all. His own sister's well being was at stake. My little daughters were his nieces. How could he refuse to help me in this situation?

On Zamenhoff I was surprised to find the door to Yoinne's store closed. I ran across the street and pressed my face against the glass of the display window. I saw no one. The back of the store was hidden by a large red curtain, drawn like a partition. I knocked on the glass and shouted his name. Yoinne stuck his head out from behind the curtain.

"Yoinne!" I shouted again, waving my hands to catch his attention. "It's me, Schloime!"

Yoinne, motioning with his finger to his mouth for me to be quiet, ran to the door. He unlocked it, pulled me in, and quickly locked up again.

"Come in the back," Yoinne said, holding on to my arm. "Don't say anything. Just come with me."

I followed him behind the curtain.

"Did you see those bastards out there?" Yoinne raved as if he were speaking to himself.

"Who?" I asked. "What are you talking about?"

"My creditors! They're all out there," Yoinne said, suddenly beginning to pace back and forth in front of me. "They want to take the merchandise back. They want to cut my throat, those bastards! They don't give me a minute's peace!"

Yoinne's face was unshaven, his eyes were sunk, his hair stuck out wildly as if he had been pulling it. He looked as if he hadn't slept for days. "How did this happen?" I asked him.

"How?..." Yoinne moaned, his eyes wide and empty wandering across the racks of his stock, "I don't know...I'm not selling...Nobody comes in anymore...Nobody has money...Those lousy anti-Semitic Poles with their slogans against buying from Jews! And the rent on that apartment is killing me. Elke doesn't know when enough is enough. I keep telling her we can't spend so much...." Yoinne stopped pacing and grabbed me by the lapels. "Are you working yet? Lend me some money."

I couldn't help laughing, although the situation was more tragic than funny.

"It's a joke, is it?" Yoinne shouted, letting go of me with disgust.

"Yoinne, I'm so sick—"

"Ah! So that's it! Still sick are you? I bet you want me to give you money!" Now Yoinne began to laugh, letting out a demented cackle. "Listen, Schloimele, I'm not my stupid sister. You can't fool me the way you fool Shifra. When you married her you took on the responsibility to take care of her and your children—"

"Yoinne, go to hell." I stood up to leave.

"Wait, don't leave through the front," Yoinne said. He opened the back door, which led into a courtyard, checked to make sure no one was watching and pushed me out.

Yoinne had convinced himself that I was using my illness as an excuse to avoid work. No doubt his brothers, Khiel and Nachme, and Uncle Ksiel felt the same way. I didn't bother to go see anyone else from Shifra's family for help.

I stopped off at the raincoat factory to let the young man know that I couldn't go on working for him and to collect the few zlotys he owed me. When he heard my problems, the young man, who could hardly afford it, threw in another ten zlotys to the ten he owed me.

I debated whether to ask for Ruchele's and Zygmunt's help. I knew that with the birth of their daughter just a month earlier they had plenty of their own problems. But I had to think of my wife and two little daughters.

When I entered my sister's apartment and found Zygmunt at home, I knew at once that they were in bad shape. Ruchele introduced me to my little niece, who looked no different from Zlatele, a reddish bundle of delicate life, with a head of dark hair, and a tiny mouth which somehow managed to bellow out the world's greatest sorrows. When Ruchele and Zygmunt asked me how I was doing, I told them that I was starting to feel better and that I hoped at the end of the summer to return to Warsaw and my old job. Zygmunt warned me that I might find the job situation in Warsaw difficult. He had been out work for two weeks already and had decided to give up on finding tailoring work and take any job he could get.

My last hope in Warsaw was Borenstein, my old boss, even though I already owed him fifty zlotys. I was shocked when I came into Borenstein's kitchen and found that only one of the tailors was still working there. Business was quickly going from bad to worse, Borenstein told me. The fear of war in Europe was destroying business. Even so, my old boss lent me another twenty zlotys. Back on the street, I began to feel keenly the creeping sense of despair that had been following me that whole day in Warsaw.

When I returned to Miedzeschien, I sat down at the kitchen table with Shifra and gave her the forty zlotys I had scraped together.

"I have to stop working again," I told Shifra without looking at her. "This money will have to last us to the end of the summer."

Although Shifra said nothing, her silence was a worse accusation than any words could be.

The following morning, when I stepped out for a walk in the woods, I noticed our neighbors loading their luggage into a car. People were beginning to go back to the city.

Over the next few weeks, as the weather in Miedzeschien quickly grew colder, more and more tenants packed up and left. By the middle of October, we were the only family still living in the building.

One morning at the end of October, I ran into Aleck, the stocky manager, in the lobby. "Good morning," he said, respectfully tipping his cap. "Well, Mr. Schmer, this is how it is." Aleck spoke slowly, scratching his head under the cap. "As you can see for yourself, the season ended a month ago. I've been waiting for you to leave. I have to lock up the building."

"So soon?" I asked. "The weather is still warm—"

"Mr. Schmer," Aleck cut in, "I have my job to do."

"Does the landlord have to know everything? Why don't you shut down the building and just leave our apartment open a little longer? I'm sure the two of us can come to an understanding." I had very little money left, but we had nowhere else to go, and I was ready to let Aleck have a few of our precious zlotys.

"Excuse me, Mr. Schmer," he said "but I have a family just like yours to feed and I cannot risk my job. I ask you kindly to move out as soon as possible."

Aleck tipped his cap and, looking at the floor, quickly walked off.

"What did he want?" Shifra called from the door of our apartment.

I had hoped that Shifra hadn't overheard Aleck, to give me a little time to think things through.

"He's throwing us out, isn't he?" Shifra asked.

"He says that he has to shut down the building," I told Shifra as I walked back to our apartment.

Shifra looked at me blankly, her dark eyes drowning in her calculations of our future. I closed the door and we sat down at the kitchen table across from one another. Shifra automatically took the money purse from her apron and pulled out a thin roll of bills. As she smoothed each one on the table, I counted with her. After twenty-three zlotys there was nothing left to count.

Orphans

"WE CAN RENT OUR ROOM BACK FROM GOLDE," I said.

"And pay her with what?"

"I'll ask for credit. Golde is our friend."

Shifra laughed.

"Just for a while," I insisted. "In a few weeks I'll get back on my feet." But I couldn't even convince myself of what I was saying.

"I hate it when you talk like an idiot." Shifra's blunt words hurt me like a slap in the face. "Where will you get money?" she continued. "Who's going to give it to you?"

"Nobody has to give it to me. I'll go back to work."

"And leave me a widow with two small babies?"

What difference does it make, I thought to myself. I already feel half-dead.

"I have a better idea," Shifra said. "I'll go to work."

"What can you do to earn enough money?"

"I'll do anything. I'll wash dishes in a restaurant, I'll clean houses. I'll take in wash like Golde. I'll sell myself!"

"Stop it!"

"What choice do I have? Your great love dragged me to this black grave. Now I just have to jump in!"

"Enough, Shifra!" I slammed my hand on the kitchen table, grabbed a few zlotys, and ran out of the apartment.

The morning air cooled me off. I walked quickly through the woods to the train station.

On the ride to Warsaw, as my anger faded, I began to feel sorry for Shifra. She was terrified by our situation and with good reason. I couldn't go back to work. I was still sick. I felt it in my bones. If I pushed myself, I would be committing suicide. Shifra was right: I had dragged her to this abyss. I wished I had never gotten married or brought children into the world. I should have remained alone. My life was cursed. From the day my father abandoned us in Lublin, my life had been cursed.

Shrill whistles jarred me out of my grim thoughts. The train had arrived in Warsaw.

Stafke Street on a gray day in late October looked drabber than I had ever seen it. The usual bustle of activity as business got going again after the summer months was missing. The faces of the people I passed showed despair. At the newsstands the papers carried Hitler's name in bold blood-red letters. I realized that what I was seeing was the fear of war stamped on every face. I had been so deeply immersed in worries about the survival of my family, I had not seen that the survival of the whole country was threatened.

I climbed the stairs at 18 Stafke Street. From the third floor landing, I saw the door to Golde Karp's apartment open and heard her singing over the water splashing in the large tub in which she did laundry. Golde, startled as I walked into the kitchen, whipped around and almost threw a wet shirt at me. "Schloime!" she let out a shriek. "You almost killed me with fright!"

"I'm sorry, Golde. I didn't mean to frighten you."

"Sit, sit down," Golde said, pointing to a chair near the kitchen table. "Let me catch my breath a minute. How is Shifra? Don't I owe you a mazeltov?"

"We had a litte girl: Zlatele."

"Mazeltov," Golde said, said wiping her wet hands on the apron. "Mazeltov. And is Shifra well?"

"Golde, we're all well, but we have to leave Miedzeschien. We need a place to stay."

"The room is rented. I rented it as soon as you left. I can't get by a week without the money. You see what's going on in the world. That Hitler, may he burn in hell, will attack yet. Some of my best customers have already left Warsaw."

"Did you rent to a single man, maybe? Could there be room for another bed?"

Golde shook her head. "I have a family, with two children."

On the street I realized I didn't know what do to next. I couldn't go back to Miedzeschien without some arrangement in Warsaw for our return. Without money, however, what arrangements could I make? I began to walk aimlessly, lost in my hopeless thoughts. Suddenly, I heard the shouts of children. I picked up my head. Across the street from where I stood, behind a chain-link fence, I saw a yard full of boys and girls of all ages. What school was this? Where had I wandered off to? As I approached, I saw that not all children were playing. Some boys and girls stood sadly on the sides, clutching wooden wagons and rag dolls to themselves. A few children were even crying. A teacher, a young woman of twenty or so, crouched next to a weeping boy and tried to cheer him up.

"Excuse me," I said to the teacher. Immediately a flock of curious children flew up to the fence. "What school is this?"

"It's the Children's Shelter," the young woman answered.

"We're orphans!" a boy piped up.

"I'm not an orphan!" another boy shouted in a plaintive voice.

"No, you're an abandoned bastard!" a third boy answered, and brought on noisy jeers from other boys.

"Everybody away from the fence!" the young woman commanded the brood of children. "Go! Go!" She followed hem to the center of the yard.

My clothes were pasted to my skin by a cold sweat as I walked away from the Shelter. What would happen to my little girls if I died? Would they end up standing in such a courtyard, alone, clutching toys, crying? I couldn't afford any pride. Yoinne had to help me. I had to make him see how desperate my situation was.

On Zamenhoff, as I crossed the street, I noticed that the display windows of my brother-in-law's store were completely covered with old newspapers. I pressed my face against the glass, cupped my hands around my eyes and tried to look in. I still couldn't see a thing. I knocked on the door. I called Yoinne's name. No one answered.

I ran to Yoinne's house. His apartment was locked. A young woman, with a child in her arms answered the door.

"Excuse me. I'm looking for my brother-in-law, Yoinne Schneidleider."

"You mean the old tenant. He moved."

I was numbed by this news. "Would you know where?"

"So many people come asking that same question, but I really don't know."

Yoinne's brothers, Nachme and Khiel, were still at work. I waited a few hours and went to see them. They rented the rear of a basement on Krochmalna Street. At the back of the apartment I found, to my amazement, my elderly mother-in-law.

"Nachme?" Sarah Leah asked from the bed where she sat. "Who is this?" She asked again, squinting, straining to see me at a distance.

I walked closer to the bed. "It's me."

"Schloime?" Sarah Leah finally recognized me. "It's been such a long time since we saw you. Is my Shifrale with you? I heard she had a little girl, God bless her. Mazeltov."

"Shifra's still in Miedzeschien with the babies. What're you doing here? Where's Nachme?"

"Working. The poor boy comes home so late every night and earns nothing. I've been here for a month already. Didn't you know?"

"No. What happened?"

"What didn't happen? Yoinne lost everything. Not only his money. He lost all of Nachme's and Khiel's money too, even Ksiel got mixed up in it. Yoinne owed so much, the merchants wanted to kill him. Don't ask. You should have heard that wife of his screaming at him…at me…at her own mother. Such screaming…a sin. I couldn't stay with them."

"Where's Yoinne living now?" I asked.

"He had to give up the flat. They moved in with Ksiel and Lotte. There wasn't any room for me anymore. I'll tell you the truth, I'm happier here with Nachme and Khiel. It's crowded, but at least no one screams at me."

As I listened to my mother-in-law's lament over Yoinne's troubles, I couldn't help lamenting over my own. There would be no help for us here.

"When are you coming back to Warsaw?" Sarah Leah asked me.

"Soon," I answered distractedly. "I have to go now."

"Tell my daughter that I miss her and my granddaughters," Sarah Leah said as I began to back out of the room.

It was useless to visit Ksiel and Lotte, but I went anyway. I left with twenty-five zlotys and the knowledge that I couldn't expect anymore help than that from Shifra's family.

I arrived in Miedzeschien late at night. I could barely see my way as I walked through the deserted woods. In the darkness I went past our building. I didn't know where I was until I stepped on the pebbled path that led to the grocery store. I realized that the veranda light in our building, which usually burned all night long, was off. In fact, not a single light was on in our building.

I walked into the pitch-black lobby. Feeling with my hands along the wall, I found the light switch and flipped it. No light came on. With outstretched arms, I countinued to feel my way across the lobby to our door. I turned the knob. The door was locked. As I felt my pockets for the key I heard a floor board creak inside the apartment.

"Shifra?" I said softly.

"Schloime?" my wife whispered inside the apartment.

"Open up."

Immediately the door opened. As soon as I had stepped in, Shifra pushed the door close and locked it again.

I reached for the light switch but no light came on in the apartment either. "What's going on?" I asked.

"Aleck came back this afternoon," Shifra whispered. In the darkness I could clearly hear the panic in her voice. "I was lying down with the children. I heard a loud knock outside and suddenly I saw him at the window. I jumped out of the bed and I asked him what he was doing. He didn't say anything. He just took out the window. I couldn't stop him. I was afraid to be here by myself. He also shut everything off. There's no more light or water."

I walked into the darkness. When I came close to the window, I saw that a blanket was now covering it. The wind blew the blanket as if it were a curtain and I felt the cold air and saw the dark woods outside.

"I've been scared all night," Shifra said. "We can't stay here anymore. I've packed already. I would have left, only I didn't know where to go. Where have you been all day? What did you accomplish?"

I embraced Shifra and held her tightly against me. I couldn't tell her that we had no money, no place to live, and that there was no one who could help us.

"You didn't accomplish anything," Shifra said, letting me hold her.

I didn't answer. There would be enough time tomorrow to tell her the bad news.

In the morning, I waited for Aleck. All I wanted from him was that he leave us alone for a few days so I could make some arrangement in Warsaw. I also wanted to ask Aleck to turn our water and electricity back on. The building manager, however, didn't show up. By late afternoon, Shifra and the babies desperately needed water. I went to the small shed next to the building. The wood around the padlock was rotted. It took one blow with a large stone and the lock went flying to the ground. Inside the shed, I found an open water well.

The following day I waited again, but again Aleck didn't come. On the third morning I dressed and left to look for work and an apartment in Warsaw. As soon as I arrived in the city I went to the Union. I was told that there were no jobs, not even for pressers. I stopped at a newsstand and checked the advertisements in the papers. The few jobs that were listed were temporary, paid almost nothing, and weren't jobs I could count on to feed a family. Soon, it began to rain. For the rest of the wet day I went to visit every acquaintance I had in the city. No one had any work or knew of any.

In the late afternoon, I stopped off at a grocery and bought food for my family and candles. Then, tired, and soaked through and through, I took the train back to Miedzeschien. As I watched a gray barren landscape disappear under the constant rain, I thought the world was drowning.

At home Shifra prepared dinner for Liebele, breast-fed Zlatele, and put the babies to bed. As my wife and I sat eating our meal at the kitchen table, a burst of wind suddenly blew open the blanket which covered the window and the apartment filled with freezing air. I quickly fastened the blanket around the window, but it made little difference. The wind seemed to blow right through. That night we shivered more than we slept under the blankets. In the morning, our babies were sick; Zlatele woke up with a stuffed nose, and Liebele woke up coughing. Over the next few weeks, as the autumn weather grew fouler, our little girls got sicker and sicker, until Shifra and I became afraid that we would lose them to illness.

"Do something, Schloime," Shifra begged me with tears in her eyes. "Do something before it's too late."

Even though Aleck had not bothered us again, I was only able to find minimal work in Warsaw—a day or two each week. It was enough to keep us going in Miedzeschien but nothing else. In early November, as I rode into Warsaw, I formed one last plan. When I got off the train, I walked to Leszno and Okopowa like a man who no longer has a free will. At the Children' Shelter I asked to speak to the Director.

A woman brought me into a small office where a middle-aged man with a short beard and a kind face sat behind a desk, writing. He looked up as I walked in.

I waited for the woman to leave the room and close the door. The Director took off his glasses, put his pen down and looked at me with a sympathetic face. He seemed to guess everything before I had even said a word.

"I have a wife and two small babies," I began the story of my miserable situation.

The director listened without interrupting me. As I spoke I could see the sadness deepening in his eyes.

"….I'm begging you. Save my children's lives. Let them stay here. Not for long. Just until I can get back on my feet. My wife can work for you. She's young, healthy. She would work for nothing. Just for a place for her and our children. If you could help me this much I would be grateful to you for the rest of my life."

When I had finished the director thought a long time. "We have never been more overcrowded," he said. "We don't even have place for the orphans." He looked at me, at the desk, out the small window of his office. "I can't help you now, but come back in a few days. If a place opens up, you'll be the first."

Unfortunately I had no time to wait. My children's lives were in danger. Another week would be too late. On the train ride back to Miedzeschien a more drastic plan began to take shape in my mind.

At the kitchen table, by the light of a sputtering candle, I told Shifra what I had done. "I thought that if they gave you a job there, you could be with the children. At least the three of you would be safe. I didn't know what else to do…"

"They'll help us after we're dead…" Shifra had summed up our situation exactly.

"There's only one way the Shelter will take the children," I said. I couldn't bring myself to speak the words, but Shifra understood and began to cry. "For a short time, Shifra. What else can we do?"

My wife laid her head down on the table. I tried to comfort her, but Shifra shook me off. For a long while, I sat next to my sobbing wife unable to do anything for her. After she had cried herself out, Shifra wiped the tears from her face and slowly stood up. With bowed heads and trembling hands, we picked up our babies. Liebele and Zlatele were both so sleepy they felt like dolls. We dressed them warmly. While they lay on the bed, I wrote on a sheet of paper, "Zlatele, 3 months old. Please hand this child to the Jewish Children's Shelter." My hand shook so badly, the writing was barely legible. On another sheet of paper, I wrote, "Liebele, 3 years old," and again I asked that she be placed in the Children's Shelter. Shifra gave me Liebele's winter coat and I sewed the letter to the inside lining. I sewed Zlatele's letter to her covering blanket.

While Shifra wrapped Zlatele in the blanket, I put Liebele's little arms through her winter coat. Both children continued to sleep. Shifra carried Zlatele in her arms, and over her shoulder, a bag with our belongings. I carried Liebele in one hand, our valise in the other, and the large sack slung across my back. And that was how we left our room at last.

Late at night we sat in the small, dimly lit Miedzeschien station waiting for the train to Warsaw. After an hour, we began to think that we might have already missed the last train. We were almost ready to return to our room when we heard a faint rumbling in the distance. The train came at last and we got on.

Shifra and I sat together, each of us holding a child. We didn't exchange a word all the way to Warsaw.

In the city we walked through the streets, careful not to be seen by anyone who knew us, carrying our children and baggage. We couldn't bring ourselves to do what we had decided. We started to cry. We looked at each other in the eyes, and tears kept pouring from us without a stop.

The night grew darker. We were exhausted from our aimless wandering and half frozen from the cold. Liebele began to stir in my arms. Soon she was awake, wriggling this way and that, questioning with her whole little body where we were.

I turned to Shifra and said, "She's up. We can't wait anymore."

We were now on Djelazna Street only a few blocks away from the Children's Shelter. Across the street from where we stood I saw a fancy, three-storey building with balconies. The large windows were covered with expensive lace curtains. Through some windows, I could see chandeliers on the ceilings. A well dressed couple suddenly walked into the building. After they had gone in, Shifra and I crossed the street.

The door to the building was open. We stepped into the lobby. I looked around quickly to make sure no one was coming. There were three apartments on the first floor.

"Put her down here," I whispered to Shifra, pointing to the door of the first apartment.

Zlatele was still asleep as Shifra, trembling and crying, laid her down on ground. I rang the bell to the apartment and we left quickly. Liebele turned wildly in my arms, looking in disbelief at her parents and back at her little sister. We crossed the street and waited around the corner to see what would happen to our abandoned child.

After a few minutes, a group of people gathered at the entrance to the building where we had left Zlatele. Soon a police automobile arrived and took our child away.

As we began to walk, I couldn't tell whether the shivering in my arms was Liebele's or my own. As if she sensed what was about to happen, Liebele clung to my neck. On Karmelistka, another street where wealthy people lived, we chose again a luxury building. It had a small vestibule at the entrance with a few steps leading up to the lobby doors, which seemed to be locked.

We waited until we were sure no one was coming, then we ran across the street and walked into the small entrance. I pulled Liebele away from myself and sat her down on the steps. At once she began to cry.

I motioned to Shifra to leave the building while I tried to calm Liebele.

"Do you want chocolates?" I asked.

Liebele, through her tears, shook her head yes.

"Then don't cry. Just sit here and wait. I'll come right back with chocolates and candy."

I looked up and saw Shifra outside the glass doors crying as she looked in at us. My plan was to ring as many bells as I could in the vestibule before I walked out. The outside door was heavy and I didn't think my little daughter would be able to open it. I stood up quickly, but before I could get away, Liebele caught my coat and wouldn't let go. I had no choice but to pick her up again.

Shifra and I continued to walk the empty streets of Warsaw while my daughter cried herself to sleep in my arms. When Liebele was fast asleep, I walked back with her to the same luxury building on Karmelitska. Shifra folded Liebele's blanket on the steps of the vestibule. Gently, I put my sleeping child down on this makeshift bed. Liebele was too exhausted to wake up. Shifra and I rang every bell and we left to watch from across the street.

Within minutes a crowd had gathered at the entrance to the building. A woman stepped out into the street, holding our crying Liebele in her arms. Soon a police car arrived and took our child away.

Shifra and I looked at each other. In my wife's eyes I saw the same question I kept asking myself, What had we done?

The Wet Nurse

SHIFRA AND I WANDERED through the dark streets of Warsaw wrapped in our own bleaker darkness. We were in such turmoil, we couldn't speak. Late at night, with nowhere to go, we ended up back at the train station. The large, hollow building was almost deserted now. We sat down on a bench. Shifra leaned against me. I put my arm around her and we fell asleep.

I woke up with a start as a train rumbled into the station. I looked around quickly. By some miracle the police had not bothered us. People going to work were already rushing back and forth. Shifra, who had stretched out on the bench with her head in my lap, also woke up. Her hair was disheveled; her face had red welts and creases; her clothes were rumpled.

"My God, what did I do?" Shifra whispered, her black eyes filled with anguish.

"Shifra, stop," I begged her.

"We have to get them back." Shifra stood up and began to wander away from me. "How could I agree to such a thing?"

I slung the sack over my shoulder, gathered up our valise and bag and followed my wife.

"Shifra, listen to me," I said trying to hold her back. "We did the only thing we could. They were getting sick in the country. At least they didn't have to spend the night in a train station."

But Shifra wouldn't stop. "Do you see a policeman?"

"Why do you want a policeman?"

"I want to know where my children are."

"Shifra, we'll get arrested. Calm down. You have to eat something. Come, let's go someplace and eat."

"I don't want to eat."

213

"Shifra, come with me," I said. "Let me at least look into a newspaper to see if I can get a job. Maybe someone will give me an advance. If we can rent a room somewhere, I'll go with you to the police and get them back. But come and eat something first."

Shifra allowed me to guide her out of the train station.

It was just a little after dawn, but the underbelly of the sky was already bloated with dark clouds. At a newsstand, I bought a paper and folded it into the pocket of my jacket. Then I led Shifra into the first cafeteria we passed.

The steam from the boiling pots in the kitchen was a welcome relief from the cold. I sat Shifra down at a table, placed our luggage at her feet, and went to the counter. We had very little money. All I could buy was a cheese sandwich and a cup of coffee for Shifra and a glass of tea for myself.

As I brought the tray to our table, Shifra looked at me with such grief-striken eyes, she frightened me. I wasn't sure whether the pain hadn't driven her mad.

"Eat something," I said, putting the tray down and sitting next to her.

"What do you think is happening to them?" Shifra whispered to me.

"We'll find out but eat first. Please."

Shifra picked up the sandwich. Even though she hadn't eaten for a long time I could see that she had no appetite. I was glad when she finally took a bite and then a sip of her coffee.

I took the newspaper out of my pocket. As I was leafing through the pages looking for the job advertisements, my eye was caught by the names Liebele and Zlatele in a small column of type. From the excitement and lack of food I began to feel dizzy.

"They're safe," I whispered to Shifra. "They're safe."

Shifra pulled at my arm, "How do you know? What did you see?"

In a low voice, as the type swam before my eyes, I read the brief paragraph to my wife. "Two Girls Abandoned. Two Jewish girls, by the name of Liebele and Zlatele were found. One child was abandoned in the lobby of a building on Djelazna Street and the other in a building on Karmelitska Street. Each child had a pinned note giving her name and age. Both children have been handed over to the Jewish Children's Shelter."

Shifra covered her face with her hands and cried. "Thank God," she whispered.

We were greatly relieved by the news article. I had no doubt that the Children's Shelter was taking much better care of our babies than we could. I reopened the newspaper. There was hardly any work available.

Shifra pushed half of her sandwich at me. "Here, you have to eat something."

I was too starved to resist. I took a bite as I kept reading the advertisements.

"What do you see?" Shifra asked.

"Not much," I quickly read the few advertisements to Shifra. We agreed that the best job was at a small factory of men's suits which was looking for a cutter.

"We have to go right away," I said, "or the job will be taken." I picked up our luggage and we left the cafeteria.

The factory, on Krolenska Street, was far from where we were on Djika. We walked as fast as we could. When we got there I left Shifra waiting in the street with our luggage while I ran up to the fifth floor.

I came back down almost at once. The job was already filled.

Next, I tried an advertisement for a helper in a leather factory. I picked up our belongings and we rushed over to that address. Again Shifra waited outside with the luggage while I went in. That job had also been taken.

By noon I had gone through all the advertisements. I had also gone to see my old bosses, and I had even dragged our luggage to Nalefky Street to the union headquarters. There was no work to be had anywhere. At the union as always I was promised a job as soon as something came up. Unfortunately, we couldn't wait even a day. We stood on busy Nalefky Street, tired and hungry, the luggage at our feet, unable to think of what to do next.

"There's one advertisement we didn't try yet," Shifra said. My wife was referring to an advertisement for a woman to breast-feed a baby for a family.

"I don't want you to do that kind of work," I said.

"We don't have any choice."

"That's not decent work for a married woman."

"You're talking of decency to me?" Shifra asked. "Was it decent what we did? We have to eat and we have to get our children back."

I picked up our luggage and we began walk again. This time to Novolipke Street, number 14.

At the address we found a two-story building of gray stone. As we were about to ring the bell, a man in his mid-thirties, heavy and bald except for a fringe of graying hair around the base of his skull, opened the door. He was dressed in a business suit, black overcoat, and had a briefcase in his hand.

"Are you looking for someone?" he asked.

I showed him the advertisement for the wet nurse in the newspaper.

"We're not looking for a couple," he said, pointing at our lugagge.

"The work is only for my wife," I said.

"In that case," he said, stepping aside, "please come in."

The polished floor creaked softly as we walked through the hallway into the living room. A polished cherry-wood table stood in the middle of the room. Against one wall there was a china closet with crystal glasses and fancy dishes. A grandfather clock ticked softly in a corner. White silk drapes hung from the ceiling to the floor, covering the windows in the warm room.

"Sit down". The man pointed us to the chairs around the table. "Let me call my wife." Just then, a woman in her mid-thirties, wearing a blue velvet house robe, walked in. "Dora, I was just going to call you."

"Are you here about the advertisement?" the wife asked us. She was thin and at least a head taller than her husband.

"Yes," I said.

"I am Dora Beckerman," the woman said, "and this is my husband, Kalmen."

I introduced myself and Shifra. Kalmen took off his overcoat and excused himself for a moment.

Dora sat down on at the table next to Shifra and smiled. "Can you breast-feed a baby?"

Shifra nodded.

"Is that your luggage?" Dora asked me. "Have you just arrived in Warsaw?"

"We are from Warsaw," I said. "We were living in Miedzeschien for a few months and we just came back to the city."

"Where do you live?" Dora asked.

As I was thinking how to answer this question, Dora's husband entered the living room carrying a tray with a pot of tea, four cups, a bowl of sugar, and a plate with slices of cake.

"We don't have an address yet," Shifra said.

Dora and Kalmen exchanged a troubled look. "You don't have an address?" Kalmen asked. "How do we know who you are? We would like references."

"Tell them what happened," Shifra said.

216

The couple turned their eyes on me.

I was ashamed but I told them the truth.

When I had finished, Kalmen said, "What a fantastic story."

"Look," I said, pulling the newspaper out of my pocket, "you can read it for yourself."

I handed the opened newspaper to the couple. They bent their heads over the article.

"It is true," Kalmen said.

"Would you be willing to be examined by our doctor?" Dora asked Shifra.

Shifra nodded.

"We can go right now," Kalmen said, standing up and pulling on his overcoat.

"Our doctor is not far from here," Dora said. "They'll be back soon."

After Kalmen and Shifra had left, Dora picked up the teapot and poured a glass for me and one for herself. "Have some tea and cookies," she urged me.

"What is your husband's profession?" I asked.

"My husband is now a bookkeeper. He goes from business to business, wherever he can find work these days, and adds up columns of numbers. When we were first married, we had a little money which our parents had left us. But thanks to my husband's passion for speculative business investments we've lost almost everything."

A baby suddenly began to cry in another room and interrupted Dora's story.

"There he is," she sang out as she left. "Arele is awake. Mama is on her way."

I looked around. I noticed now that the top of the table was chipped and blistering. The silk curtains had patches. The carpet under my feet was worn down to holes in spots.

Dora returned holding the baby wrapped in a blanket. Her son whimpered as she paced back and forth rocking him back to sleep. I wondered why a healthy woman like Dora couldn't nurse her own child, but I was too embarrassed to ask.

As soon as the baby stopped crying, Dora sat down again, and said, "I had enough milk the first month, then it just stopped. I should have become a mother at a younger age. That's the reason my poor little son was born in the seventh month and why my milk dried up. I've been to see the best doctors in Warsaw. Not one could help me, but they all agreed that because Arele is so small, he has to have breast

217

millk. Kalmen only wants to hire a Jewish woman. I've begged him to advertise in the Polish newspapers, but when he makes up his mind…"

Finally the front door opened and Kalmen and Shifra walked into the living room. Kalmen went to his wife and kissed her. "Everything's fine," he said. "Shifra's healthy and can start nursing Arele at once. Now we just have to settle on a salary." Kalmen turned to us and asked, "How much were you expecting?"

Shifra looked to me. I didn't know what to ask for anymore than she did. "We leave it up to you," I finally said. "I trust you'll treat us fairly."

"I can offer you fifteen zlotys a week. If all goes well and my business improves, I would like to raise the amount. But remember, your wife will have the best of food and there's a comfortable bed in the baby's room for her. All we ask is that Shifra help us bring up the child. There will be no other work for her."

I looked at Shifra. She agreed.

"Where do I put my things?" Shifra asked Dora.

"Come with me," Dora said. "Let me show you the room."

After the women had left Kalmen took out his wallet and pulled out some money.

"Here is fifteen zlotys," he said, giving me the money. "I'm sure you can use it."

I thanked him.

Our wives returned almost immediately.

"It's a good room," Shifra told me. "Take your things in the suitcase and leave everything else here with me."

I opened the suitcase on the floor, took out Shifra's and the girls' clothes, and piled them on the large table. The suicase was much lighter now that it only had my own clothes in it.

I said goobye to Kalmen and Dora. Shifra walked out of the house with me.

The day, which had started with cover of dreary gray clouds had grown darker.

"Did he give you some money?" Shifra asked.

"Fifteen zlotys."

"Go and find a room first," Shifra told me. "Then find out how the babies are doing. In a week, come back and I'll give you the fifteen zlotys."

I wanted to embrace and kiss my wife, but she walked quickly back into the house and closed the door.

Alms for a Beggar

I LEFT MY WIFE WITH THE BECKERMAN'S on Novolipke Street to feed the milk which belonged to our Zlatele to another child. On the street, carrying the lightened suitcase, I soon felt the cold gnawing into my bones. I had to find some place to spend the night. With the fifteen zlotys Kalmen had given me I figured I would be able to rent a bed for at least a week. I opened again the newspaper which seemed to have all the sad answers to our lives, the same newspaper which had told us that our babies had made it safely to the Children's Shelter, and which took us to the Beckerman's, and found myself a bed with an elderly Jewish couple on Zamenhoff Street. My new landlords must have sensed that my story would not be a happy one and didn't ask me much. I was grateful to them for not prying. The corner of the room they rented to me had no more than a narrow bed, a night stand, and a slim chest of drawers. I paid them ten zlotys in advance for the week, slipped my suitcase under the bed, and went to sleep.

My night was filled with nightmares of walking along dark Warsaw streets with Shifra, holding our babies, looking for a safe place to leave them. In my sleep again I went through the wrenching torture of putting Liebele and Zlatele down on the steps of strange buildings. As Shifra and I ran away, our hearts torn by our babies' cries, we found we were still carrying our Zlatele and Liebele in our arms and that we had to abandon them again. Over and over I had to hear the cries of our babies. I woke up many times during the night, drenched in sweat and tears, and everytime I fell asleep the same nightmare returned.

In the morning as soon as I had gathered my wits, I dressed and ran to Children's Shelter. I waited outside the building, until I saw a young woman with a kind face about to enter.

"Excuse me," I stopped her, "but do you work here?"

219

"Yes," she said.

"The two little girls that were found yesterday, how are they doing?"

"Do you know them?" The interest on the young woman's face alarmed me. Had she guessed so quickly that I was their father?

"I may know the parents," I said, unable to think of anything else.

She led me away from the entrance to the building. "What has happened to the parents?" she asked. "You can tell me."

I guessed from her tone of voice that she knew who I was. Still, I felt I could trust her. "The father has been very sick," I said, "unable to work. The parents had no money, no place to sleep, and nowhere to turn. Believe me, the parents will come for their children the moment they're able to take care of them again."

"The children are upset now," the young woman said, "the older one especially. But they're safe and healthy. I'm glad you spoke to me. Now we can tell Liebele that her parents will come for her and her sister as soon as they can."

I couldn't speak. I simply nodded. I was sure the young woman understood how grateful I felt. Shifra was the only person in the world with whom I could share this good news. Without thinking, I ran immediately to Novolipke Street. I knocked on the Beckerman's door and waited. Dora, dressed in her blue velvet house robe, answered. Her expression, when she saw me, was far less friendly than the day before.

"I'm sorry to bother you," I apologized, "but I have some important news for my wife."

"Shifra is busy right now," Dora said not looking at me.

"I can wait. I promise I won't keep her long. It's about our children."

"Let me see," Dora said. "She may be done."

I waited at the door. A few minutes later Shifra came out. "What are you doing here? She thinks you want to move in already."

"Shifra, I've just been to the Children's Shelter."

It took Shifra a few moments before she could ask, "How are they?"

"Liebele and Zlatele are safe and healthy."

"How do you know? Did you see them?"

"I spoke to a girl who works there. I told her I was a friend of the parents but I'm sure knew who I was. She's going to tell Liebele that we'll come for her as soon as we can."

Even though Shifra said nothing, I saw the relief on her face.

"How are they treating you?" I asked.

"When the baby feeds on my breast I can only think of Zlatele. I feel that my heart is being sucked out along with my milk."

"This won't go on for long," I said.

"Did you find a room?" Shifra asked.

"I'm renting a bed from an old couple on Zamenhoff."

"Don't take work as a presser. You'll kill yourself," Shifra said. "Come back in a week and I'll give you the fifteen zlotys." Without saying anything else, Shifra walked back into the house.

There was no danger that I would kill myself by going back to work as a presser. Towards the end of 1938, there was no work to be had anywhere in Warsaw. We did the best we could. Shifra survived as a wet nurse to the Beckerman's child; I survived on my wife's salary; and both my wife and I survived on the news from the Children's Shelter that our girls were healthy. Early in 1939, under these strange circumstances, my left lung seemed to finally heal. In the summer of 1939 another miracle occurred. The union found a job for me as a finisher in a coat factory. My salary, twenty zlotys a week, was not much, but at least Shifra and I were able to start saving. Whenever I visited my wife, we counted our money and calculated how much longer we had to wait before we could rent our own room and take our children back from the Shelter.

I hadn't seen Ruchele and Zygmunt for almost a year. I knew that they too had been facing difficult times and I didn't want to add to their burdens. But now that I was working again, I decided to visit them. They were still living on Sherakovsky Street, sharing the same noisy apartment with Hersh the cobbler, his wife and brood of children.

Both Zygmunt and Ruchele looked thin. They were dressed in old, patched clothes. I had always expected my brother-in-law with his vigor and intelligence to become a successful man. Instead, it seemed to me, Zygmunt was struggling almost as much as I. He took whatever tailoring jobs he could find, but mostly he was forced to work as a porter in order to feed his wife and little daughter.

When I told them what Shifra and I had gone through, my sister and her husband were shocked. I was sure they were upset not only for what had happened to Shifra and me but for what could happen to them. They insisted that I visit them often.

On such a visit one Sabbath afternoon, I found Ruchele alone in the house with her little daughter. The cobbler and his family were out, and for once it was quiet in the apartment. Zygmunt still had not returned from visiting his friends. As I sat at the kitchen table talking to my sister, Dvoirale, my two year old niece, came wobbling towards me, carrying her story book. I lifted her to my lap and opened the book. Together we looked at pictures of kings, queens, and wizards and read a fantastic story.

While Dvoirele was occupied, Ruchele moved to the kitchen stove to prepare a meal. But almost at once she was interrupted by a knock on the door. Ruchele answered it.

"Who is it?" I asked my sister as she walked back from the kitchen.

"A poor lady begging for alms. I don't have any change."

"I'll give her something," I said.

Holding my little niece in one arm, I went to the door. With my free hand, I reached into my pocket for some groschen. When I saw the poor woman, a dry, bent twig with white hair, I almost fainted. She also recognized me at once and burst into tears. Ruchele came to the door and looked at us as if we had both gone mad, and suddenly she too understood.

"Mamme...?" Ruchele murmured. "Is that you?...Mamme?"

I remembered the last devastating meeting between my sister and our mother, and I didn't know whom to comfort first.

Our mother suddenly turned and began to run away.

"Don't let her go!" I cried out to Ruchele.

My sister ran after our mother and threw her arms around her. "Don't go," Ruchele cried holding on to our mother. My sister led our mother, too weak to resist, into the apartment and sat her down at the table. I closed the door. My little niece, frightened by the commotion, was crying in my arms. In the midst of this chaos Zygmunt returned.

"What's going on here?" he asked.

"Please don't ask," I said as I held Dvoirele out to him.

He took her at once. In her father's arms, Dvoirele began to calm down. I sat down at the table, next to my mother and sister. All the crying had finally stopped and a heavy silence filled the apartment. Dvoirele, completely exhausted, fell asleep in her father's arms.

"Put the child to bed," my sister said to her husband.

Zygmunt took Dvoirele to her crib.

Now I saw why Ruchele hadn't recognized her own mother. Mamme's face was drawn and wrinkled as if she were an old woman; her hair was completely gray; her clothes were torn and dirty. Our mother had truly become a beggar.

Zygmunt came back to the kitchen.

"Please make us some tea," Ruchele asked her husband. "And bring some food to the table."

"Is that your mother?" Zygmunt asked in a whisper.

Ruchele nodded without looking at her husband.

"Mamme, are you sick?" Ruchele asked.

Our mother lifted her head for the first time and looked at us. Her once green eyes were now gray. We waited for her to speak, but she didn't say anything.

"Why do you live with that man?" Ruchele asked. "Look at you. You're still young but your hair is white. And you're so thin."

"What can I do?" our mother said in a voice worn out by grief. "That bastard won't stop drinking. He promises that now he's going to stop, now he's going to stop, and then he starts again."

"Stay here with us," Ruchele said.

"I have small children to feed," Mamme said. "I can't leave them. My life ended many years ago, when I abandoned you. The only reason I'm still walking around is to atone for my sins."

"If you left that horrible man you could still rescue yourself!" Ruchele burst out unble to contain her anger.

I knew it was useless, but I couldn't help wishing that Ruchele would have some effect on our mother.

Zygmunt returned to the table with a plate on which he had four glasses of tea. He set it down on the table and returned to the kitchen.

"Is that your husband?" Mamme asked Ruchele.

"Yes. His name is Zygmunt, we have a little girl, Dvoirele."

"And you, Schloimele, do you have a family?"

"I have a wife and two little girls," I said. I simply couldn't bring myself to add to our mother's grief by telling her how my own family had been broken up by my illness.

"You were always such good children," Mamme said. "You were such a small boy when you left cheider to help me. I always felt so guilty that your childhoods were stolen from you. Your father... I will blame him for everything to the day I go to my grave."

I couldn't bring myself to tell her about the few letters we had received from our father.

Mamme stood up as Zygmunt came back from the kitchen with a plate of buttered bread and cheese.

"Don't leave," Ruchele said and jumped up from her chair.

"I beg you not to stop me," our mother said as she walked to the door. "At least I know that my children have found some happiness."

1939

THE START OF 1939 in Poland smelled of war. The streets were filled with unemployed men and I was constantly afraid of being laid off from my job as a finisher. Every week, after paying for my bed and food, I brought my left over money to Shifra. In our desperate attempt to rent a room and get our children back from the Shelter, we counted each grosch. But just as we were getting close to having enough money, my work began to dry up. Instead of working a full week, I suddenly had work for only a day or two, and I was forced to use our savings.

By the spring, the situation in the country had worsened. Even though no one could afford to buy a newspaper, the newsstands were crowded with the curious who read only the headlines and front pages. And every day there were fresh horrors to read. Hitler's brutal treatment of the Jews shocked us. While innocent men, women and children were being beaten and killed, there wasn't a country in the world interested in stopping Germany's government of terror. It wasn't until the Germans had overtaken Czechoslovakia and turned their attention on Poland, that Britain and France offered to help. Poland gladly accepted this assistance. Britain and France, however, felt they needed the Soviets' alliance. The Soviets knew that if Germany was not stopped it would simply step over Poland into the Soviet Union. Stalin offered to build military bases and airfields in Poland. The Poles, afraid of a Soviet takeover, refused. Smigly-Rydz, Poland's leader, said he wouldn't let a single Russian boot step on Polish land.

Those who could afford it began to stock up on food. Products disappeared from grocery shelves as merchants hoarded their goods expecting prices to rise. And the poor were soon going hungry.

Every Sabbath, when I saw Shifra, we would take a walk past the

Children's Shelter. We couldn't go in, but it reassured us to see the building where our girls were being cared for. One Sabbath in late Spring, when the weather was warm, Shifra and I were surprised to see children playing in the yard of the Shelter. There were so many boys and girls running back and forth it was hard to find our little daughter.

"I see her!" Shifra shouted suddenly grabbing my arm. "I see her! Liebele! Liebele!"

"Mamme!" came a piercing cry, and with a sobbing face our Liebele ran up to the fence. "Please take me home!" she cried. "I don't want to stay here! The boys scare me! The ladies don't let me play!"

The teacher on duty, a young woman, came running to the fence. I recognized her at once, just as she recognized me. "What's the matter?" she asked "What's going on here?" She saw Liebele crying and picked her up.

"As soon as we have a home," I said to Liebele, "we'll take you back."

"Didn't I tell you that they would come for you?" The young woman said to Liebele. She calmed our little daughter down and took her back inside.

Shifra and I walked away from the fence without a word. When we looked at each other both our faces were wet with tears.

The next Sabbath, Shifra and I again went to visit the Shelter. This time Liebele was waiting for us, her face pressed against the chain-link fence.

"Do you have a home yet?" Liebele asked as soon as she saw us.

"Not yet," I said, "but we brought you some cookies."

Liebele took them from my hand and began to eat one.

"When will you have a home?" Liebele wanted to know.

"Soon," Shifra said.

Liebele ate two cookies and hid the other two in the pocket of her white apron.

"Why don't you eat the rest of your cookies?" Shifra asked.

"I have to give some to Zlatele," Liebele said. "Frau Faige told me that Zlatele is my sister and I have to take care of her. When Zlatele learns to walk, I'll take her to play in the yard."

The bell rang and the teacher took Liebele in with the rest of the children.

On a Sabbath in August of 1939, when I came to visit my wife, Mrs. Beckerman invited me into the house. Mr. Beckerman soon joined us in the living room.

"We have good news," the husband said. "The doctor says that our baby can start nursing from a bottle."

His wife thanked Shifra for her help.

Shifra and I looked at each other. This was hardly good news for us. I barely had work. We had less than twenty zlotys saved. And the world was on the brink of disaster.

I helped Shifra pack and took her to my room on Zamenhoff Street. I asked the elderly Jewish couple from whom I rented if my wife could join me in the apartment. All they wanted was another five zlotys a week. Shifra and I spent most of our time looking for work.

On September 1, 1939, the Germans finally attacked Poland. Suddenly, all the shelves of the stores were completely bare. To buy a loaf of bread, we had to stand in line a whole night. In the morning, when the bakeries opened, only those who were close to the front of the queue were lucky enough to be able to buy something. The rest went hungry. And when people couldn't stand their hunger anymore, they paid outrageous prices in the black market.

Within days, the assault on Warsaw started. As people stood in line for food, German airplanes dropped bombs and killed them like insects. Warsaw began to burn more fiercely every day. People ran every-which-way as if they had lost their minds. The barricades which had been thrown up in haste to stop the Germans only made it impossible for us to get from one street to the next. Old men and women, mothers with children, whole families abandoned their apartments to hide in cellars. Under the endless German bombing, buildings collapsed and thousands of human beings were buried alive. The cellars in which people hid for safety became their graves.

One afternoon, after Shifra and I had spent the day scavenging for food, we returned to Zamenhoff Street to a sickening surprise. The building in which we lived had been bombed. In the mountain of brick before us, we couldn't even find our apartment.

We ran immediately to Shifra's uncle. The door to Ksiel and Lotte's flat was locked and no one answered the bell. On the street, a neighbor told us that the Schneidleiders had moved to the cellar. Shifra and I walked down the steps. In the overcrowded basement we found not only Uncle Ksiel, Lotte, and their children, but also Frau Liebe, Sarah Leah, Yoinne and Elke with their three children, as well as Khiel and Nachme. Ksiel told us that it was too dangerous to stay in the apartment and invited us to join them.

There were many other families in the basement besides our own. I had never lived in such packed quarters before. Hunger drove me out of the basement as soon as there was a letup in the bombing.

Late at night Warsaw flickered eerily. As I ran through the ravaged city looking for scraps of food, the only light came from the flames of burning buildings. On Zamenhoff, I suddenly heard an inhuman cry, a mournfull bellowing as if an ox were being slaughtered. A young man, burned and bloodied, came running out of the rubble. He was naked to the waist and had a four-year-old boy in his arms.

"Save us!" the young man screamed wildly. "People! Save my child!"

"Wait!" I called out as I ran towards him.

"Where is Twarda Street!" he asked when he saw me. "Show me the way! Please!" he begged.

"Follow me," I said and began to walk quickly.

The young man was covered with ashes. His left shoulder had a deep, bleeding gash. His hair and skin were burned. He smelled as if he were still on fire. Tears poured from his eyes. He trembled as he pressed the small boy to his chest and kissed the small, dazed face over and over.

"The Germans captured our village," the man suddenly began to speak. "They murdered everyone. I saw with my own eyes how a German soldier, a man no older than me, with one hand picked up a baby by its feet, a little Jewish girl less than a year old, and swung her in the air as if she were a doll. He laughed as his comrades applauded him and then he smashed the baby's head against a lamppost. I saw it with my own eyes. Could a man do such a thing? What kind of men are the Germans?"

These words spoken by a man who was little more than ashes himself, as we ran through the flaming streets of Warsaw, made me think that we were no longer in the world but in hell.

"I barely escaped with my wife and son," the continued. "We roamed for days. We got here just a few hours ago. My brother lives on Zamenhoff. We were so exhausted we fell asleep like the dead. We didn't wake up even when the house began to burn. A flaming log fell on me. When I opened my eyes the room was collapsing. I grabbed my son who was lying in my arms and jumped through a window. I don't know how we got out alive. The whole building caved in as soon as we were out. I called my wife and brother. Nobody answered. And now I'm running to a cousin's house on Twarda, No. 5."

"It's only a block away," I said as we rushed along.

"What is your name?" the man asked me.

"Schloime," I said.

"I will never forget you," he said.

I knew that as long as I lived I would never be able to forget him either.

"Your mother has been burned to death!" the man suddenly cried out to the child in his arms. "God!" he screamed, lifting his face to the black sky. "God! Where are you hiding?!"

We were finally on Twarde Street. The building he was looking for was still standing. "This is it," I said. I couldn't listen to his screams anymore and I left quickly.

The siege of Warsaw didn't last long. The Polish Army, unable to stand up to the Germans, retreated after the first week. In the last few days of fighting, it was impossible to walk the city's streets. All day long the Germans dropped bombs from the sky. At night they shelled the city with heavy artillery. Warsaw was wrapped in flames and her streets were heaped with dead people, dead horses, dead dogs and cats. Streams of blood flowed down the gutters. The wails of children rose from cellars. Thousands of people, hungry and frightened, lost their minds. Some committed suicide.

In the cellar where we were hiding, the food ran out. We lived on cold water. During the days of fighting many more families had moved in. At night the air was so stale I felt I was suffocating. Finally, I couldn't stand it anymore. I asked Uncle Ksiel if he would let me sleep in his flat. He looked at me as if I were mad but he handed me the key. Shifra wouldn't join me.

I walked up to the apartment and began to search for food. In the kitchen, in the corner of a shelf, I found two pieces of dry bread covered with green mold. I started to scrape it off, but I realized that if I scraped much longer there wouldn't be any bread left. I devoured the moldy bread with a glass of water. As I ate, I tried to imagine that I was chewing a tasty piece of roast turkey. After that delicious meal, I got into Uncle Ksiel's large, soft bed and fell soundly asleep.

It was Shifra who woke me up the following morning. Still groggy, I looked up from the bed where I had been sleeping and saw her face above me.

"Thank God you're alive," Shifra said. "Weren't you afraid of the shelling? I thought for sure they had killed you.

"I didn't hear a thing."

"What happened here?" Shifra was pointing to the window next to the bed. "My God! Look at this!"

I sat up. At my feet on the bed, amidst the broken glass, lay a black iron cylinder. I jumped up and we ran down to the cellar.

We told Uncle Ksiel what we had seen and followed him quickly upstairs. Uncle Ksiel approached the bed, saw the black iron object, and stepped back.

"You should say a prayer of thanks," he said to me. "That's a live bomb. You're lucky it fell on the soft mattress and didn't explode."

That was the last time I slept in my uncle's apartment. I resigned myself to the crowded basement. That same night, I went back out into the street to look for food. I had only walked a block when I noticed a house on fire and people running out, carrying boxes, cans, and sacks.

"What've you got there?" I asked a boy dragging a bucket stuffed with canned goods.

"Food!" he said as he ran away with his loot. "There's a grocery back there."

Stores such as these were burned by the hundreds. The owners had hoarded their products, hoping for better times when they would be able to make from a grosch a zloty. Instead, their goods went up in flames. I walked into the burning rubble. The smoke and heat made it impossible to see. I grabbed a large, heavy can and ran out. I returned at once to the cellar and showed my find to Shifra.

"What is it?" my wife asked.

The label had been burned off. "We'll soon see," I said, as I struggled to pry the lid off with a knife. Finally, it popped open. We couldn't believe our eyes at the treasure inside.

"*Herbatnicks*!" Shifra cried out.

There were fifty long packages of tea biscuits in the can.

Drawn by Shifra's cry, Uncle Ksiel, his wife and children surrounded us. They were as astounded by my find as Shifra. Those biscuits sustained us for many days.

Poland surrendered in less than a month of fighting. Warsaw began to fill with two revolting colors, the green and black of the German soldiers' uniforms. One of the first orders these conquerors issued was that within three days the streets of Warsaw had to cleared of the rubble which the Germans' own merciless shelling of the city had created. Anyone who refused to work, the Germans shot dead on the spot. For three days every man and woman worked at clearing the streets, not even the oldest and sickest were spared.

Warsaw was cleaned up. The German Army marched in triumphantly and turned Warsaw, which had been called the Paris of Eastern Europe, into a city of horrors. Jewish men who were caught in the streets were beaten and had their beards cut off on one side. The Germans looked at this handiwork, laughed, and threatened their victims that if they shaved the other half of the beard off they would be shot. I saw a young German soldier attack an elderly Jew who was trying to sell a pair of worn shoes in the market. Like a wild animal the German pulled the shoes out of the old man's hands and threw them away. Other German soldiers, machine guns in their hands, looked on with self-satisfied smiles as the young German grabbed the old Jew by the beard and started to drag him along. The old man struggled to free himself from the German's sadistic hands. The young German pulled out his revolver, aimed it at the old man's forehead, and shot him.

As soon as I could, I went to the Children's Shelter. I approached Leszno Street with great apprehension. The bombing of the city had been so devastating, I was afraid of what had happened to the building full of children. A great wave of relief washed over me when I saw that a miracle had spared it from the bombs. The moment I stepped inside, however, my heart stopped. In the corridor which had always been full of children's shouts and laughter, I heard only the echo of my own footsteps. The Shelter was deserted. As I ran from empty room to empty room a middle-aged man stepped out of an office. "What do you want?" he asked.

"Where are the children? What happened here?"

"Calm down," he said. "Who are you?"

"I'm looking for my two little girls, Liebele and Zlatele."

"The children are being relocated to a safer place."

"Where?"

"I can't tell you yet," the man answered.

"What do you mean? Don't you know?"

"Calm yourself. The staff is with them and taking good care. It's for the best. Come back in a week or two and maybe I'll be able to tell you more."

I realized from his tone of voice that he was trying to protect the children and that I shouldn't press him. I left, my heart torn by fear and hope.

From the Children's Shelter, I went at once to look for my sister. The cobbler at Sherakovsky Street told me that Ruchele and Zygmunt had taken their baby and left Warsaw on the first day of the war. They were headed for Russia. I was glad to hear they at least had escaped and I hoped they were safe.

Before invading Poland, the Germans had made a pact with the Soviets and between them they had divided Poland. The Germans took the Western part, which bordered on Germany, and the Soviets took the Eastern part. The pact also allowed Germans living in Russia to return to Germany and for Russians living in Germany to return to Russia. This agreement gave Polish Jews a small opportunity to leave Poland. While many working class Jews tried to get into Russia, many businessmen, still hoping for the return of the good old days, didn't want to leave.

The road to Russia was not an easy one. In Eastern Poland the railways had been destroyed. All day and all night long Jewish people wandered on the highways. Some made it to Russia. Many were caught on the way by German soldiers and shot in mass graves which the Jews were forced at gunpoint to dig for themselves. The few young people whom the Germans spared were sent to labor camps to suffer slower deaths. In spite of these hardships Jews kept trying to escape and some were able to tear themselves out of the blood-soaked hands of the Germans. I saw that no good would come of our staying in Warsaw and decided to leave.

At night I pulled Shifra to a corner of the basement. "We can't stay here anymore," I said to her in a low voice. "The Germans are going to kill everybody. Ruchele and Zygmunt already left to Russia. Let's not wait."

"How are we going to get to Russia?" Shifra asked.

"The same as everybody else."

"It's going to be worse wandering on the streets and roads," Shifra said. "Here at least we have a place to sleep."

"Don't you see what they're doing?" I asked. "They won't let us live!" I couldn't believe that my wife would even think of staying. "The Germans aren't human. They're devils."

"It'll stop now that the fighting is over," Shifra said. "Yoinne isn't going anywhere. And neither are Nachme and Khiel."

"How do you know? Maybe they're afraid to speak up. Let's ask them."

"You want to get everybody killed," Shifra said.

I turned to the other members of our family. "Listen to me," I said to them as they sat on the makeshift stools and folding cots. "What's the good of sitting here? We won't hide out from those bastards for long. Let's take a few things with us and let's leave for Russia."

Everyone stared at me as if I had lost my mind.

"Schloime," Yoinne said, "things are bad enough without your crazy plans. Sit down and stop talking nonsense."

"Wait a minute," Nachme said, "maybe it's not such a crazy plan. How do you propose we get there?"

"Anyway we can," I answered. "Even if we have to walk all the way. There are plenty of people on the road to follow. Ruchele and Zygmunt have already left."

"And so has Tsutel," said Frau Liebe. "I just found out yesterday. May God lead her safely to Russia."

"I can't go anywhere," Sarah Leah said. "I'm too old. They won't bother with me, an old woman."

"Mother-in-law," I pleaded with Sarah Leah, "the Germans are not human. They take pleasure in killing people."

Ksiel and Lotte's two older girls understood what I had said and started to cry.

"Stop scaring everybody," Uncle Ksiel said, angry at me. "Don't worry, my children, don't worry." Ksiel embraced each child. "Tatte won't let anything bad happen to you. Schloime is just talking nonsense as always." He turned back to me and said, "Look, no one's stopping you. But we're not going to follow. We have old women and children here. Another week and everything will quiet down. It's already better than it was. The bombing has stopped. Little by little we'll get back to normal. You're too impatient."

"Nachme? Khiel?" I asked. "What about you? You go out everyday to look for scraps of food. You see what's going on."

"It's bad here," Khiel said, "but I think it could be worse on the road."

"My friend Seveck keeps talking about leaving," Nachme said. "He thinks we could get across the border. But I'm not sure. Maybe we should wait a few weeks and see if things get better."

"See," Shifra said. "Nobody is running, except you."

"I still think it's a mistake to stay," I said. "I'll wait a little, a few days, but no more. If I have to, I'll go alone."

Life under the Germans grew worse by the day. The rabid anti-Semites inflicted more and more terror on the Jewish people. Whenever German soldiers saw a Jew standing in line for a piece of bread, they pulled him out by his hair and beat him senseless. I kept looking at the Germans and asking myself what kind of animals were they? They couldn't be human, I was convinced, these killers of old men and women, of little children and babies. They were the greatest cowards and the lowest form of life I had ever seen.

Finally, two weeks after I had proposed that we escape, Nachme announced that he and Seveck had decided to leave for Russia.

"When does your friend want to go?" I asked.

"He's ready now," Nachme said.

I looked at the gray faces of Shifra's family and said, "What are you all waiting for? Open your eyes! It'll never get better under these murderers!"

But no one else was interested in leaving.

"If you want to go so much," Shifra finally said in disgust, "go."

The Lost Relative

ONCE NACHME AND I MADE UP OUR MINDS, we prepared to leave Warsaw as quickly as possible. Our destination, if we managed to escape into Russia, was the house of Nachme's uncle Moishe Schneidleider in Baranovitch. We promised to write as soon as we got there.

On the morning of our departure, while my brother-in-law waited, I ran to Leszno Street to find out if there were any more news about our girls. The Shelter was still empty, but I found the same middle aged man I had seen there on my last visit. This time he told me at once that the children were on their way to Russia, although he didn't yet know exactly where. I would have embraced him if he hadn't been sitting. This was the first hopeful news I had gotten since the war started. I took his hand and pressed it with all my strength.

I ran back to the basement. Nachme's friend, Seveck, had already arrived. My brother-in-law introduced me to the short, husky young man with muscular arms and a face of stubble. I told Shifra the good news about our children. There was a brief look of elation on her face, an expression I hadn't seen from my wife in years, but it lasted only a moment.

"How will they get through all the bombing of the roads?" Shifra asked.

"They will get through," I said with determination. "The Shelter wouldn't endanger the children's lives if they didn't think they had a good chance. Our girls will soon be in Russia. Come with me, Shifra. I beg you."

She looked back at her family, all of whom except Nachme were staying, and said, "I can't go. Besides, the children haven't arrived in Russia yet. If they come back, at least I'll be here."

Again and again I tried to convince Shifra to leave with me, but my

234

words were useless. I asked my wife to keep checking at the Shelter for our children's address in Russia and to send it to me at her Uncle Moishe's home. Finally we said our good-byes.

It was still early in the morning when Nachme, Seveck and I took to the road. The sky had a mournful, gray face. God had plenty to cry about, I thought to myself. We had a long journey ahead of us and we set off at a quick pace.

An hour out of Warsaw, on a road of gravel between two grassy fields, we saw a young man ahead of us. He looked nervously behind his back as we drew near him. For a while, the four of us walked side by side. The young man was no more that seventeen years old. He had a slight build, bent shoulders, and was carrying a large knapsack.

We introduced ourselves. The young man's name was Nussem. He was hesitant to trust us at first, but once he began to talk we couldn't stop him. "My parents are elderly people," he told us. "That's the only reason they're staying in Warsaw...." For a moment he seemed to choke on his words and then, suddenly, he exploded. "Those German fiends shot my two older brothers!" and he began to cry.

Nachme, Seveck and I didn't know what to say to comfort the poor boy. When he regained control of himself, Nussem continued, "We owned a soap factory. A week ago four Germans, may they all be blotted out from the face of this earth, came into our plant and started to carry out everything we owned. Our stock, our machinery, anything they could lift, they took. My brothers tried to stop them, but the four German gangsters pulled out their guns and shot my brothers in cold blood." Again Nussem was unable to hold back his tears.

"After this," he finally went on, "my father urged me to get out of Poland. He wanted to have at least one son left. He gave me a little money and some bars of soap. I didn't want to take the soap but my father insisted. He said that in times like these, soap was better than money. Now I have a knapsack full of soap."

For a long time, all we heard was the crackling of the gravel of the road under our boots. Suddenly the noise of creaking wagon wheels and the clip-clop of a horse's hooves made us stop and look back. A woman driving a wagon piled with bales of straw was quickly approaching. As she passed us, Seveck greeted her in Polish and asked, "May we know where you're headed?"

"Yadova," she said.

The four of us exchanged looks of hope. Yadova was a town on the way to the border.

"How about giving us a lift?" Seveck asked. "We'll pay you."

The woman slowed the horse down to a crawl and looked around the fields as she considered Seveck's offer. "I'm afraid of the Germans," she finally said. "They'll take the wagon from me for carrying Jews." She slapped the reins on the horse's haunches and started to roll away from us.

We looked at each other in despair. "Wait a moment!" I shouted after the woman and began to run. As I caught up to the wagon, I said to her in Polish, "We have soap."

Abruptly she pulled in the reins and brought the horse to stop. "Quick," she said. "Climb up and tell your friends to hurry."

As we sat sat on bales of straw, being jostled from side to side, Nachme asked me, "What did you tell her?"

"I had to promise her soap." I looked at Nussem. "What do you say?" I asked him. "We'll repay you as soon as we get to Russia."

"My father was right," Nussem said. "Soap is better than money."

After about an hour, the wagon started to slow down.

"Hide!" the woman whispered. "Quick!"

We dropped to the floor of the wagon and covered ourselves with straw. Soon we heard the gallop of another horse.

A German officer in a black uniform, pistol drawn, rode up to the side of the wagon. Shoving the straw aside, he shouted, "Get up!" He looked down at us from his horse, his face bursting with rage. "Out of the wagon! Stand there!" He pointed with his gun across a field.

Against a large brick wall, we saw a mass of Jews being held prisoners by German soldiers.

We jumped off the wagon and put our hands up in the air.

"And you!" the German shouted at the Polish woman, "Leave! Go on! Move!"

As we crossed the field, I noticed that the German officer who had caught us had quickly turned his horse around and had ridden off. Ahead of us, the young German soldier who was watching our approach had a dazed, sickly look on his face. A few hundred meters down the road the Polish woman had slowed her wagon and stopped. She was reluctant to give up her payment of soap. I raced up to the German soldier. "She's pregnant!" I said, pointing at the woman in the wagon. "She needs a doctor! We're taking her to the hospital!" He waved me away with his hand. I took that as a sign that I could go. I began to run. Nachme, Seveck and Nussem followed me. We scrambled back up on the wagon. The woman slapped the reins down on the horse and it took off at a gallop.

We lay on the floor of the wagon, staring at each other, awed by the miracle that had just saved us. None of us understood how my words could have had any effect on the German.

"Did you see how many people they had caught?" Nussem asked, trembling. "There must have been at least five hundred Jews there."

The gray sky had turned to black by the time we arrived in the small town of Yadeva. We couldn't see a moon or stars above us. Nussem opened his knapsack and paid the woman with five bars of soap. Now that he knew its real value, Nussem parted with the soap reluctantly.

We found an inn to spend the night. The owner, a small, fat Polish man, demanded to be paid in advance. Seveck, Nachme and I looked at each other. I had no money at all. Seveck and Nachme had sewn their few zlotys into the shoulder pads of their coats. The three of us turned to Nussem.

"Can you lend us some money?" Nachme asked him. "We'll pay you back as soon as we get to my uncle's house."

Nussem had little choice. He needed us as much as we needed him. He excused himself for a minute and stepped into a corner of the inn to get the money out of its hiding place. When he returned, he paid eight zlotys to the innkeeper.

We ate a good supper, for which we again thanked Nussem, and afterwards, the innkeeper showed us to a room behind the kitchen, with two beds. Exhausted from the day's traveling, we fell asleep at once.

The following morning as we prepared to get back on the road, Nussem told us to go on without him. "I think I'll stay here a while longer," he said as we stood outside the inn ready for the march. "I may have relatives here."

I guessed that he was afraid we would use up all of his money and soap. Nachme gave him Uncle Moishe's address in Baranovitch. "When you get to Russia, come and see us," Nachme told Nussem. "I promise that you'll get back every grosch we owe you."

We wished Nussem luck and began to look for the road that would lead us to Russia. The border was still far away and we had a long walk ahead of us. Before we were out of Yadeva, however, a Jewish man in his early twenties, dressed like a businessman, ran up to me and shouted, "You're here too? What luck! A miracle!" He embraced me as if I had been a long lost relative. I had never laid eyes on him before in my life, but before I could say anything, he invited me and my companions to have breakfast with him. We were too hungry to say no. As we walked to the young businessman's hotel, he began to pour out questions about his family. How was this one, he asked, and how was that one? I didn't know what to answer. I shook my head this way and that way, sometimes yes, sometimes no. This somehow satisfied him.

My new friend brought us to the restaurant at his hotel. We sat down at a table covered with a white lace table cloth and a waiter took our order at once. Another waiter suddenly appeared and called out, "Telephone call for Herr Chaim Blatt!"

The young man at our table jumped up. "Excuse me for just a minute," he said and left.

Nachme, Seveck and I looked at each other as if we were all caught in the same crazy dream.

"Who is he?" Nachme asked me.

"I know him," I said, "like I know the President of America."

"Let's hope the food gets here before he comes back," Seveck said. "He'll makes us pay for our breakfast yet."

"Do you know how much this must cost?" Nachme said.

But Chaim Blatt returned almost immediately. "By the way," he said to me as he sat down again, "I recommend this hotel to you. The rooms are large, the service is first class, and business here in Yadeva is not bad."

"We're not spending another day with the Germans," I said. "We're on our way to Russia."

"Russia?" Chaim exclaimed. "What are you saying?"

We told Chaim what was happening in Warsaw. Our account shook him up. "I had no idea things were so bad. Are you all on your way to Russia?" he asked.

We assured him that we were. Chaim considered our words. "I'm going with you!" he said slapping the table with his open hand.

When the waiter brought our food, Chaim ordered drinks for a toast. We wiped our plates clean and drank down a tumbler of vodka for our safe deliverance from the German devils.

"Come up to my room," Chaim said after he had paid for our meal. "Help me pack."

In his room, Chaim closed the door. "I have a little money with me," he said, "and I'm afraid that if the Germans find it, they're going to take it away. If each of us carries a little of it, I think it'll be easier to get it across the border. Can I count on you?"

"Of course," I said.

Without any further ceremonies, the young man pulled a suitcase out from under the bed, opened a false compartment on the bottom and showed us bundles and bundles of zlotys. Each one of us took at least a thousand zlotys. We hid the money in the linings of our jackets. Chaim packed the rest of belongings and we went back down to the lobby. We waited while Chaim went up to the front desk and settled his bill.

"How are we getting there?" Chaim asked when we were out in the street.

"We're walking," Seveck said.

"I have a better way," said Chaim. "We'll hire a horse and wagon. I know someone we can trust. Wait for me here outside the hotel." Chaim left his suitcase with us and ran off.

"I'm sorry that Nussem didn't stick around," I said. I wished we could repay the young man for his kindness.

Chaim soon returned riding on a wagon next to a broad shouldered, middle-aged, Polish peasant.

"Peter wants ten zlotys for each of us," Chaim said to me. "I think it's too much, but he won't take any less. What do you think?"

"This is no time to bargain," I said. "We have to move as long as we're able. The only trouble is that we have to borrow our share from you. We can pay you back as soon as we get to Baranovitch."

"Get on," Chaim said. "Peter's also restless to get going."

We loaded up Chaim's suitcase and climbed on the wagon. Chaim slapped Peter on the back, winked, and pointed him to the road ahead.

We rolled quickly out of Yadeva. Like the day before, the sky was full of dark clouds. Our luck, however, seemed to be holding up and it still hadn't rained. A few kilometers out of town we were stopped by a small group of Jews.

"Help us!" one of the men shouted. "Show compassion!"

Chaim asked Peter to stop.

"We've been walking four days," another man said. "The men can take it, but my wife, Leah, keeps fainting. We've nothing with us to revive her. I'm afraid she could die. Have God in your heart," he pleaded, "help us. We'll pay whatever we can. But your reward from God will much greater for this good deed. God will spare you from the hands of the Germans."

Chaim turned to Peter and and asked him if he could take these people with us.

"It'll slow us down," the wagon driver said. "But if you don't care, why should I?"

Nachme, Seveck and I immediately helped the woman and the five men up on the wagon. They couldn't stop thanking us.

We rode the whole day, stopping only to relieve ourselves. Towards evening, I noticed Chaim fall into a serious discussion with the wagon driver.

"Listen," said Chaim to us, turning around from his seat next to the driver. "My good friend here tells me that if we try to cross the border at the official point the Germans will send us all to slave labor camps. He can take us to a small forest near the Soviet border. The crossing area is covered with barbed wire but it's deserted except for two old German farts. He says that if we can get past the two Fritzes, we'll find the Soviets on the other side of the forest. According to Peter it's our best chance."

We quickly agreed that the little forest was the way to go.

"To the forest," Chaim told the driver.

"Look, we're nine men," Seveck said. "If the German bastards try to keep us back, we can tie them up."

"We can kill them," said one of the Jews we had picked up along the way. He was a man in his forties with a face so drawn and marked by grief that I knew just by looking at him that he had lost his closest family to the German murderers.

As darkness was setting in, the wagon stopped at the edge of a wood. The driver whispered something to Chaim, who then turned to us and said quietly, "This is it. He can't go any farther."

We jumped off the wagon. The driver pointed out the direction we should take into the forest. Then he crossed himself, turned his horse around, and left.

At the edge of the forest, darkness thickened around us like a black fog. We had to act quickly because soon we wouldn't be able to see a thing.

"We need a plan of action," Seveck said, taking charge. "Let's send two men up first. The rest of us will follow from behind. If the Germans give the two men any trouble the rest of us attack."

"Who will go first?" Chaim asked.

"Let's make a lottery," one of the men we had picked up on the road said.

Chaim pulled a small notebook from the breast pocket of his coat. He quickly scribbled numbers from one to nine on a blank page. Then he tore the paper into nine small pieces, folded them, and said, "Whoever gets the numbers three and seven will go first."

He shook the small pieces of paper in his cupped hands and each of us drew a number.

I unfolded my slip and saw the number four. I could tell from the sudden shock on Nachme's face that he had drawn a bad number. "Seven," he said in a whisper to the group.

"Three," said one of the five Jews we had picked up.

The woman immediately let out a wail. "Oh, my God! Moishe, I don't want to lose you!"

"Don't worry, Leah," the man told his wife. "If there's any trouble there are seven men to back us up. Stop crying."

We begged her to quiet down or we would all be lost.

Nachme and Moishe entered the forest first. The rest of us waited a minute and followed. We moved as quietly as we could but the twigs kept crackling under our feet. Ten minutes later, unexpectedly, we saw the barbed wire.

"Halt!" we heard a scream in German.

The Hasid's Dance

NACHME AND MOISHE, naked to the waist, appeared holding their shirts and coats over their heads. Behind them, two Germans soldiers were pointing long rifles with bayonets at their backs. The soldiers, one tall, the other short, looked like a strange father and son pair, except that both were heavyset middle-aged men. Their heads were covered by large green helmets not unlike overturned night pots.

"Who showed you this way!" the short German barked. "Who brought you here!"

"No one showed us the way," a Jew from our group who spoke German answered. "We're lost. We've been walking for days."

As the tall German approached us and looked at our luggage, the short one continued the interrogation, "Where do you want to go?"

Our interpreter looked at us. We agreed quickly that he should tell the truth. "We want to get to Russia," he said to the Germans.

"Russia!" the short German screamed. "If you don't tell me who brought you here, I'm going to shoot you like dogs!"

"We've been following our eyes," our interpreter said.

When the short German saw that he wasn't getting anywhere with us, he yelled, "Everybody, hand over your money!"

We reached into our empty pockets and turned them out. Anyone who had a zltoty certainly didn't keep it in his pockets.

"What have you got in your suitcases?" screamed the taller German.

There were only four suitcases among the ten of us. Chaim opened his, and three of the other Jews opened theirs. The rest of us spilled out the measly contents of our cloth sacks.

"Step back!" ordered the tall German. While he stood guard over us with his rifle, the short German fell to his knees and began to scatter the clothes, looking for valuables. In a few minutes he had thrown out every rag that been in the suitcases, without finding a single thing of value. Infuriated, the short German shouted, "Go to the devil! Go to the Russians! We'll find you there soon enough!" And with this, the two Germans disappeared back into the forest.

Leah threw her arms around her husband and wept. We reminded her that we had no time to lose. Nachme and Moishe pulled their shirts and coats back on. The clothes that were strewn on the ground were hastily thrown back into the suitcases and sacks.

As we approached the barbed wire, Nachme and Seveck carefully grabbed hold of it and pulled it apart. One by one, we crept through. From the other side, Chaim and I held the wire apart for Nachme and Seveck. In almost complete darkness, we marched across the forest until we came to a clearing, a strip of no-man's-land. Beyond it we saw the woods again. We looked up. The clouds were blowing away letting the light of the half-moon through. We began a wild run towards the other side.

We heard Russian voices as soon as we reentered the forest. We had escaped the hands of the German murderers. We let out a shout of relief and began hugging each other. Russians soldiers in brown uniforms, rifles up on their shoulders, appeared from every side. We began to embrace them for joy too. Those embraces were the only language we had in common. We didn't understand a word of Russian and the soldiers didn't speak Polish or Yiddish. It took us a while to realize that the soldiers were gesturing and pointing to urge us to move deeper into the forest.

We followed their orders and continued our march. In less than fifteen minutes we were out on a flat field. Ahead of us, shining in the darkness, we saw the lights of a small house. We walked up to it and knocked. An elderly Jewish couple, greeted us at the door. He was a short man with a white beard, wearing a rough Russian overcoat; and she was a woman with a wrinkled face, a babushka on her head, in a flowered peasant dress. Before we had said a word, the old man welcomed us into his house.

"Did you come from the forest?" he asked us. "Did the soldiers send you here? May God bless those soldiers. You don't know what they've done for us. They saved us from death. Look there," the old man said pointing to a sack of potatoes standing against a wall of his small hut. "The soldiers gave us those potatoes to share with newcomers. Stay the night and we'll make some food for you."

"How far is it to Baranovitch," I asked.

"A long way," the old man said. "You'll have to take a train to get there. You can catch it in the next town."

In spite of the old Jew's warm welcome, there wasn't room for ten people in his hut. Besides, I was eager to get to Baranovitch as soon as possible.

"How far is the next town?" I asked.

"About two kilometers," he said.

When the others in our group heard that Nachme, Seveck, Chaim, and I were going to move on, they decided to join us. They were as eager to find relatives as we were. Our host stepped out of his home and showed us the direction to take.

Walking on Russian soil, even late at night, we felt so safe and free we began to sing. We soon reached a small town. Right at the entrance a long table had been set up in the open air at which officials sat to register the new arrivals. The Russians were expecting people like us. They even had a Polish translator. Through him we answered all questions: our names, professions, where we came from and where we were headed. The translator urged us to keep moving deeper into the country since the stream of people from Poland was great.

Nachme, Seveck, Chaim and I decided to go directly to Baranovitch. We bid farewell to our friends who had crossed the border with us, and we walked to the train station. The town was a collection of one-storey houses. Everywhere, people were celebrating. Like one large family, the whole town seemed to be out on the streets dancing and singing and drinking.

The station, a small wooden building with a few benches and a single ticket window, was packed with Jews and Gentiles. As soon as we found out that the train to Baranovitch wouldn't arrive until seven o'clock the next morning, Chaim invited us to a good meal.

We searched out the best restaurant. On Chaim's generosity we stuffed ourselves thoroughly and got drunk. Then we stumbled back out into the street ready to join the celebration.

At dawn, when we returned to the train station, it was still bursting with life. Amidst the confusion, I saw a tall, thin Hasid, with a scraggly black beard. His bony shoulders were covered by a yellowing prayer shawl, and the black leather straps of his phylacteries were wound over his left arm and around his head. He rocked back and forth as he whispered his prayers. When he was done, after he had folded his prayer shawl, rewound his phylacteries, and had safely replaced them into the worn, velvet pouch, the Hasid picked up his head and turned it to the heavens. His Adam's apple bobbed in his outstretched throat as he carried on a conversation with God. Suddenly, he flung his arms out wide, jumped up on one foot, then the other, clapped his hands and threw himself into a joyous dance. People made a circle around him. They sang, clapped their hands, and urged him on. The pious young Hasid danced to exhaustion and collapsed against the crowd. They carried him to a bench, and left him sprawled out, panting.

I was curious to know what made him dance with such passion. I approached the bench where he lay, head thrown back, staring at the ceiling. I waited until he had caught his breath and asked him what had driven him to such ecstasy. The tall young man pulled his head up, stared back at me with a bewildered look, and burst into tears. It dawned on me that he was mad. Whatever reasons he had for dancing, would never make sense to anyone else but him. I was ready to leave, when he said, "I'm from Rodom. When the German murderers took over our city, I ran to escape from Poland. Two weeks I wandered, till I got to the border. There the Germans captured me. There must have been at least fifty other prisoners with me. The Germans shot every one. I saw it with my own eyes. German soldiers shooting bullets into the heads of women and children and old men. Human brains were flying in the air. Why was I spared, I wondered. A few hours after the murder of the fifty people, the Germans packed me into a transport of cattle wagons with other Jewish men to be shipped off to slave labor camps. I considered myself a dead man already. I would have said kaddish for myself if it weren't a sin. On the way, the train stopped somewhere near a wood so we could relieve ourselves. The train wouldn't stop again until Berlin, we were told. Everyone left the wagon. The Germans stood on the wagons with their rifles, revolvers, and machine guns watching us, ready to shoot anyone who made a move to escape. In a few minutes, the train whistle blasted a signal for us to return. I walked slowly. As everyone else was climbing on, I bent down pretending to tie my shoelaces. Suddenly there was another blast of the whistle and the train started to move. I began to run away. The Germans shot at me. I threw myself down into the tall grass and didn't move as if I were shot. They must have thought I was dead. I didn't get up until the train had completely disappeared."

As he started to tell me how he crossed the border into Russia, an announcement was made that the train to Baranovitch had arrived.

"You know something," I told the young Hasid as we rushed off to catch our train, "you didn't dance enough."

Sitting on the train, crowded between civilians and soldiers, I kept thinking about the young Hasid's courage.

Four hours later we arrived in Baranovitch. It was a crowded city, overflowing with newcomers from all Europe. Chaim looked for the best hotel and took a room. We returned the money he had asked us to carry for him across the border. To celebrate our escape, he invited us to eat with him. During the meal I revealed to Chaim that I had never met him before we ran into each other in Yadeva. He was stunned. He had been sure that I was a cousin of his. We drank a toast to our new freedom and after the meal we parted ways.

Nachme, Seveck and I found Moishe Schneidleider's house without trouble and were warmly received by him. Uncle Moishe was a man in his sixties. He looked youthful and strong; his wife, Toube, unfortunately, was bedridden. Even though Uncle Moishe was happy to see Nachme and me, he was greatly disappointed when we told him that we were the only ones from the family who had left Poland. Why had everyone else stayed behind, Uncle Moishe wanted to know. We told him how much we had pleaded with them to leave.

"They think they might be able to get along under the Germans once the situation stabilizes," Nachme said.

"No one can live with those Germans," Uncle Moishe said. "They're butchers."

"Let's hope it won't take long before everybody gets out of Warsaw," I said. "Not just our relatives but all Jews."

That same evening I wrote to Shifra that we had arrived in Baranovitch and had been well received at Uncle Moishe's house. The full meaning of my separation from my wife and children struck me now with all its force—Shifra in Warsaw, our two girls somewhere in transit, and I in Russia. Would we ever see each other again? I blamed myself for our scattered lives and felt a sudden urge to run back to Poland. I knew that if I allowed myself to dwell on these thoughts I would go crazy or do something foolish and get myself killed. I reminded myself that I had left exactly because I wanted to draw Shifra and the others out of Warsaw. Again I pleaded with my wife to join me and urged her to convince Yoinne and Khiel to get out while there was still time. Uncle Moishe added a few words to his brother Ksiel begging him to take the whole family and move to Baranovitch as soon as possible.

Uncle Moishe put Nachme, Seveck, and me up in his house. We realized, however, that because of Aunt Toube's illness we wouldn't be able to stay too long. Baranovitch was so crowded that getting a job there was out of the question. The city government was helping all the new arrivals find work in other parts of the country. Nachme, Seveck, and I went down to city hall and registered for work. We had no idea where we would be sent or what the work would be, but we were ready to accept anything.

Within a few days we were taken to a village in White Russia near a small town called Klitchev. At the village we were given just enough time to put down our belongings in a large hall where bunk beds had been set up, and we were immediately driven by horse drawn wagons to a forest. The three of us looked at each other as we were handed axes. Our job, we found out, was to chop down trees. None of us was happy to have suddenly become a lumberjack, but we were glad to be out of the Germans' hands.

Late in the afternoon of our first day of work an official from the government came along, took back our axes, and made us follow him. Since we didn't speak Russian, we couldn't fathom what was going on. We were taken back to the village, to a large hall, where about one hundred men were already gathered. Since many of them were Jews we were able to find out what was going on. Managers from factories in Klitchev, who had heard of newcomers arriving from Poland, had come looking to hire craftsmen.

When I was asked what my trade was, I said tailor and was hired on the spot. Nachme and Seveck unfortunately had no trade, both had been porters in Poland, and neither one was hired. Our little group was being broken up. We said our goodbyes. Nachme and Seveck returned to chopping trees in the forest, and I was taken to Klitchev.

As soon as I arrived in the town I was taken to the tailoring factory and put to work sewing military uniforms. I wondered where I would sleep. Later that night, after work, my boss asked me to follow him. He took me to a house, just a few blocks away from the factory, where the Blausteins, an elderly Jewish couple, lived with one married daughter, her husband and their two small children, and one unmarried daughter. It was a small house with two rooms. The front room, which belonged to the elderly couple and the unattached daughter, had a small iron bed, a small table with a few chairs, a wide wooden bench, and a *pieckolick*, a baker's over, on top of which the Blausteins had made a bed for themselves where they slept. The back room belonged to Dobche, the married daughter, and her family.

I was given food and while I ate, Dobche's husband laid a thin mattress down over the wooden bench and turned it into a bed for me. After dinner, as the others prepared to go to sleep I wrote two letters. One was to Shifra telling her where I had moved, what I was doing, and again urging her and her family to leave Warsaw at once. The other letter was to Uncle Moishe in Baranovitch to give him my new address and to ask him to let me know at once if he had any news from my wife.

Rivka, the unattached daughter, took a liking to me at once. She was well into her thirties, much older than me, but a very attractive woman. She told me that she worked as a secretary in a government office. She also told me that her sister's husband was the manager of a produce warehouse.

I became quite uncomfortable when it was time to go to sleep. Rivka's iron bed was very close to my wooden bench, and the thought of undressing next to her and sleeping just a few meters apart was a bit alarming. Late at night, long after Rivka's parents had gone to sleep on top of the *pieckolick*, I kept myself awake waiting for Rivka to turn off the light and go to bed. Unfortunately, Rivka kept waiting for me to do the same. For the first week, neither one of us slept very much. This couldn't go on forever, of course, and we soon became more at ease with each other. I was careful, however, not to become too friendly with her. I still had a wife and two children. Rivka, on the other hand, liked my company and schemed to be with me as much as possible. She invited me to the cinema. When I excused myself from that, she invited me to take a walk. Soon, I heard very clear hints in our conversations that she would be willing to become more than friends with me. I reminded her that I was a married man with two children. This not only cooled Rivka's passion, it threw her into a sullen silence which was also not good since I depended on the goodwill of her family for my survival. So I tried to break the silence and lift her spirits with a few good jokes.

After a while, Rivka's married sister, Dobche, started to work on me. At first she tried to find out what I thought of her unattached sister. I told Dobche that I wasn't a free man. Dobche told me that I was now in Russia and my wife was in Poland. Dobche tried to convince me that Shifra and I wouldn't get back together again. I told Dobche that no one could tell what time would bring. Soon, I had

Rivke's mother trying to convince me to marry her daughter. I became concerned that Rivke might simply slip in next to me on my wooden bench some night. I was, after all, only human and I wanted to avoid the temptation. I began to work longer hours at the factory and I also started to look for another place to live.

One Sunday, a few weeks after my arrival in Klitchev, Nachme and Seveck came to visit me. I was appalled at how haggard they looked. I hardly recognized them. The work was impossible, they said, and they had decided to move to a larger city to look for something easier. I asked Nachme to write to me as soon as he had settled down again.

A week later I received a letter from my brother-in-law. Nachme and Seveck were now in the city of Minsk, working at whatever manual labor came their way. It wasn't easy they wrote, but it was the same for most Jews from Poland. I read Nachme's letter and I thought to myself that no matter how hard life was in Russia, it was a thousand times better than life in Poland. Here Jews weren't being herded into mass graves and shot to death.

Six weeks after my arrival in Klitchev I received a telegram from Uncle Moishe. Shifra had arrived in Baranovitch.

The Coal Mines of
Bobrick Danskoi

I WAS ECSTATIC over this news. I was especially glad that I hadn't allowed myself to be seduced by Rivka. On the same day I received the telegram from Uncle Moishe, I asked the foreman at the tailoring factory for permission to travel to Baranovitch to get my wife. My boss, who was a decent man, told me that I could go but cautioned me to return in a day or two. Otherwise, he said, he would have to report me to the authorities and I could be arrested. The penalty for leaving my work without permission, my boss warned me, could be hard labor in Siberia.

The next morning I took the train to Baranovitch. As we were approaching the city of Minsk, military police boarded the car and began to check papers. My boss had failed to tell me that in order to travel to the newly occupied territories, I needed a permit from the military. When the police found out that I had no such permit, they arrested me.

In Minsk I was taken off the train and led to the military station. It was crowded with Jews, most of them recent arrivals from Poland. They had originally been sent deep into Russia, but many soon found they couldn't bear the cold weather and hard labor, and were now trying to get back to the Polish occupied territories. When I came up to the officers's desk I was told that if I wanted to travel to Baranovitch, I would have to go back to Klitchev to get a permit from the military there.

As I left the station, a Jewish man followed me. He had overheard my conversation with the officers, and he told me not to bother going back to Klitchev. Because of overcrowding in the Polish territories, no permits were being issued anywhere. I thanked him for this information.

I was at a loss for a direction to take. Fortunately, I had Nachme's address in Minsk with me, and I decided to visit him.

My brother-in-law was surprised and happy to see me. When I told him that Shifra had arrived in Baranovitch, Nachme immediately helped me to send a telegram to her at Uncle Moishe's house. I told her that I was in Minsk, staying with Nachme, and since I couldn't get a permit to travel to Baranovitch, she should come to Minsk as soon as possible.

I decided to wait for Shifra in spite of my boss's warning not to stay away too long. Nothing mattered to me more than seeing Shifra again, and I was afraid that if I returned to Klitchev I wouldn't be allowed to leave again.

Nachme put me up in his room. A week after I had sent my telegram, I received a letter from my wife. She couldn't travel to Minsk, she wrote, without a permit from the military and they refused to giver her one. At once I wrote back and told Shifra not to worry; I would try to find a way to get to Baranovitch.

I went back to the military station and pleaded with the officers to allow me to visit my wife. Again, I was told that I would have to return to wherever I came from and get a permit there. From the other Jews who gathered every day at the station, however, I found out that there was a rumor that any day, they might be given permission to travel.

I began to haunt the military station morning and night. One morning, a few days later, when I got there, the station was empty. The Jews had all disappeared. I ran to the officers and asked them what had happened. They told me that only three hours earlier, the Jews had been given permission to leave.

I ran to the Minsk Station. Although everyone was already on the train, it hadn't taken off yet. I jumped on. Within a few hours I had arrived in Baranovitch.

The joy that Shifra and I felt seeing each other again was overwhelming. We couldn't stop kissing and crying. When we had calmed down somewhat I was happy to see that Uncle Ksiel and his wife, Lotte, were also in Uncle Moishe's house, and so was Khiel.

"Where's Yoinne?" I asked.

"He didn't want to come," Shifra said. "He was afraid he wouldn't be able to cross the border with the children."

"What about our babies?" I asked. "Did they tell you at the Shelter where they took them?"

"The Shelter couldn't get the children out of Poland," Shifra said close to tears. "I had to take Zlatele and Liebele back."

"Where are they now?" I asked.

"With Yoinne, in Uncle Ksiel's apartment."

"Why did you leave the babies?"

"Everyone told me not to take them," Shifra cried. "They said the way to Russia was dangerous," she sobbed, "and I'd get myself and the children killed. Mother and Frau Liebe are taking care of them. As soon as the war lets up, Yoinne says he'll cross the border and bring the rest of the family here."

"I'm going back to Warsaw," I said. "I'm getting the children out of there now!"

"Schloime, don't even think of it!" Uncle Ksiel said.

"It's suicide," said Khiel.

"We were almost killed," added Lotte.

"The Germans, may they burn in Hell," said Uncle Ksiel, "caught us at the border and held us for three days. We bought our lives with all our valuables. But in truth, it was only a miracle that saved us, nothing else. I was sure the Germans were going to shoot us."

"Schloime," Lotte said, with pain in her voice, "we had to leave our children with Yoinne also."

"If I can find a way to get my children out of there," Uncle Ksiel said, "I promise you, I'll get yours and Yoinne's out as well."

Shifra and I stayed with Uncle Moishe as long as possible. After a few weeks, however, our money ran out. I knew that I had to find work at once. In Baranowitch that was impossible. The city continued to be flooded with refugees from Poland. As for Klitchev, I had been gone for so long now, I was certain I'd be arrested if I returned there. I was equally afraid to go back to the authorities in Baranovitch and register again. If they discovered that I had already registered once and had left my job, they could suspect me of being a spy and send me straight to Siberia.

Uncle Moishe's acquaintances advised me to go to Bialistock. There, they told me, people were being signed up for work in other parts of the country.

Shifra and I arrived in Bialistock in January of 1940. The area was already deep in winter and everything was frozen. We saw immediately that Bialistock, like Baranovitch, was overflowing with refugees and there would be no jobs here either. In fact, the only work for which people were being signed up was coal mining in the city of Tulla. We didn't think we would survive such hard labor.

We spent our first day in Bialistock, half frozen, roaming the streets. As night fell, we still didn't have a place to sleep. We kept wandering from one unfamiliar street to another, until, close to midnight, we came across a large synagogue. The lights were still on inside. Here, at last, I thought, we would get help. We walked in at once. When I saw what was going on in that synagogue, I knew it was useless. The large hall was so packed with people, there wasn't room for a pin. Along all four walls, from floor to ceiling, wide wooden shelves had been built as bunks. These were occupied by old people and women with children. Everyone else was lying on the floor, one up against the other.

Shifra and I looked at each other. We simply couldn't continue to roam the freezing streets for the rest of the night. We forced our way in and over much grumbling from those around us, we squeezed out a spot on the floor. We may have gotten out of the cold but we couldn't sleep. Children cried, the sick moaned, and the healthy argued all night over a bit of space.

By morning, Shifra and I knew that we had no choice. We would have to register for the coal mines. If we didn't turn out to be such good coal miners, no one would prosecute us. I was still sure that as soon as we got out of the crowded Polish occupied territories we would have no trouble settling down.

At the military station where we went to register for the coal mines, we were told that the next transport would not leave for four days. If we signed up, however, we would get an advance and we would be given a place to sleep. Shifra and I registered. We were given money and papers authorizing us to buy provisions at government prices. We were also taken immediately to a house where other families were waiting for the transport to the coal mines.

Shifra and I were no longer hungry or cold, and we had a place to sleep. At the house we befriended two other couples who also came from Warsaw. The husband of the younger couple, also named Schloime, was a barber; his wife, Tavel, had no trade. The husband of the older couple, Chaim, a man in his forties, had been a fruit peddler; his wife, Sureh, was a dressmaker; and they had a twelve-year-old son with them. We became such good friends that when it was time to leave Bialistock we decided to stay together.

The train ride to the coal mines was long, but we were comfortable. The Soviet authorities provided all the food and medical help we needed. Since we had nothing else to do, we talked. Schloime poured his heart out to me.

"You see this young girl?" he said, pointing to his wife, Tavel. "We have known each other since childhood. We went to the same school in Warsaw. I've wanted to marry her since I turned eighteen, but my parents wouldn't allow it because her parents ran a night club which had rooms in the back.

"'Why blame Tavel?' I asked my parents. 'Like father, like son; like mother, like daughter,' my father answered.

"There was no way I could change my parents' mind. When the war started, Tavel and I got married and ran away."

So this was the good this miserable war had produced, I thought to myself.

"Chaim and Sureh have an even more interesting story," Schloime said to me. "They've been lovers for a long time. She was married to another man for thirteen years, a bastard who gave her nothing but grief. Well, actually, the first few years she had with him weren't all that bad. That's when her son was born. But then her husband changed; or maybe he just stopped hiding what he really was. He would disappear for months at a time. She had to keep up the house by herself. When he was around, he wouldn't work; he drank; he slept with other women. She asked him for a divorce. He refused. Why should he give up his easy life? She was ready to kill herself. That's when she met Chaim. He saved her. Chaim was a widower. After his wife's death, he thought he would never marry again. But when he met Sureh and learned what she was living through, his heart went out to her. They became friends and soon they were lovers. No matter how much Sureh begged her husband for a divorce, he wouldn't give it to her. This went on until the war started. Then Sureh told Chaim that she was running away and they ran off together..."

"How do you know all this?" I asked.

"I've known Sureh a long time," Schloime said. "She used to live in the building next to ours and she was my mother's best friend. She would always come to visit and tell my mother all her troubles."

The world is full of stories, I thought to myself. Everyone carries around his own bundle of miseries.

After two days of traveling through vast Russian fields and forests, we arrived at the coal mines. The small town was called Bobrick Danskoi. It was near the city of Gomel and had twenty-nine coal mines.

We were about four hundred newcomers. As soon as we stepped off the train, we were taken to a great hall. Foremen from the twenty-nine mines had assembled there, each waiting to receive his share of new workers. Shifra and I were assigned to mine number twelve and so were our friends, Schloime and Tavel, and Chaim and Sureh.

Our foreman took charge of us and led us to the mine, about two kilometers from Bobrick Danskoi. First, we were given a room. Then our foreman took us to a cafeteria for a good hot meal. We were happy to hear that from now on we would eat all our meals there.

We had arrived on a Thursday, and for the rest of the week we were shown around the mine. Before being assigned specific tasks, we had to go through a medical check-up. It was the doctor's duty to approve the kind of work each person could do. Shifra went into the examination room first. When she came out, she told me that her job would be to distribute lamps to the workers going down into the mine, and then to collect and wash the lamps after the workers came back up.

When I entered the examination room, the doctor, an elderly woman with a shrewd smile, looked me up and down. She shook her head slightly. She didn't seem too keen on sending me down into the mines.

"Do you speak Russian?" she asked me.

"I've learned a little."

"Good," she said. "Take off your shirt."

I obeyed.

She probed along my chest with the cool stethoscope. "Have you ever had trouble with your lungs?" she asked me.

"Yes, but it was a few years ago."

"What kind of work did you do in Poland?"

"I was a tailor."

"We need tailors," said the doctor. "I'm going to recommend that you be allowed to work at your trade."

I was deeply thankful to her.

The following day I reported for work at the nearest tailoring factory, in the neighborhood of mine 13, about two kilometers from where we were living. My wages were low, but the work wasn't bad, and as long as Shifra and I were both working we managed. My greatest problem, I soon discovered was getting to work in the morning and returning home at night. It was bitterly cold and the snow was always piled high. Anytime I went out, I almost froze to death. Still, I couldn't forget that we were out of the Germans' hands and for that we had to be grateful.

As soon as we had settled down, I sent out three letters. One, to Yoinne in Warsaw, another to Uncle Moishe in Baranovitch, and the last to Nachme in Minsk.

The first answer I received was from Warsaw. Yoinne wrote that the Germans had sealed off the Jewish quarter. Day and night the area was surrounded by German soldiers and it was impossible to get in or out of it. The children were hungry all the time. Food was hard to find and Yoinne begged us to send whatever we could.

Shifra and I went immediately to the supply store in Bobrick Danskoi. We bought as much as we could afford of canned goods, dry noodles, salami and immediately shipped the package to Yoinne.

From Minsk and Baranovitch, I received no answer. After a few weeks, another letter came from Yoinne. He thanked us for the food. The conditions in the Jewish quarter, he wrote, were getting worse every day; finding something to eat was impossible. Poles smuggled food in every now and then, but the prices they charged were so high, no one could afford to buy anything from them. The Poles claimed they had to pay off the guards and that's what drove the prices up so much. Above all, Yoinne wrote, he was trying to take care of the children, but he needed our help and he begged us to send another package.

Again Shifra and I bought whatever products we could afford and sent it to Yoinne. In our letter to him we begged him to continue to look after our Liebele and Zlatele. We kept sending a fresh package every few weeks but months passed without an answer.

As long as we had been getting the letters from Warsaw, Shifra and I still hoped to get our daughters back. But when Yoinne stopped writing, we began to despair. The longer we went without a letter from Yoinne the more frantic we felt. Soon, we couldn't close our eyes at night. We kept on trying to figure out ways to find out what had happened to our children.

One of the new friends we had made at the mines was Avrum Peszak. He was around my age, twenty-eight, and had wiry red hair and a pale complexion. He liked to talk and came to see us often. He was originally from Lodz, in Poland. His parents, however, were now in Warsaw and he was in correspondence with them. I wrote down Yoinne's name and address and begged Avrum to ask his parents to find out what had happened to my brother-in-law and my children.

Avrum soon had an answer. His parents couldn't find anyone named Schneidleider at the address I had given. Most likely, they wrote, Yoinne had been forced by the Germans to move out of his apartment. Avrum's parents promised to continue looking and to let us know as soon as they found something out.

Unfortunately this was the last letter we ever received from Avrum's parents. Our worries and fears continued to grow. The people in the tailoring factory wanted to know why I walked around with such a sad face. I told them what was eating at me. A woman suggested I write to Moscow, to the Department of Foreign Affairs. Minister Molotov, she said, might be able to help me.

That same night I told Shifra of the woman's suggestion. I didn't think that a Minister of the Soviet government would bother with our problem, but Shifra urged me to try. I sat down and wrote a letter to Moscow. I wrote to Minister Molotov that my wife was working in a coal mine and I, in a tailoring factory. I explained that we had been forced to escape from Poland but that our two little daughters had been left behind with my wife's brother. I included Yoinne's name and address in the letter, and the name of my two daughters, and I pleaded with the Minister of Foreign Affairs to help us find our children.

A few weeks later I got an answer from the Soviet Authorities. They were trying to reach an agreement with the German Government to reunite families separated by the war. As soon as arrangements were completed, we would be informed where we could go to reclaim our children.

The answer from Moscow reawakened our hopes and calmed us down somewhat. After a few weeks had passed without a letter from the Soviet Government, I wrote to Moscow to ask whether an agreement had been reached yet with the Germans. The answer that came back asked us to be patient. Arrangements were soon to be completed and we would be notified.

Shifra and I continued to live and work drawing our hope from those two letters from Moscow.

We didn't receive another letter from anyone until the summer of 1940. One evening, when I came home from work, Shifra handed me an envelope. I saw at once that it wasn't from Moscow. My first thought was that Nachme or Uncle Moishe had finally answered. This letter, however, came from the city of Gomel. I tore open the envelope and couldn't believe what I saw. The first words were, "Dear Brother." The letter was from my sister. Ruchele had run into Nachme in Gomel and he had given her my address. Nachme was returning to Baranovitch to be near his brother Khiel and Uncles Moishe and Ksiel. Much had changed in Ruchele's life. She and Zygmunt had divorced soon after their arrival in Russia. Zygmunt had remarried almost immediately after the divorce and had taken their little daughter. Ruchele had also remarried. Her husband's name was Sucher Papier.

I answered my sister's letter at once and we began a steady correspondence. In July of 1940, I received a letter from Ruchele in which she wrote that she had given birth to a boy, Valerie.

In the fall of the same year, on November 17, Shifra gave birth to twins, Moishele and Ninale. My wife couldn't return to work and my wages alone weren't enough to support us. To feed my family, I was forced to start working at home in the evenings. I took on tailoring work from our neighbors. The extra money I earned made our life a little easier. But there was one problem. Communist law required that anyone working for himself pay a tax. This tax was so heavy, it wasn't worthwhile to work for oneself. I couldn't afford to pay the tax and I certainly couldn't stop working for myself, so that I no choice but to work without a permit. I was aware of the danger I faced for breaking the law and I lived in constant fear of being found out. Every evening, before I sat down to work, I locked the door and drew the curtains across the windows.

One night, as I was working, someone knocked on our door. We didn't answer.

"Open up!" A man shouted. "This is the police! Open up at once!"

We ran around the room trying to hide all traces of my work. When we opened the door, we pretended to have been asleep. As soon as I saw the policeman, however, I knew that I was in deep trouble. He must have recognized the fear on my face.

"Don't be afraid," the policeman said. "I came to tell you to be careful. We've been informed that you're working for yourself at night without paying taxes. You're obviously not doing this to get rich. We know that your wife can't work because of your newborn twins. We don't want to harm you. If someone hadn't informed on you, I would have never come here."

"Who informed on me?" I asked.

"That I can't tell you," the policeman said. "What I came to tell you is, be more careful."

I thanked him. In spite of the policeman's warning, however, I continued to break the law.

Near the end of the 1940, I received another letter from my sister. Her son, my sister wrote, was sick, and the doctor had told her that the air in Gomel was bad for the child. Ruchele was preparing to relocate to the Caucasus region, to the city of Naltchick.

In her next letter, Ruchele wrote that she was already in Naltchick. Sucher had found work there, and they were comfortably settled in. Her son was feeling better from the change of air. In the same letter, Ruchele asked me if I had our father's address.

Although I still carried the photograph of our father which Ruchele had brought from Lublin, I had long ago lost his address. Searching my memory, however, I seemed to remember: 25 Actiaveska Street, Fergana. I sent this address to Ruchele and told her I wasn't sure it was right. My sister and I both wrote letters to our father, but neither of us got an answer, and I began to doubt whether I had remembered his address correctly.

The winter of 1940 ended. I continued working at home, earning the few extra rubles we needed to survive. One morning, in the spring of 1941, we received a short letter from the authorities. I was being called to the Tax Office to answer some questions.

The Cursed Sands of Makhatschkala

I WAS TERRIFIED AS I WALKED to the government building in Bobrick Danskoi.

At the Tax Department I sat down on a bench in the hallway and waited. Soon a middle-aged man appeared with a folder in his hands. He called my name and led me into a small, bare room.

"Sit, sit," the official said with a casual wave towards the only chair across his narrow desk. "Why are you trembling?" he asked, as he sat down himself. "Don't be afraid, we don't eat people here. We know that you've been working at home. Yes, yes, we know everything. Look, you want to go on working? With our blessings! Just one thing, you have to pay taxes. You worked all winter without paying. We'll overlook that. But you can't go on breaking the law. Is that clear?"

I nodded nervously.

"You realize that we could send you to Siberia for what you've done?"

I nodded again.

"All right, then it's settled." The official closed my folder. "If you weren't an immigrant, we would have punished you long ago."

"Excuse me," I said gathering my courage now that I knew that I wasn't being arrested, "but how am I supposed to feed my family? I don't earn enough from my job."

"We have a solution for that. Let your wife go back to work," the official suggested. "Then you'll have more than enough."

"But we have two babies," I said. "How can she go back to work?"

"We have a solution for that, too." The official smiled, obviously pleased that he had all the answers to my problems. "Use the nursery which the government provides for all workers. Bring your children there in the morning and pick them up at night. The nursery won't cost you a kopeck and your wife can go to work without a worry."

I wasn't all that happy with his solutions. My children were just five months old and I didn't think it would be good for them to be dragged back and forth everyday to the nursery.

Shifra was relieved when I returned from Bobrick Danskoi. She had been sick with worry that I would be arrested. When I told her what the official had said, my wife agreed sadly. "We have no choice," she said. "I'll have to take the children to the nursery. If they catch you working at home again, you'll be arrested for sure."

Shifra returned to work. In the morning we took the babies to the nursery and in the evening we picked them up. For a while, that seemed to solve our problems.

At the tailoring factory where I was employed there were two shifts: the first, from eight in the morning to five in the afternoon, with a lunch break at noon; the second, from five in the afternoon to one in the morning, with a dinner break at nine. Our supervisor's hours, from ten in the morning to eight at night, overlapped both shifts so he could prepare work for everyone. The staff was split into two groups. Since I was newly hired my assignment was to work one-week days and the next week on nights.

I hated the night shift. As soon as the manager left the factory, everyone started to drink. They guzzled liquor as if it were water. Since I never joined in these binges, the workers were afraid I might inform on them. No matter how I tried to reassure them that I just wanted to mind my own business, they didn't trust me. As soon as they got drunk, they started to call me ugly names. My only friend was Tania, a heavy woman in her fifties, who sat near me. She was as much of a drinker as the rest of workers, except that Tania could hold her liquor better than most men.

One night, one of the workers, Ivan, an old drunkard with a menacing face, insisted I take a swig. The other workers had nicknamed him Ivan the Terrible in honor of his miserable temper. No matter how I tried, I couldn't shake him off. I finally saw that if I didn't drink with him, I would be in trouble. Ivan poured a shot of liquor for himself and one for me. I lifted my glass as if to drink and while the old buzzard had his head tilted back, I quickly poured the drink over my shoulder.

"I saw you!" the bastard screamed. "You dirty Jewish dog! Wasting precious Soviet liquor!"

"I have a bad stomach," I said. "The doctors have forbidden me to drink."

He swung at me. I stepped out of his way, and Ivan went flying across the factory. The other workers, who were just as drunk as the old man, laughed.

"*You* ruined Mother Russia!" Ivan shouted, turning back to me. "*You* murdered the Czar and stole our mansions! *You're* responsible for the Revolution!" Suddenly, he grabbed a long pair of shears from the cutting table. "I'll get even with you!" he shouted as he lifted the shears and lunged at me. Tania saw that Ivan was about to kill me and quickly gave him a good shove. She laid the drunk flat on his back.

"Go to sleep, you old goat," Tania said with disgust as she pulled the shears from Ivan's hand.

The old man was so exhausted by then that he simply curled up on the floor and started to snore.

In the morning, I went to see the manager and asked him to take me off the night shift. I told him that I didn't feel well working nights. My health was suffering; I worked more slowly; and I couldn't earn enough.

The manager said he would see what he could do.

At noon, there was a knock on my door. I opened it and there was Ivan the Terrible, sober, holding his hat in his hands and a sad look in his bloodshot eyes.

"I beg your forgiveness," he said looking at the ground. "Please don't tell the manager what happened. I didn't know what I was doing."

"Don't worry," I reassured him. "I'm not going to say anything." As he turned to leave, I said, "By the way, you accused me last night of murdering your Czar. You should know that I was five years old when you had your Revolution."

After that incident I became even friendlier with Tania. I had always been curious why she drank so much and a few nights after she had saved my life, as we were working, I asked her.

"I've been married to the same louse for fifteen years," she began. "He's a tailor. Works over in mine ten. We have four children. Every kopeck he makes he spends on drink. He's nothing but a drunkard. He runs around with other women, disappears whole nights at a time. And if I say anything to him, he beats me like a dog. Look here," she said pulling away the gray hair from her forehead to show me an ugly black and blue stain on her temple.

"I would have run away from him long ago if it weren't for the children...What am I saying? You see? I'm a liar, too. That bastard beats the children the same way he beats me. So why *do* I stay with him? I don't know why. I could have him thrown in jail for the way he treats me. I have a weakness for him, and that bastard knows it and takes advantage of me. Is that a good enough reason to drink?..."

A week after the incident with the old drunk, the manager told me that he had arranged for me to work only the day shift. This solved a big problem for me.

In June of 1941, the Germans invaded Russia. The Russians, however, weren't the Poles and the Germans soon had a good fight on their hands.

I decided to move my family deeper into the country for safety. I didn't want the Germans to capture anymore of my children. I went to the management of the tailoring factory and asked for a permit to travel to the Caucasus region, where my sister had settled.

The answer to my request came in a letter. We weren't in any danger yet, the management advised me. There was no reason to fear for the safety of my family. And if the situation should change, everyone would move out of the area together.

The Germans kept advancing. They took city after city. Soon we heard they were about to overrun Tulla. I went to see the factory managers again. "I've already lost two children to the Germans when they invaded Warsaw," I said. "My wife and I are afraid of losing another two children."

"Where do you want to go?" one of the men who sat on the management committee asked me.

"We want to join my sister. She lives in Naltchik, in the Caucasus region."

"We'll review your case," the committee member said and I was dismissed.

In August, I received another letter from the management committee. I expected them to have turned me down again. This time, however, the letter had a travel permit to the Caucasus attached.

I lost no time. That same day I sent a letter to Ruchele telling her that we were leaving Bobrick Danskoi for Naltchick.

When I said goodbye to my fellow workers at the factory, the old man who had blamed me for the Russian Revolution poured out two shots of whiskey. "Better drink up," he said. "I'm sober now and I'm going to watch carefully what you do with that liquor."

"*L'chaim!*" I said. Ivan and I gulped our drinks down together. Then he shook my hand and wished me good luck.

When we were ready to leave, the manager of the tailoring factory provided a driver with a horse and wagon to take us to the train station. The driver even helped us pack.

This time we didn't have to cross any borders and we didn't have to watch out for the German monsters at every step. Even so the way to Naltchick was not easy. The trains weren't running on schedule and the deeper we traveled into Russia the longer we had to wait from one train to the next. Since there were masses of people running from the Germans, when a train would finally arrive, it was usually overcrowded. Shifra and I had two tiny babies in our arms and couldn't squeeze into the packed cars. Because we were often forced to wait for an emptier train. It took us two weeks to get to Naltchick. By the time we arrived at my sister's house, both of our babies had caught colds and were running high fevers.

We took the children to the hospital. The doctors told us that Moishele and Ninale had developed pneumonia and would have to be hospitalized. After two weeks in the hospital, Moishele died.

An elderly Jewish woman, who lived in the neighborhood, carried my child to the cemetery. I dug the grave with my own hands and buried my son.

Two weeks later, our little daughter recovered and Shifra brought her home. I hoped that we would slowly return to some kind of normal life. My wife, however, was strongly affected by Moishele's death. Out of grief, Shifra became quite ill. She was constantly depressed and couldn't stop crying. Almost anything could provoke her to fits of rage. She threw whatever came into her hands. I couldn't leave the house. I was overwhelmed by my wife's illness. Ruchele and Sucher tried to spent as much time as they could with Shifra and me, to help us get over our loss.

I didn't return to work for a few weeks, not until I saw that Shifra was feeling better. Once I was earning a living again, we began to feel more settled. I was hoping at last to find some of the peace we desperately needed in our lives. The Germans, however, kept advancing into Russia. In the summer of 1942, we heard that they were close to Naltchick.

Again we had to escape deeper into the country. This time the only open way was through Makhatschkala, a city on the Caspian Sea. When we arrived there, thousands of people were already waiting at the shore for a ship to cross the Sea. Families had simply put their luggage down on the sand and were living on the beach. Shifra and I, and Ruchele and Sucher had no choice but to join them. It was a sad existence. For the young it wasn't quite so bad. The old and sick, however, suffered.

And for mothers with small children it was sheer torture. Although the days were warm, the nights were cold, and the small babies got sick. There was no medical help. Mothers wrung their hands in agony as they listened to the helpless cries of the ailing children. Soon babies and old people began to die. One young mother couldn't bear to watch her little son's agony and lost her mind. After her child died, we saw the young woman running naked, gesturing madly along the edge of the sea. Suddenly she jumped into the water. People ran into the sea after her and barely pulled the distraught woman out alive.

By talking to those around me, I found out why no ship came to take us off the cursed sands of Makhatschkala. The shipping authorities were busy with the arrival and departure of warships and the transport of war supplies to the front. We were the lowest priority.

Our greatest fear was that the Germans would overtake the city before we could get across the Caspian. All day and all night, religious Jews gathered at the edge of the water to pray. It seemed to me they were praying for the return of Moses, so he could again part the waves. The prayers didn't help. I thought to myself, either God is deaf or pretends not to hear. At the same time I remembered that God helps those who help themselves.

Finding something to eat was our greatest problem. The citizens of Makhatschkala had special cards which allowed them to buy food from the grocery stores. Those of us living on the beach had no such cards and we had to deal with the black market where everything cost ten time as much. The rich, as usual, got by. I saw a man give a gold ring for a loaf of black bread. Shifra and I, however, had no gold and almost no money. After the first week on the beach, we began to starve. I took whatever clothes we didn't need, sold them, and bought some bread and cheese. I also went to the government building in the center of the city to ask for help. All they gave me were promises.

After a month of waiting, I saw notices posted around the government buildings. The military authorities were directing all men to register at draft centers. Those who didn't register, the notices said, would be court-martialled as deserters. When the women found out that their husbands were being taken away into the army, there was such loud wailing on the beach that it drowned out the waves of the Sea. The mothers with tiny children were the most pitiful. Some of these desperate women tore at their hair and clothing. Their frightened children began to scream. It looked as if everyone on the beach had been caught in a blaze of fire. The shipping authorities tried to relieve the chaos. Through microphones, they announced, "We beg you to calm down! We promise to get ships to you as soon as possible!"

Sucher and I went to register. At the draft board, all our documents were taken from us. Then we listened in stunned silence as we were given two hours to say goodbye to our families.

Shifra was pregnant and I didn't want to leave her alone with a two year old child. I decided to desert. Shifra and Ruchele, however, were firmly against my plan.

"If you desert," Shifra said, "you'll get caught sooner or later and that will be the end of you."

"And if you do go to the military," Ruchele said, "they probably won't send you to the front. I'll help Shifra as much as I can."

Ruchele's promise calmed me down.

My sister had a friend who lived in the Ural region, Kaile Masler. Before we separated each of us copied this friend's address. We agreed that wherever we ended up we would write to Kaile.

At last, in tears, we said our goodbyes.

A few hours later, while Sucher and I stood at the Makhatschkala Station waiting with hundreds of other men for the Army train, we heard the sudden roar of airplanes above us and the explosion of bombs. A cry went up. The Germans were attacking. Without giving a second thought to the consequences, Sucher and I bolted out of the station. As people were fleeing wildly through the streets, my brother-in-law and I ran back to the shores of the Caspian Sea to be with our wives and children. When we got there, the beach was empty. The last of the women and children were boarding two ships. Even though we couldn't see Shifra or Ruchele, we were certain that they had gotten on board. Sucher and I quickly returned to the train station.

In the evening our train, packed with recruits, finally pulled out of Makhatschkala. As we passed near the Caspian Sea, I saw two ships leaving the port. I pointed them out to Sucher. We felt relieved. Our wives and children would be safe on the other side of the water.

Late at night, on the train, we could hear the distant sound of gunfire. I wondered whether I wasn't slipping back into the bloody hands of the Germans. I felt so exhausted from the events of the past few weeks, from the sleepless nights on the beach, from the shock of being separated so suddenly from my wife and daughter that the moment I closed my eyes I fell asleep and had an amazing dream.

I was in the Polish Army. A Polish officer had trained me to operate a tank. While I sat in the mess hall eating dinner with my company, I heard an alarm. The officer suddenly banged open the door and rushed in screaming that the Germans had attacked. He ordered all soldiers to prepare at once for war.

"You," the officer said pointing to me, "follow me."

We ran out of the mess hall and boarded a tank.

Inside the tank, the officer said, "We've received orders for a surprise attack on the Germans. You and ten other men will hide in your tanks in the woods. When I give the order, you'll charge. We're going to chase these German bastards out of our country."

At night, we got into our tanks. Our commanding officer jumped on his horse and we followed him. Deep in the woods, the officer showed each man where to hide his tank.

"Wait for my signal," the officer reminded us.

We saluted from our tanks.

Full of suspense, I waited an hour. Suddenly the officer reappeared. "Charge!" he cried from his horse.

As our tanks rolled out from their hiding places, we heard the roar of the German airplanes and violent explosions tore the earth out in front of us. Behind us, Polish soldiers on horses rode up to join the fight. Our assault on the enemy was relentless. After firing the whole night, we finally surrounded a German battalion. The defeated Germans surrendered their ammunition to us. We continued to roll against the German forces. Battalion after battalion of the enemy fell to our ferocious strikes. Within a week, we had captured Berlin. I wept for joy when I saw Hitler hanging from his neck in the center of the city, his black tongue hanging grotesquely out of his mouth.

A jolt suddenly woke me up. It was the middle of the night. The brakes had been thrown and the wheels of the train were grinding against the rails with a deafening screech. I felt my face, it was covered with tears.

We stopped at a small station. The officer in charge of us, a tall, rugged man with a face of granite, ordered our unit off the train. About two hundred men got off. In the darkness of the deserted station we lined up and began to march. No one told us where we were going. We marched for three hours, until we came to a field. Here, our officer told us, we could rest. As we collapsed on the soft grass, a fine rain began to fall. Slowly, while we slept, it soaked us through and through.

The rain finally let-up at dawn. The sun came out. We had just begun to dry off when our commander appeared before us. He marched us into nearby woods and ordered us to build shelters for the night. At once we started to gather large tree branches. Two wagons, driven by Russian soldiers came rolling into our camp as we worked. They set up a kitchen. At night we lined up to be served our only meal of the day, soup and bread.

We spent the night in our newly built shelters. We had to sleep on the ground and even though the tree branches offered some protection, we were more awake than asleep. In the dark, I heard, someone complain to our commander.

"Our hotel is not exactly first class," our commander agreed in a sarcastic tone of voice. "Tomorrow we'll put some straw down and you won't have a thing to complain about."

At dawn we lined up for roll call. After the commanding officer had made sure that no one deserted during the night, each of us received a piece of bread the size of a man's fist and a cup of tea. We were give five minutes to eat our breakfast. Then we were handed picks and shovels, and we marched half a kilometer to an area of hills and rocks where we were ordered to dig trenches.

I plunged my shovel into the earth and immediately heard a clang as it hit rock; the pick was of no use either. I threw my tools down and began to pull the boulders out of the earth with my bare hands. After I had cleared my area, I began to dig again.

It was a hot day. By noon, all the men were unbearably thirsty. Our mouths and throats were dry and dusty. We asked the commander for water.

"It's coming," he said. "This area has no water and we have to bring it here."

An hour later, amidst the noise of our shovels and picks hitting the stony earth, we heard the wheels of an approaching wagon. We stopped working. A soldier on a horse drawn wagon was carting a large wooden barrel of water. We dropped our tools and rushed forward like crazed men. The barrel on the wagon was resting on a wooden platform. Five of our strongest men lifted the platform with the water off the wagon and set it down on the ground. Tin cups hung from chains around the barrel. One after the other we took turns dipping the cup into the water and gulping it down. I had never tasted such foul water. It was warm, yellow, and smelly. My thirst was so powerful, however, that after I had finished drinking one cup, I immediately had a second. I would have drunk a third if the man next to me hadn't pulled the tin cup from my hand. We didn't stop drinking until the last drop was gone. Then we went back to work.

Soon two more soldiers arrived in a wagon and began to prepare food. An hour later, at about one o'clock in the afternoon, we were each given a bowl of soup. That was our midday meal. After a short rest we went back to work. We worked until dark. For dinner, we were given a baked potato and a cup of hot tea. We returned to our shelters and went to sleep.

A few days later, men began to fall ill. I was one of them. In the heat of the midday sun, I was in a cold sweat. My teeth chattered so violently I expected them to break. After three hours, when the shivering let up, I began to burn up with fever. I had attacks of diarrhea. I became so weak, I could barely stand on my feet. In my dazed condition, I heard men around me speak of malaria.

There were about thirty sick recruits. Our commander ran to the closest town to fetch a doctor. A few hours later he returned alone. All doctors had been called to the front. The hospital authorities had promised to send us someone within a few days. In the meantime, our commander had been given medicine. I took the pills which he handed out, as did the other sick men, but none of us got better. I lost all appetite. The piece of bread which I received every morning, I gave to my brother-in-law.

After waiting for a doctor two days, a young man who had been lying next to me died. I wasn't sure I would survive either.

Four days after he had been promised to us, the doctor finally arrived. By then another three men had died. The doctor examined us and immediately ordered that we be moved to a hospital.

We were loaded into wagons and taken to Darbend. An emergency facility had been set up there because the main hospital in Kiev had to be evacuated when that city was overtaken by the Germans.

We waited in the wagons while our commander went in to arrange our admission. A half hour later he strode angrily out of the hospital.

We're turning back." our commander said. "They can't take us. There's no room."

From Baku to Fergana

BEFORE THE WAGON STARTED TO ROLL BACK TO CAMP, I stood up and jumped off. My legs were so weak that I fell to the ground in a heap.

"I refuse to leave!" I shouted feebly as I stumbled to my feet. "I'm not going to die in the field! Do what you want with me! I don't care!" I ran towards the hospital and collapsed against the building. I began to hallucinate. I saw the funeral of the man who had died next to me in the forest. He had been no more than 20 years old. Two soldiers had wrapped the dead man in rags, laid him in a grave, and covered him with earth. There was no ceremony, no prayer, not even a marker was put up. After a few days no one would even know where he had been buried.

"Who's yelling?" came a voice from the window above me.

Moments later, a doctor, a lanky man with unruly white hair, in a long white smock, a stethoscope dangling from his neck, came rushing out into the yard. "What's going on?" he asked. "What's that man doing on the ground?"

Our commander jumped down from his wagon. "My men are dying," he said, "and your hospital won't accept them."

"*I* will accept them!" said the outraged doctor. "Get them inside at once! Let's go! And I want to know who turned you away."

I was taken into a room with a large tub. An elderly woman, an assistant nurse, washed me clean. Then I was put into a bed in the hall of the hospital. Just lying on a fresh linen again gave me hope.

That same evening a nurse came and gave me an injection. It put me to sleep at once. In the morning, when I woke up, I was no longer in the hall but in a large room with other patients. I overheard nurses talking: another three men from my company had died. For the second night, I was given another injection and again I slept soundly. In the morning, I felt much better. On the third night, however, after I received my third injection, I suddenly had such a severe attack of convulsions I almost fell out of bed. The nurse came running and tried to help me. I was too sick, however, and she was forced to call the head nurse who called a doctor.

A woman in her fifties arrived. She was dressed in a white gown. She examined me carefully and when she was done, she looked at me with deep sympathy in her eyes like a mother looking at a dying child. The doctor gave me an injection, ordered the nurses to put two hot water bottles at my feet, and the doctor herself wrapped me in two more blankets.

"Don't worry, my child," the doctor said to me as she stroked my face. "If you survived the first two injections then the third one will definitely make you well. Rest. You'll soon fall asleep and wake up in good health."

As the doctor caressed my face and soothed me with kind words, my shivering finally stopped. I took the doctor's hand in both of mine, squeezed it with the little strength I still had left, and I fell asleep.

In a dream I saw Babbe Zlate standing at my bed. She leaned over me and put something sweet into my mouth. "Swallow this," she said softly, "it will help you." Babbe Zlate placed something under my pillow and then without saying another word, she faded away.

The next morning, I woke up and felt as if I had never been sick. I didn't believe in miracles, but I couldn't explain this in any other way.

I spent another week at the hospital regaining some of the weight I had lost. Then I was taken before a committee of doctors. They examined me and I was given a letter to take back to my commander. Even though I was being sent back to my unit, the doctors had given me a two-week furlough so I could continue to recuperate. I thanked the doctors for these weeks of freedom.

Before I left the hospital, I went to ask the head nurse where I could find the doctor who had cared for me like a mother.

"She's not in the hospital today," the head nurse said. "She's in Baku."

"When she comes back," I said to the head nurse, "please thank her for me."

Other men from my group were discharged from the hospital that same day and all of us were taken back to our unit in a wagon.

At the camp I went to see my commander. I showed him the letter the doctors had given me.

"All right," said the commander, "you can rest for two weeks."

"Couldn't I visit my family?" I asked.

"I can't let you go traveling across the country," said the commander. "Do you have family living in this area?"

I tried to think quickly. "I have a sister living in Baku," I said.

"Baku? All right, then," the commander said "if you want, I'll give you a permit to go to your sister for two weeks. But you can't travel anywhere else."

The permit to travel named the unit from which I came, and stated that I was being allowed two weeks of furlough. The commander also told me that simply by showing my document at any food distribution center, I would receive bread for free.

That evening, when my brother-in-law returned from digging trenches, he was happy to see me back from the hospital. I led Sucher away from our group.

"I'm leaving," I said.

"What do you mean?" Sucher asked. "You're not deserting?" he whispered in a panic.

"I have a permit to travel for two weeks. I told them I have a sister in Baku."

"Who do you know in Baku?" Sucher asked.

"I made it up; otherwise, he wouldn't let me out of here. I'm going to find Shifra and Ruchele."

"In two weeks?" Sucher whispered.

"I'm not coming back."

"Schloime, it's maddness. If they catch you—"

"In two weeks I'll be far away. They won't bother looking for me. Sucher, I almost died. I won't survive these conditions."

We turned around and started back.

I spent the night at camp and in the morning one of the soldiers drove me to the train station in a wagon. With the travel permit, I was able to board any train and travel for free. A few hours later I was in Baku, a port city on the Caspian Sea. As soon as I got off the train, I started to look for a way to cross the water. I had to act quickly. I was afraid I might lose my courage.

First I went to a food distribution center to pick up enough bread to last me two weeks. I stuffed the bread into my knapsack and headed for the port. On the pier, I walked up to an elderly, bearded Jew who was about to get on a ship and asked him where he was headed. Krasnovodsk, he said. I glanced up to the deck. No one was checking papers. I mixed in with the stream of people walking up the gangway and got on.

Within a half hour the ship was full. Most passengers were civilians escaping from territories under attack by the Germans; the rest were soldiers, some of whom were wounded. On board, no one stopped me to ask where I was going.

As soon as the ship left port, I tore up my travel permit and dropped it into the sea. I was better off without it. If anyone asked me who I was and where I was going, I decided to say that I was a refugee, that I had lived in Minsk, and that I was now traveling to the Urals where I had a brother. And if anyone asked me for documentation, I would say someone had stolen all my belongings, including my papers, in a train station while I slept.

In the port of Krasnovodsk, I was relieved to see that no one was checking papers as people left the ship. On the ground, however, I noticed that the port was enclosed, and when I saw everyone crowding towards the same exit, I had a sickening feeling. At the gates, just as I had feared, military officials stood on either side stamping documents. The only passengers getting through freely without having to show any identification were soldiers in uniform. I moved back and waited until I saw a rowdy bunch of Russian soldiers. I mixed in with them and as they approached the gates, I crouched down among their legs. When I straightened up again, I was outside the port.

This city like all others was overrun with people fleeing the Germans. Everyone seemed to be heading deeper into Russia for safety. My guess was that Shifra and Ruchele had done the same. I looked for a Jew and asked for directions to the train station.

When I got there, everywhere I looked, people were boarding long trains. I decided to use the same strategy which had worked in crossing the Caspian Sea, to act as if I belonged there. I quickly boarded a train, looked for an empty seat and squeezed in next to two elderly Russian farmers. The Russians spoke to each other and left me alone. Finally I heard a whistle blast. Before we started to move, however, the conductor, a young man with a round, reddish face, entered the car and began to check papers. I closed my eyes and pretended to sleep.

Soon I heard the conductor speaking to the farmers beside me.

"Excuse me," the conductor said, shaking me. "Papers, please."

I opened my eyes. "They were stolen," I said.

"Stolen?" the conductor asked. "What happened?"

"I fell asleep at the station and someone took my suitcase and my wallet with all my papers."

"I'm sorry," said the conductor, "but you'll have to get new papers if you want to travel."

I was afraid to argue with him and got off.

A few hours later, I tried to board another train. The same thing happened. Before we started to move a conductor came around checking documents and again I was forced off. I spent the night in the train station.

For the next two days, I tried a few more times to get on trains without luck.

On the third morning, as I sat in the crowded station, feeling desperate, a young man in a conductor's uniform approached me.

"You're still here?" he asked me.

I looked at him. He was about my age, in his late twenties, with a round, well-fed, childish face. He was smiling as if he recognized me.

"Do you know me?" I asked him.

"I put you off my car two days ago. Don't you remember?"

He was the first of the many conductors who had kicked me off the trains.

"Didn't you get new papers yet?" he asked me.

I shook my head no.

"Why not?" he asked. "I'm sorry I couldn't let you travel, but I have to account for everyone in my car. I'm responsible for supplying my passengers with food. Even medicine, if they need it. If I give those supplies to someone without a travel permit, my supervisors could send me to Siberia. Why don't you go to the authorities and get new papers?"

He seemed to be a friendly person, I was desperate, and I decided to trust him. I told him how I had slipped into Krasnovodsk and why I couldn't go to the authorities for new papers.

"Where do you want to go?" he asked.

"I want to find my wife and sister. We were separated in Makhatschkala when the Germans attacked."

The young conductor scratched his head. "I'd like to help you," he said, "but I'm afraid. I certainly wouldn't be able to give you any food!"

"That's not a problem," I reassured him. "I just need to get out of this city. Every day new people keep arriving. If someone from my troop recognizes me, they could turn me in."

Again the conductor considered my case. Finally, he said, "Be here at three o'clock in the morning. The trains will be less crowded then."

I felt my courage returning. I needed to arrange food for myself. I left the train station and started to look for an open market.

A kilo of bread at the market cost 100 rubles. I was still wearing a good pair of shoes. I sold them for 500 rubles, replaced them with a cheap pair for 300 rubles, and with the rest of the money I bought bread.

In the evening, I returned to the station. I didn't allow myself to fall asleep. At exactly three by the station's clock, the young conductor appeared. He motioned me with his hand to follow him. We stopped at a train. When he was sure no one was watching, he told me to get on. At the back of the empty car, the conductor pointed me to a seat. "Don't tell anyone you don't have documents," he whispered.

Passengers continued to board the train for another hour. Luckily, no one sat next to me. At last I saw the young conductor again as he started to check the passengers' documents. When he got to me, he bent over as if looking at my papers and then quickly left. Suddenly, after a sharp whistle blast, the train started to move.

Later, after he had attended to all the passengers in his car, the conductor stopped at the back. "It's lucky you had this seat all to yourself," he whispered, as he sat down next to me. "At the next stop, the car will start to fill up. You can talk, but don't let anyone know your situation." He wished me luck, got up, and continued to do his job.

I couldn't help admiring his kindness. If only the whole world had been made of people like the young conductor.

At the next station, passengers poured into the car. A middle aged woman and her daughter, an attractive girl in her early twenties, sat down across from me. I heard them speak Yiddish to each other. They noticed that I understood them and we were soon talking.

The woman, Sonya, and her daughter, Pearl, were moving to live with Sonya's brother. "My husband," Sonya said, "was taken into the army and to this day I don't know where he is." She began to cry.

Pearl pulled a handkerchief out of her purse and gave it to her mother.

I told Sonya that I understood how she felt. I too had lost track of my family, but I wasn't giving up hope.

"That's why we're traveling to Fergana," Sonya said. "I couldn't stand to live alone, away from my family anymore. There, at least, I have a brother."

As soon as Sonya mentioned Fergana, I remembered my father.

The women noticed that something had struck me. They asked what was the matter. I told them that I thought my father was living in

Fergana. Mother and daughter started to ask me questions. As the train rushed through the Russian dawn further into the country, I told them my life story.

We became good friends. The next few days of travel passed quickly. On the fourth day, my bread ran out. I told Sonya and Pearl that I would have to get off to try to find some food.

"Don't leave," Sonya urged me. "Come to Fergana. We can share our food with you. If you find your father, he'll surely help you find your family."

I thanked Sonya and her daughter from the bottom of my heart.

By the fifth day of travel I noticed that the train was making many more stops to pick up and discharge passengers and to restock on provisions. Soon, it seemed to me, we were more often stopped than moving. My two friends shared their food with me, as they had promised. After two weeks of such travel, we finally arrived in Fergana.

I followed Sonya and Pearl to the house of Sonya's brother, Adam. He was older than his sister but seemed to be just as kind as she. Sonya explained my circumstances to him. Adam asked for my father's address. I told him what I remembered and Sonya's brother gave me exact directions how to get there.

Even though I had been only two years old when my father left us, I had gone through many feelings towards him in my life. At first I had hoped he would return to us after the war. Then, in 1918, when the trains loaded with returning soldiers didn't bring my father back, I felt disappointed. Finally, I became angry when I saw how my abandoned mother had to struggle alone for our survival. Now, as I finally walked towards my father's house, all I had left was a feeling of apprehension. Whatever had happened in the past would have to stay buried there, I needed my father's help desperately.

I came to a small house in a clean residential neighborhood. I knocked on the door. An elderly woman answered. She looked at me with questioning eyes.

"I'm looking for Baruch Renglich," I said. "Is he home?"

"Renglich? He doesn't live here anymore. He moved."

"Can you give me his new address?" I asked.

"I don't have it," she said. "But he's in Ashkhabat. At least, he was there a few years back."

I thanked her. As I was about to leave I asked her, "How far is Ashkhabat?"

"How far? Oh, I don't know," the old lady said. "But it's far, very far."

Walking back to Adam's house, I felt lost. Sonya and Pearl, however, weren't discouraged when I filled them in on my visit to my father's old address. "It's still a good thing we insisted you travel to Fergana," Sonya said.

"I'll write a letter to the Bureau of Addresses in Ashkabat for you," Pearl offered, "and they'll soon send us your father's new address."

Their optimism encouraged me. Perhaps they were right, I thought, and this was a lucky break for me. Since I now had an address where I could receive mail again, I wrote a letter to Ruchele's friend, Kaile Masler, in the Urals. I gave her Adam's address and asked Kaile to please send me any information she might have about my wife, my sister, or brother-in-law.

Fergana, too, was overflowing with uprooted people. When I returned from mailing my letters, I saw that a large crowd had gathered in Adam's one room apartment. Sonya and her daughter were not the only relatives who had come to Fergana to join Adam. He actually had fifteen people living with him. I wondered if they would have room to put me up. Soon enough, Sonya, with deep apologies, told me there simply wasn't anymore room there.

I thanked my friends for everything they had already done for me and left. I walked around the city looking for a place to spend the night. By chance I passed the post office. Even though it was closed, the doors to the building were still open. I went in, found myself a bench, and sat down. Soon other men and women who had nowhere to sleep came in. I spent my first night in Fergana there.

In the morning, I started to look for work. I walked into the first tailor shop I found. The tailor said he could give me work, but I needed authorization from the militia to live in Fergana.

I ran to the offices of the militia and asked for a permit to stay in the city. They told me I first had to bring proof that I had work.

I ran back to the tailor. I explained to him what the militia required. He wasn't convinced that he wouldn't be fined if he hired me without authorization.

I ran back to the militia offices to find out, then back to the tailor, and back to the militia again with another question from the tailor. By nightfall, I had accomplished nothing. I didn't get the job and I had to return to the post office to sleep. I was so hungry, I couldn't fall asleep. In the middle of the night, when I had finally dozed off, I was awakened by a policeman and taken with the rest of the post office sleepers to jail.

I was kept there overnight. In the morning I was questioned and ordered to leave the city. The next time I was arrested in Fergana, I was told, I would be sent to Siberia.

I was starving as I walked out of the police station. Instead of leaving the city, I went straight to the open market to look for something to chew on. This region of the country grew an abundance of fruits. Farmers came daily to the market to sell their produce and almost every farmer, competing with his neighbors, offered free tastes to attract customers. There was no lack of tasters for the fruit. Actually, there were more tasters than customers. Unfortunately, one had to be well dressed to be allowed a taste by the farmers. In my worn out, dirty clothes, I hardly looked like a prospective customer. As I passed the stalls, the brilliant colors and sweet smells of the fruits drove me mad with hunger. When I reached out to get a taste of mellon from a farmer, he suddenly pulled out a long stick from behind his table and instead of the fruit he offered me a taste of the stick across my hands. I jumped away before I got hit.

I kept circling the market. Finally I saw a farmer who was busy with a few customers. His attention, I noticed, was on the money rather than on the fruit. I quickly grabbed a pear and slipped it into my pocket. When I was sure that no one had seen me, I pulled out the fruit and devoured it.

I remained in Fergana in spite of the warnings from the police. At night, since I had no choice, I went back to the post office. Other men and women who slept there assured me that the police only came by once a week. Indeed no policeman came to bother us and I had a good sleep at last.

In the morning, a man who had spent the night at the post office asked me if I wanted work. I told him that I had already tried without success. The man told me that he knew of a cotton processing plant which was looking to hire people. He offered to take me to it.

The man led me up to the factory, an enormous, low building. Inside, the large machines made such a racket, I had to shout to ask one of the workers for the manager. The worker pointed to the other end of the floor.

The noise died down somewhat as I closed the door of the manager's office. A harried-looking, pot-bellied man in his mid-fifties, sitting at a desk, gave me a quick glance. "Yes? Can I help you?" he asked.

"I'm looking for work," I said.

He glanced up. "I need a man in the third shift. Midnight to eight."

"All right," I snapped back.

"It's hard work."

"I don't care," I said.

"Do you have a room?"

"No."

"We'll give you a place to sleep. Papers," the manager said, putting out his hand.

"I lost them. They were stolen from me. I'm from—"

"I don't want to hear stories," the manager said. He pulled out a form from his desk drawer and started to fill it out. He asked for my name, when and where I was born, and what city in Poland I came from.

"Take this letter to the police station," the manager said. "They'll give you identification papers. When you have them, come back here."

As soon as I showed the manager's letter at the police station, I was told to sit at a desk. A policeman soon came over and after he had asked me the same questions I had just answered for the manager, he wrote another letter out for me.

"Take this letter to the factory," the policeman said. "Come back in a week and we'll give you documents."

I returned to the factory. The manager looked over the letter from the police and hired me. He gave a card for bread, good for ten days, and told me that I could buy hot food cheaply in the kitchen. The manager then led me to a large hall next to the factory where there were rows and rows of beds. He showed me to bed 125; the number was written on a piece of cardboard attached to the headrest.

"This is your bed," said the manager. "Better rest up now, because at midnight you start."

I told him that I wouldn't mind a bit of food.

"Go and eat," he said.

"But I don't have any money."

"You don't need money," the manager said. "Go to the kitchen and tell them that you'll pay after you get your first salary. You can do the same thing in the store."

I didn't waste a moment. I asked the manager to show me where the kitchen was. He left me there. I sat down and had myself a meal to make up for my many hungry days and nights.

The Journey to Ashkhabat

AFTER MY MEAL, I returned to the hall with beds. For the first time since my stay at the hospital in Darbend, I had a real mattress to lay down on. At midnight, I was awakened by the workers coming off the second shift. They were now going to sleep. I got dressed and left for work feeling well fed and rested.

At the factory, the night foreman took me to a revolving conveyor belt running out of a monstrous machine which packed and tied bales of cotton. My job was to pull the bales from the belt and stack them on wooden lorries. It was back-breaking work. Each bale weighed at least 50 kilos. As I worked my shift, the cotton seemed to get heavier. No matter how heavy the cotton was, however, there was no stopping the machine. It took every bit of my strength to keep up. The night foreman saw my struggle and tried to be encouraging. "You're still new at it. Don't give up. It gets easier with time."

In spite of my foreman's kind words, as the days passed, the work only got harder. Somehow I managed to last out the week and I went back to the police station for my new documents. The policeman who handed me a passport and military identification book said, "Remember, if you leave your job, you'll be sent to the army."

I assured him that I had no intentions of quitting. To myself I wondered how much longer I would be able to last at the cotton factory.

In my spare time, I visited Sonya at her brother's house. I went hoping to find an answer to my letters to Kaile Masler in the Urals and the Office of Addresses in Ashkhabat. Nothing came back. Sonya asked her daughter to write again to Ashkhabat, and I wrote another letter to Ruchele's friend.

In November, the nights began to grow very cold. I was always sweated up from the physical strain of my job and I caught a cold. In a few days I was running a fever. I felt so weak, I couldn't even get out of bed. I was sent to the infirmary to see the doctor.

"Have you had problems with your lungs before?" the doctor asked as he examined me.

"Yes. In Warsaw."

"What kind of work are you doing now?"

"I stack bales of cotton."

"That job will kill you. I'm going to write a letter to your boss. I want him to give you lighter work."

I went immediately to the manager. "I wish I had another job to offer you," he said after reading the letter. "Let me see if I can find something."

Two days later, he called me back into his office. "I'm sorry," he said, "but I can't let you work as a stacker anymore and I don't have anything else. If you want you can use the bed until the end of the week." He counted out the money I had coming, paid me, and returned the doctor's letter to me.

I started to look at once for another job. Sick as I was, I spent the whole day going from one factory and tailor shop to the next. But now that I finally had documents, I couldn't find work.

In the evening I went to visit Sonya. Adam answered the door and after he told me that no mail had come for me, he told me that his sister and niece had moved. They were now living with another sister in a nearby town. Adam gave me the address. That same night, I wrote a letter to Sonya and Pearl to thank them for their help.

Even though I was still sick, I kept looking for work. By the middle of the week my money had almost run out. I was afraid to get caught with empty pockets in Fergana. While I still had a few rubles left, I decided to head for Ashkhabat to find of my father.

I went to the police station to ask for a travel permit. The officer wanted to know what business I had in Ashkhabat and why I wasn't in the army. I told him my father was living in Ashkhabat. I also explained that I had been let go from my job because of bad health and that I couldn't find easier work. When I saw that the officer was looking at me suspiciously, I showed him the doctor's letter. The officer read it and gave it back to me. "We can't issue a permit to Ashkhabat," he said. "I'll give you another week to find a job, after that you'll have to join the army. As for your father, if you want, we can try to find him for you."

I accepted his offer at once and provided the officer with all the information I had about my father. The officer wrote it down and suggested I check with him in a few days.

My money ran out on the same day that I was asked to give up the bed at the factory. Three days had passed since I had been at the police station. I went back. The officer told me that no information had returned yet about my father. For the rest of that day, I kept looking for a job. But I had no more luck than the day before. At night, as I passed the post office and considered sleeping there, I realized that I could no longer stay in Fergana. I walked to the train station and boarded the first train that came in.

I sat down in the half-filled car and waited to see what would happen. As the train began to move, the conductor came to collect tickets. When he got to me, I told him all my belongings had been stolen and I had no money. The conductor left and returned a minute later with two guards. One of them started to question me while the other wrote my answers down in a small notebook.

I told them that I was a refugee from Poland, that I had been separated from my wife when the Germans attacked Makhatschkala, and that I was going to Ashkhabat to look for my father with the hope that he could help me find my wife.

"By all rights, we should arrest you," said the guard who had questioned me. "You don't have a travel permit, and you're traveling without a ticket." He turned to his comrade and they moved away to have a little conference on my fate. After a short talk they seemed to come to an agreement and returned to me.

The guard who had questioned me said, "We've decided not to arrest you. Go. Find your father." And they left.

A few minutes later, one of the guards reappeared. "Didn't you say you were going to Ashkhabat?" he asked.

"Yes."

He started to laugh. "You're traveling, but you have no idea where you're going," he said. "Ashkhabat's in the other direction."

After the guard had left, I asked a Jew sitting next to me if Ashkhabat was really in the opposite direction. He assured me that it was.

At the first stop, I got off the train. It was already late at night. The station was no more than two long benches and a bulletin board of train schedules. Even so, there were a few people sitting on the benches waiting. I sat down too. A young woman next to me picked up her head and asked whether I spoke Yiddish. She was in her twenties, thin, dirty. Her dress was so large on her it seemed to have belonged to an older sister. Her feet were wrapped in rags.

"Where are you traveling?" she asked in a tired voice.

"Ashkhabat," I said.

"Your train won't come until the morning," she said.

"Where are you going?" I asked her.

She shook her head as if she were lost and it didn't matter to her. "I don't know," she said. "I'm roaming from city to city looking for my husband."

"I'm looking for my father," I said. "I'm hoping he can help me find my wife. Shifra and I were forced to separate in Makhatchkala when the Germans invaded. She had our little girl with her and she was pregnant. My sister was with us there, too, with her own child. Now I don't know where any of them are."

"I doubt that my sister or parents are even alive," the young woman said. "We came from Budapest. When the Germans, may they burn in Hell, attacked I ran with my parents and my sister to Russia. We were working on a collective farm near Pultave until the Germans invaded that area. They killed almost all the Jews they caught; the rest they deported to German labor camps. I don't know by what miracle I escaped. I hid in the forests during the day and at night I ran. In Samerkand, I found work as a waitress. Then I met a boy from Romania, Alex. He was the supervisor of a shoe factory. We fell in love and got married. It's a lucky thing we didn't have children. A few months after our marriage, the shoe factory burned down. Alex and two other Jewish men were accused of setting the fire and sentenced to five years in prison. They were innocent, decent, honest men. But those anti-semitic Russian bastards did such a good job setting them up that nothing helped. Now I don't know where they sent Alex. So I travel from city to city looking for some trace of my husband."

She began to cry softly. After a while she stopped.

"There isn't enough room to stretch out on these benches," she said. "I know a place where we could get a little sleep, but I'm afraid to go there alone."

"Is it far?" I asked. "I don't want to miss the next train."

"No," she said. "Do you want to see it?"

I picked up my knapsack and we left. She took me to a small, deserted house, only minutes away from the train station. We entered a narrow corridor which led to a waiting room of sorts. It had a long bench pushed up against one wall. Above the bench there were three small windows covered with red curtains. On the opposite wall there were portraits of Marx, Engels, and Stalin. There was also a door which seemed to lead to the inside of the building. I tried it but it was locked. I guessed we were in a government office.

"You see?" The young woman pointed to the long bench. "I've slept here for the past three nights."

We sat down. I offered her a piece of black bread from my knapsack. The bread was dry and stale but we ate it as if it were a fine pastry. Then we lay down on the bench and went to sleep.

We woke up at daybreak and immediately returned to the station. We soon heard a train approaching. The young woman wished me luck in my search.

"Aren't you getting on?" I asked her.

"Not yet," she said. "I heard yesterday that there's a jail nearby. I want to see if my husband is in it or if someone knows where he could be."

I wished her luck and ran to board the train.

Before I sat down, I asked a Jewish passenger whether the train was going to Ashkhabat. It was, he said. I sat down glad to be heading in the right direction at last.

I didn't feel glad for long, however. When the conductor came around to collect tickets and found out that I didn't have one, he called two guards. I tried telling my story to them, but it did me no good. At the next stop, I was taken to the police station. I repeated my story there. The policemen weren't interested. They jailed me, but luckily, after a few hours, they let me go.

I immediately walked back to the station and boarded the next train towards Ashkhabat. I was ready to take any risk to find my father. Only minutes after the train started to move, I was arrested again. At the next stop, I was taken to the police station. This time I was held the whole night. As soon as I was let out, I went back to the station and got on the next train. I repeated this cycle of traveling a station and being arrested, over and over.

One night, a week after the start of my journey, I noticed a coal transport headed towards Ashkhabat. I jumped into a wagon, found myself a clear corner next to a mountain of coal, and sat down leaning my back against the wooden boards. When the train started to move the dust from the coals began to blow in the wind and to hit me from all sides. The faster the train hurled through the night, the stronger the wind churned up the bits of coal. I was pelted as if I had been caught in a storm of black hail. I tried hiding my face in a corner of the wagon, but the dust flew up from underneath. I didn't know what to do with myself. Soon the sharp iciness of the night wind began to cut into me like a whip. I decided to jump off. I walked to the edge of the open wagon and looked at the ground streaking away in a dark blur. I couldn't jump. I would be torn to pieces.

Hours after I had boarded it, the train finally came to a stop.

When I got off, in the middle of the night, I was shaking violently from the cold. I looked around in the moonlit darkness. There wasn't even a station where I could warm up. All I saw was a long wooden bench next to a sign in Russian with the name of the town. When the coal transport finally rumbled away, I was sitting alone, surrounded by empty fields and the cold night. Nothing moved. Far off, in the distance, I saw small fires no bigger than stars. I was tempted to walk towards these lights. But I was afraid of losing my way and missing the next train. I lay down on the bench and using my knapsack as a pillow tried to catch some sleep.

I was awakened by the sound of voices. The darkness was dissolving into a pale light. I sat up and saw three men and a woman holding a boy by the hand. They were carrying bundles and suitcases. As they approached me, I noticed strange expressions on their faces. They looked at me as if I had been something inhuman, a ghost. I glimpsed down at my hands. Black. My clothes. Black. I touched my lips with my tongue and tasted the gritty saltiness of coal mixed with sweat. From head to foot, I was covered with a layer of black soot.

The people sat down at the other end of the bench. I tried to tell them as best I could in Russian what had happened to me. They nodded with understanding. I asked them when the next train to Ashkhabat would arrive. In about half an hour, said one of the men.

When the train arrived I was the first one to get on board. The conductor who came to ask for my ticket was frightened by my looks.

"Why are you so black?" he asked me.

I started to tell him the story. He didn't even let me finish. He took me into another wagon where two guards were playing cards. They stopped the game and began to question me. When I told them my story, one of the guards said, "You'll have to repeat your saga at the next police station."

As soon as the train stopped, the guards turned me over to the local authorities. I was taken to the police station and interrogated once more.

"Go into the bathroom and wash up," said the policeman who had listened to my story. "You look worse than a chimney sweep."

I washed a long time but I still couldn't get all the soot off. When I had done the best I could, I came out off the bathroom. The policeman walked over to me and ordered me to take off my jacket.

"Couldn't you clean yourself a little better?" the policeman asked with disgust. "At least wash that ugly stain off your arm."

For the first time in weeks I laughed. That ugly stain, I told the policeman, was a birthmark. It was the only thing on me that I could *never* wash off.

He didn't seem to find it funny. "Take off your cap," he said.

I did as he told me. He looked me over from head to foot, then reached out, grabbed a handful of my hair, and gave it a yank. I wondered whether he thought that I was a German spy in disguise. When he was convinced that the hair was mine, he freed me.

As I continued to travel, I met other Jews from Poland, and they helped me out, some with a piece of bread, some with a few kopecks or a ruble. I dragged myself like this, from train to police station, from police station back to the train. After eighteen days, dead tired, I arrived in Ashkhabat.

According to the station clock, it was three in the morning. Even at that hour, the immense railroad terminal was packed with people. Not only was every bench occupied, most the floor was covered with men, women and children sitting on their luggage. The dress of these people was so diverse, it was obvious that they came from all parts of Europe. And all were running from the German murderers. I began to look for a Jewish face. A fellow Jew, I figured, would take an interest in my problem. I soon spotted a man in his fifties, well dressed, an expensive gray felt hat on his large head, and a nose just as large as mine, so much like mine in fact I was sure he had to be Jewish even though he was clean-shaven and dressed like a dandy. He was sitting next to an elegant woman, having an intimate conversation.

I approached the man and in Yiddish asked him, "Can you tell me where I can find the Bureau of Addresses?"

The couple looked up at me with annoyance and returned to their conversation.

I excused myself and repeated my question, this time in my best Russian.

The man glanced over his shoulder and told me, "It's too early now. All the offices are still closed. Go into the city during the day and you'll find what you're looking for."

I stood where I was. I hoped even though he wasn't Jewish that he might still ask me for whom I was looking. He didn't seem interested, however. He spoke a few more quiet words to the woman, looked back at me with revulsion, then both got up from the bench and walked away.

I wasn't surprised that I repelled people. How could I have made a good impression on this middle-aged, Gentile dandy and his elegant girlfriend? Here it was December already and I was still wearing the same clothes I had been wearing in August when I was drafted to dig trenches in Makhatschkala. Everything on me was ragged and dirty. I had exchanged my shirt and shoes many months ago for much cheaper ones and a bite of food. The shirt was now torn. And the shoes which I had bought in Krasnovodsk had come apart long ago. To avoid losing them, I had tied them around my feet with heavy string. My face went unwashed for weeks at a time. Ulcers had formed on my skin. I was hurt but not surprised by the reception I had received. As I watched them go, I wondered how people could be so heartless. All the same I took advantage of the empty bench which the couple had left me and stretched out on it. It fit exactly my short frame. Within moments, I fell soundly asleep.

The train station was already flooded with daylight when I woke up. It was 8 in the morning by the station clock high up on the opposite wall. As I prepared to leave, I noticed the well-dressed dandy who had snubbed me a few hours earlier. For a while, I enjoyed watching him run desperately from one ticket window to the next, apparently unable to get a ticket.

On the street, I began to ask for directions to the Bureau of Addresses. When I entered the office, a young woman, standing behind the counter, was so frightened by my appearance, she dropped the papers she had been holding, and ran to the back of the office.

She reappeared with a man. "What do you want?" he asked bluntly, trying to scare me off.

"Excuse me," I said politely, " but I was told that this is the Bureau of Addresses. I need to find someone who lives in Ashkhabat."

The man turned to the young woman with an exasperated look and said, "Please help this man with his question," and he left.

The young lady approached the counter with an apologetic face and asked, "Who are you looking for?"

"I would like the address of Baruch Renglich."

Suddenly she seemed interested in me. "What do you want with citizen Renglich?"

"He's my father," I said.

"Your father?" the astonished young woman asked. "It's not possible. I happen to know his children well."

I was in no mood to tell her my life story. "I'm not in the best of health," I said. "I've been traveling for almost twenty days. Could you please give me the address?"

"Of course," she said. "Please forgive me." She immediately picked up a blank sheet of paper from her desk, wrote down the address, and handed it to me.

"Svoboda Street," the young woman said, "No. 109. It's not far from here. I'll walk out with you and show you the way."

We stepped outside of the office and she pointed me to the right. Then she wished me luck.

As I was walking, a fine rain began to fall.

No. 109 Svoboda Street turned out to be a large house in a row of attached houses. I knocked on the door. It was opened by a short woman in her mid-forties, dressed in a long flowered house robe. She took one look at me and shut the door in my face.

I had frightened her, just as I had frightened the young woman at the Bureau of Addresses. I knocked again. She opened the door and asked, "What do you want?"

"Is this 109?" I asked. The rain was falling more strongly now and I tried to step into the vestibule.

"Yes," she said, blocking my way. "Who are you looking for?"

"Baruch Renglich," I said.

I was getting drenched. The lady finally took pity and allowed me to take a step into the vestibule.

"Why are you looking for him?" she asked.

"I must see him."

"Well, he's not home now."

"When is he coming back?"

"Much later," she said. "At night." I could tell from the way she spoke, her eyes lowered, her voice strained, that she was lying.

"Could I wait for him here?" I asked. I was still sick. Outside the cold rain was washing down the dark day. Inside it was warm and the smell of cooking filled the air. Being in the vestibule felt so good to me just then, that I thought I could have stayed in that house forever.

"No, you can't wait here," she said. "I have to go to the market." She began to push me out the door.

"Father!" I shouted into the house. "Father, it's me!" I reached into my pocket and took out my father's photograph. The picture which my sister had brought with her from Lublin when she first arrived in Warsaw. I held it up and said, "This is my father!"

The woman stepped back. From a room inside the house I heard a young woman's voice shout, "Papa, get up! Your son is here!"

Risen from the Dead

THE BEWILDERED WOMAN eyed me as if I had risen from the dead. I heard a man's quick step approaching over the wooden floor in the house. I ran past the woman, who no longer tried to stop me. As I entered the living room I saw coming towards me, wearing pajamas, arms outstretched, the same middle-aged dandy who had shunned me at the train station. He saw me and stopped as if a cannon ball had been fired at his chest. His arms dropped. A look of shock distorted his face. I was just as stunned. No wonder I had taken him for a Jew. I looked at his face again and now I recognized my own features: my nose bulging out of his face, my thin, wide mouth, my large ears, my high forehead, my shock of hair on his large head. The man before me studied my face as intently as I studied his. Did he remember now the two year old son he had left in 1914? Did he recognize the beggar he had ignored so cruelly at the train station? He started to lift his arms, took a step towards me, and collapsed.

"Papa!" a young woman shouted running into the living room and dropping to her knees to help the unconscious man.

"Boris!" cried the middle-aged woman, clutching her hands to her chest. She ran past me and also fell to the floor to help the man. The two women opened the buttons on his pajama top, fanned him with their hands, and patted his face.

The man revived slowly. He sat up on the floor and looked at me.

"What is your name?" he asked me in Yiddish now. "Where are you from?"

"Schloime," I said. "I was born in Lublin. We lived on the Volye…"

"My God," he said. "Can this really be you?"

"Ruchele is my sister and my mother's name is Roise Schmer."

"Enough," he said. "Enough." He tried to get up but was still shaky.

290

"Help me," he said in Russian to the two women. They took his arms, one on each side, and raised him to his feet.

He stood before me with tears in his eyes, put out his hands, and embraced me at last. I cried as my father held me and pressed me against himself.

"You have to wash up," he said finally letting go of me. "But eat something first." He turned to the middle-aged woman. "Lena, give him some food right away and then bring him a towel and fresh clothes. Marta," he said to the younger woman, "heat up water for a bath."

"Yes, Papa," she said and left.

The older woman disappeared into the kitchen.

"Sit down," said my father to me. "That was my wife, Lena, and my daughter, Marta." He didn't look at me as he told me these facts.

My father sat down next to me at the table. "Who else is with you in Russia?" he asked in a hushed voice.

"Ruchele," I said. "And my wife."

"And your mother?" he asked.

"She didn't come with us," I said. "She…"

We heard footsteps coming from the kitchen.

"We'll talk more of that later," said my father.

Lena, my father's second wife, brought me a hot plate of vegetable and dumpling soup.

I took a spoonful of the soup. I hadn't tasted anything so good in months. My stomach, no longer used to such rich food, rebelled for a moment, but I soon felt better.

"I have another son," my father said as I ate. "Mareck. He's in the Army. When Marta shouted that my son was home, I was expecting to see him. We're worried about him. We haven't heard from him for many months now. Marta's husband was killed last year, and now I don't know what to think about Mareck. Why didn't you write and tell me that you were in Russia?"

"I did write," I said. "And so did Ruchele. But we didn't know that you had moved from Fergana. Why didn't you send us your new address? I wrote many letters to you from Warsaw, but you never answered. Why did you stop writing?"

"The bath is ready!" Marta shouted from another room.

"We'll talk later," my father said with a weary sigh.

Lena came back with my father's freshly-laundered underwear, black socks, a white shirt, and a blue pair of pants.

I took the bundle of clothes from Lena and my father showed me the way to the bathroom.

I was left alone. I peeled off my dirty clothes and slowly eased into the tub. I had forgotten how soothing a hot bath could be. As I lay back in the large porcelain tub, the warm water covering my sore body, I wanted desperately to go to sleep. I rested awhile, then I began to wash myself.

After I had finished the water in the bathtub was dark. I dried myself off, put on my father's clean clothes, and went back into the living room.

My father, his wife, and daughter were sitting at the table waiting for me.

"You look much better," said my father. "Come. Sit down with us and let's have breakfast now."

I took the seat next to my father. His wife and daughter, on the opposite side of the table, kept their eyes on their bowls of kasha as they ate. Suddenly, my father's wife lifted her face out of her plate and said to me in Russian, "He came home dead tired. He didn't get a wink of sleep last night. That's the only reason I said that he wasn't home."

"Why didn't you tell me who you were looking for at the train station?" asked my father, as I helped myself to kasha and milk and bread with honey.

"How could I tell you anything?" I asked. "First you acted as if you didn't understand Yiddish, and then you got up and left."

My father's face turned red with shame. I wanted him to know that he had hurt my feelings. Even if I hadn't been his son, he still shouldn't have treated me as he did in the station. "Nobody knows what time can bring," I said.

My father lowered his head. I wasn't exactly pleasing him with my words.

"I'm sorry," my father apologized. "I was having a very bad night. I waited for a train from seven in the evening to eight in the morning. And I still wasn't able to get one. In the meantime the factory for which I'm responsible sits idle. Sixty-four workers have nothing to do because I can't get on a train to arrange for supplies."

"Is it a shoe factory?" I asked my father.

"Yes," he said with surprise. "How did you guess?"

"Mamme told me what a good shoemaker you were. And so did Sruel Kopitch, when I worked for him."

"Sruel Kopitch?" asked my father with astonishment. "I haven't heard that name in thirty years. *You* worked for Sruel Kopitch?"

"I had to start working when I was eleven years old. Mamme couldn't take care of us by herself."

My father looked nervously across at his wife and daughter. They continued to eat as if the conversation between my father and me had nothing to do with them.

"I'm the director of the shoe factory here in Ashkhabat," said my father to change the subject.

I understood this wasn't a good time to talk of the hard times we had endured in Lublin after he deserted us. I felt strange sitting so close to my father and yet not being able to speak to him freely.

We finished eating in silence. At the end of the meal, while Lena and her daughter cleared the table my father asked about my health.

"I have a bad cold," I said. "I caught it in Fergana working in a cotton factory."

"What you need is a steam-bath," said my father. "A good sweat will drive the cold out of you. Let me give you a warm coat to wear and let's go."

I had no interest in a steam-bath. I didn't want to leave the warm house. I could tell, however, from the way my father had proposed this idea, that he was bent on going. He dressed quickly, picked out a long winter coat for me, told his wife that we were going out, and we left.

The rain had stopped, although the sky had remained gray and it looked as if the rain could return at any moment. Now that I was finally alone with my father, all the questions which I had accumulated for him over the past twenty years came rushing into my mind.

"Where did Sruel Kopitch have his workshop?" my father asked before I had a chance to ask him anything.

"In a basement," I said.

"What was the address?"

"I don't remember."

"Well, what did Sruel look like? What do you remember about him?"

I felt as if my father were interrogating me. "He was a tall, thin man." It suddenly struck me that maybe my father thought that I was an impostor. "Sruel took me to the theater. He told me that he used to meet you at the theater with Mamme."

As soon as I brought up my mother, however, my father immediately changed the subject again and asked me where I had lived in Warsaw.

I gave my father Frau Liebe's address, the address I had sent him in my letters. But before I could ask him why he had stopped writing to us, my father pointed me into a large red-brick building, the bath house.

When we were undressed, my father took hold of my right hand and looked for the large brown mole on my forearm. He had remembered my birthmark.

"You still have that mole," my father said, smiling.

I realized that this was the real reason my father had wanted to take me to the bathhouse. The birthmark had finally convinced him that I was his son.

"Why are you limping?" asked my father. Now that I had my shoes off my limp was much more noticeable.

"My leg was broken when I was a small child."

The intense heat of the steam made it hard for me to breathe, and I wasn't able to say anything more. Afterwards, however, while we were dressing again, I felt refreshed and much stronger than when we first went in.

On the street, as we walked back to Svoboda Street, I turned to my father and asked, "Why did you leave us?"

He reacted to my question as if I had slapped his face. He gave me an angry look, as if to say, How dare you put such a question to me? But this expression was quickly replaced by a look of shame. He turned his head away. We walked for a block in silence. He obviously didn't want to speak about this painful part of his life. I promised myself, however, that I would not let him get away without answering my questions. I was about to ask him again, when my father began to speak.

"If war hadn't broken out in 1914, I never would have left. What could I do? Every man who could lift a rifle was drafted. Those years of fighting in the trenches changed me. I don't know how to explain it to you. I realized my life wasn't worth much. I knew that any day I could get killed. Everything I had once valued lost its meaning to me. Do you understand what I'm saying?"

I understood that he was blaming the war for the fact that he had abandoned a wife and two small children. I didn't believe the war excused his actions. But I said nothing. I simply waited for him to continue.

"I was wounded three times. Twice I recovered and was sent back to the front lines to fight. Towards the end of the war, I was hit by a bullet which went in through the front, tore up my guts, and went out my back. Somehow my comrades were able to drag me to a field hospital. The doctor who stopped the bleeding didn't think I would survive the night. Only in the morning, when the doctor realized that I still wasn't dead, did he send me to a hospital. I lay near death for a long time. If not for a young nurse, who watched over me like an angel, I never would have survived. I was still in the hospital when the war ended. Not until many months later was I finally able to leave. By then Lena, the young nurse who had saved my life, and I had fallen in love. I wasn't strong enough to travel back to Poland yet. Lena had a small apartment and invited me to stay with her while I recuperated. I shouldn't have accepted that invitation. I thought I would stay with her until I felt stronger and then go back home. Well, in less than a month Lena was pregnant." My father stopped talking.

We continued to walk aimlessly through the murky afternoon.

"I know what's going through your mind," my father finally said, his voice full of irony. "You're thinking how conveniently everything turned out for me; that I never had to suffer as you did for my actions. Well, you're wrong. I despised myself for what I'd done. I thought about you, your sister, and your mother every moment. If Lena had not been pregnant, nothing could have stopped from going back to Lublin. I kept telling myself that I had to figure some way out of this mess without hurting Lena's feelings. But once Mareck was born, Lena needed me more than ever. Even so, I didn't marry her for many years, not until I found out that your mother wanted a divorce."

"Mamme never wanted a divorce!" I said angrily, unable to contain my feelings. "She only asked for it because she heard that you weren't coming back. She waited four years after the war for you. A rich American proposed to her. He was ready to take us all to America, including Babbe. Mamme turned him down, even though she could barely earn a living and even though we were going hungry, because she still considered herself your wife!"

"Khumale wrote me that Roise wanted a divorce so she could remarry," my father said.

"Your sister's a liar! She hated us! Whenever we turned to her for help she insulted us. How could you have believed her over Mamme?"

Again my father fell silent. We had reached an isolated part of town where there were few houses and no stores. "I didn't know my sister's true nature then," my father finally said in a defeated voice. "For years I sent money to her that she was supposed to give your mother. Your lives wouldn't have been so difficult if you had received that money. When you finally wrote to me from Warsaw and I could finally help you directly, a law came out that no money could leave Russia."

295

I listened in silence as my father tried to defend himself. I wondered if he knew how his actions had ruined my mother's life. I guessed that he must have heard the tragedy that had befallen her, because not even once had he asked me a question about her.

"Do you remember that you wrote that you would help Ruchele and me to move to Russia?" I reminded my father as we walked.

"Yes," he admitted.

"Why did you stop writing to us after you had made that promise?"

"I was waiting for you to ask me that question. I don't want you to feel uncomfortable in my house, but I can't lie to you. At first when I received your letters from Warsaw my family was glad that I had found you. They knew that I couldn't get you out of my mind and they thought that if I could send you some help, it would make me feel better. But when my wife and children found out that I was preparing to bring you over, they became afraid that you and Ruchele would take me away from them. Lena started to cry and fight with me. My children took their mother's side. They accused me of being cruel. The misery in the house was unbearable. Marta happened to be working for the post office, and she began to intercept and hide your letters. I had to spend long months away in Moscow for my work. I thought you had simply stopped writing, and I thought maybe that was for the best considering what was going on with Lena and the children. By accident I came across a bundle of your letters a few years ago. I was angry at Lena and Marta for having fooled me, but what could I really do then?"

None of my father's answers satisfied me. But I was a father myself now, and my biggest problem was to find my own wife and children as soon as possible. "I need your help," I said to my father. Then I told him what had happened at edge of the Caspian Sea in Makhatschkala. "I'm worried about Shifra and Ruchele. They each had a small child with them and Shifra was pregnant."

"Of course I'll help you find them," said my father said as he looked at his watch. "But first we have to get you a permit to stay in Ashkhabat. It's not so easy. This is a sensitive area. We're only fifteen kilometers from the border with Iran and the law forbids newcomers settling here. You need a special permission which isn't easy to get. Let's go back and let me see what I can do."

We turned around and began to walk towards Svoboda Street at a brisk pace.

As soon as we were back at my father's house, he asked to see my documents. I pulled the bundle of papers out of my knapsack. My father began to examine them.

"What's this!" he shouted, suddenly upset. "Why are you called Schmer in these papers? How can I claim you as my son if you don't have my last name?"

"It's not my fault," I said. "Mamme changed our name many years ago to her maiden name."

"These documents are no good. If the authorities see these, we'll both be in trouble. I'll never be able to convince them that you're my son." I found that laughable considering how alike we looked, but my father knew these officials better than I did.

"We have to discard these papers." he said. I had gotten rid of documents before and I wasn't too concerned as my father tore up my papers, put the pieces into a large ashtray, and set them on fire. "Now we have to arrange new identifications for you," said my father. "Let's go right away."

We left the house again. This time we didn't have far to go. A few blocks from Svoboda Street, my father led me into a three-storey building. We walked up to an apartment on the second floor. My father knocked. The door was opened by an elderly, distinguished-looking man, with snow white hair, dressed in a brown silk robe. The gentleman greeted my father warmly and led us into the living room.

My father and I sat on the sofa while the man took an armchair across from us. My father wasted no time telling him my story.

After my father was done, the man thought deeply and said, "If you want your son to remain in Ashkhabat, it's going to cost you a bundle. But that's not all. Don't forget that your son is still a young man. Even if he gets the right to stay in Ashkhabat, they will almost immediately draft him into the army. And when it comes to that, you know, we have no recourse."

"What should I do?" asked my father.

"The best advice I can give you," the gentleman answered, "is that your son leave Ashkhabat and go to a smaller city. Some place where you can get a little more cooperation from the local boys. You understand what I mean?"

"Yes, of course," my father said at once. "Someplace like Marie?"

"Exactly," the gentleman smiled. "You won't have any trouble getting your son signed up there and by comparison with what our friends here charge, it will be a bargain."

While my father was pleased with this advice, my own heart sank. I was completely exhausted from tramping around Russia and had been looking forward to living in my father's comfortable house while I searched for Shifra and Ruchele. I desperately needed a warm bed and decent food so I could recuperate. But my father seemed all too eager to send me off again. I suspected that he was also attracted to the idea of not having to spend too much money on me.

My father looked at his watch. "It's getting late," he said, standing up. He shook the old gentleman's hand and we left.

On the street, I turned to my father and asked him, "Why can't you hire me in your own factory here in Ashkhabat? If you told the authorities that my job was important they wouldn't draft me."

"I wish I could do that," my father said. "But I couldn't even keep Mareck out of the army with that excuse. If I tried it, there are so many spies in that factory that we would be denounced in a day and both end up in jail."

I was not convinced. Not only was my father well-off, but from the visit we had just made, he was obviously well connected politically. "What about my wife and children?" I asked my father. "I'm afraid for what could have happened to Shifra. I left her pregnant and carrying a small child in her arms. And I'm also worried about Ruchele. I need to find them soon."

"I understand," my father said. "Believe me, I want to meet both your wife and my daughter. But today we can't do anything else because I have to catch a train and arrange the leather supplies for the factory. Just as soon as I come back, I'll try to take care of everything."

At his house, my father explained to his wife and daughter what we had found out. I wasn't surprised that they also liked the idea of my being sent away.

My father got his suitcase, checked his papers, his ticket, then he turned to me and said, "I'm not sure how long it will take me to complete this business. I'll be back as soon as possible. In the meantime, be careful if you go out. You still don't have any documents."

"I understand," I told my father. "I won't take any foolish chances. I'll stay in the house."

My father was pleased to hear that.

I was given a small room behind the kitchen. It seemed to have been once a maid's quarters. The bed, however, was soft and the room was warm. I was exhausted and went to sleep soon after my father left.

I was awakened in the morning by the noise of someone beating eggs in the kitchen.

I got dressed, washed, and joined Lena and Marta for breakfast.

The two women seemed to be as uncomfortable as I was. We spoke little as we ate. They asked me how I had slept. I told them, "Well, thank you." And that was the extent of our conversation.

After breakfast, I asked Marta for a few sheets of paper and envelopes.

"To whom are you going to write?" Marta asked when she brought me the paper.

"To a friend of my sister's in the Urals. We agreed to write there before we were separated."

"Who do you mean when you say 'we'?" Marta asked.

Lena, who had been in the kitchen, suddenly appeared in the living room, absentmindedly drying a plate as she listened.

"My wife, my sister, and my wife's husband. We were all together in Makhatchkala when the army drafted the men."

"Your sister is also in Russia?" Marta asked and looked at her mother.

"Is she also on her way here?" Lena asked.

"No. I don't know where my sister or my wife are. I'm trying to find them."

Lena suddenly put the plate and the towel down on the table and sat down next to me.

"Please be careful what you write," she said. "Your father is in a very delicate position. There are many people who envy him. They would like nothing better than to accuse him of some offense and see him in trouble."

"I wouldn't write anything to hurt my father," I said.

"Please understand," Lena continued, "it's not just what you could write. Just your being here could hurt him terribly. You see, the situation in the country is very dangerous now. Everywhere the authorities are looking for spies. If your father is suspected of doing anything wrong, it could cost him everything."

"What my mother means," said Marta, "is that you don't have to wait for your father to come back. We can help you ourselves. You say that you want to find your wife and sister and you probably need money. We can give you five hundred rubles and you could leave to look for them at once."

I grew angrier and angrier as I listened to the two women try to bribe me. I looked Marta in the eyes and said, "Please stop giving me advice. I know what I have to do. I'm not going anywhere before my father returns. And one more thing. In spite of how much he made my mother, my sister, and me suffer, I'm not going to do anything to hurt my father."

Lena's and Marta's faces reddened.

"Please don't misunderstand," Lena said at once. "Heaven forbid, we weren't trying to send you away."

"And we know that you wouldn't hurt your father," Marta added quickly.

"We're very sorry for everything you and your family suffered," Lena said. "It really was not our fault. You must understand. These wars destroy everyone's life. My poor Marta's husband was killed no more than half-a-year ago. God alone knows where my poor Mareck is."

"I didn't come to blame anyone," I said. "I wanted to know who my father was. And I want him to help me find my wife and sister. I don't think I'm asking for too much."

There was little else we had to say to each other. Lena and Marta left the room and I began to write my letter.

The Lovesick Engineer

AFTER MY OUTBURST I expected Lena and her daughter to become hostile towards me; instead, they seemed friendlier. I didn't care why their feelings had changed. I guessed they must have felt guilty for the suffering my father's absence had caused his family in Poland. It was just as well I didn't have to put up with the women's anger, because my father was gone a long time. There was a telephone in one of the rooms, and I heard it ring many times. Some of those calls must have been from my father, and yet neither Lena nor her daughter ever called me over to speak to him.

Two weeks after I had sent my letter to Kaile Masler, I received an answer. To my complete surprise, it wasn't from Kaile but from my sister. Ruchele was now living in the Urals and working in a tailoring factory. Her letter continued, "When Shifra and I arrived in Krasnovodsk after crossing the Caspian Sea, we signed up for work in the Urals. Unfortunately, the authorities rejected Shifra because she was pregnant. I don't know where she was sent. When we separated at Krasnovodsk, I told her that as soon she settled somewhere to write immediately to my friend Kaile. But to this day, your wife hasn't sent a word to us. I've been worried about her. I hope our father can help you find her soon. The moment I hear from her, I will let you know. Do you know where Sucher is? I thought you were together in the army? Where did you last see him? Could you please ask Tatte if he could help me find Sucher? How did you locate our father? Tell him I look forward to meeting him."

I answered Ruchele's letter at once and told her how I had found our father. As for Sucher, I wrote to my sister, when he and I had separated, he was digging trenches somewhere near the city of Darbend. I assured Ruchele that I would ask for Tatte's help in finding

301

her husband.

The day after I received my sister's letter, my father returned from his business trip. I was looking forward to telling him the good news about Ruchele. I also wanted to stress to him how important it was that he help me find Shifra at once; and I wanted to ask him what he could do to help find Sucher. But no sooner had my father stepped into the house than his wife and daughter dragged him off for a long conversation behind closed doors.

My father finally appeared at the door of my room a few hours later. I could tell from his expression that he didn't have good news for me. He sat down at the edge of my bed and looking at the floor said, "I've made arrangements for you in Marie. It's a small town, nearby. We have a branch there, a tailoring factory. The director is a good friend of mine. I'll give you a letter of introduction. He'll help you settle down."

"When am I going?"

My father couldn't bring himself to answer. He sat with his head bowed a long time. "Today," he said at last. "There's a train this evening." He got up abruptly and left the room.

I was too startled by the curtness with which I was being bundled out of my father's house to say anything. I was sure that he was doing this against his will. His wife and daughter were no doubt forcing him to get rid of me.

I didn't see my father for the rest of the day. Lena came to my room in the early afternoon and brought me some of my father's clothing: a few pair of underwear, socks, two shirts, a pair of pants.

It wasn't until the evening, when it was time for me to leave, that my father showed up at my door again. Lena was with him. The three of us left for the train station. Marta, my step-sister, didn't even bother to show her face to say goodbye.

At the station, my father asked me to wait with his wife while he took care of some business. He went into an office and a few minutes later came back out and said everything was arranged. My father then told his wife that he was going to see me off.

"I received a letter from Ruchele," I quickly told my father when we were alone.

"Where is she?" he asked.

"She's living in the Urals. But Shifra isn't with her and I'm worried. They had to separate in Krasnovodsk. The officials wouldn't let Shifra travel because she was pregnant. Ruchele hasn't heard from Shifra since then. I don't know what to think anymore. Please, you must help me find my wife."

"I'm trying," said my father.

"One more thing," I said. "Ruchele asked if you could help her find her husband. I've written down all his information for you, and also Ruchele's address in the Urals." I handed my father the sheet of paper.

"I'll try," he said. "But I don't know how much I can accomplish. You see, I can't even find Mareck."

We were now standing on the platform. My father pulled out his wallet and gave me thirty rubles. I asked him if I could have his telephone number. He scribbled it on a small piece of paper and handed it to me. We climbed up the steps of the train. In the car, the conductor seemed to be expecting us. He came up to my father and as they exchanged a few words my father slipped something into the pocket of the conductor's jacket. With tears in his eyes my father embraced me, wished me luck, and left.

"Sit here" the conductor said to me. "I'll take care of you."

As soon as the train started to move, the conductor came back and led me to a small compartment. "Don't be afraid," he said. "Wait here until I let you out. If anyone knocks, don't answer."

He locked the door from the outside. He was hiding me from the guards, who were probably already inspecting the passenger's documents.

An hour later, the conductor returned. Smiling, he said, "All is fine. Come with me." He led me back to my seat in the car and wished me a good trip.

The train was delayed along the way. By the time I arrived in Marie, it was past one o'clock in the morning, too late to go searching for my father's friend. I was already quite used to spending nights in train stations. I made myself comfortable on a bench and went to sleep.

Early in the morning I left. Marie was a small town and I found the way to my father's friend without trouble.

As I stood at his door, Volodya Kupsov, a man the size of a bear, looked down at me and smiled. He had been expecting me, he said in a gravelly voice. He put a furry arm around me and led me into his house. Volodya, a bachelor in his fifties, shared his breakfast with me. While I ate, he read my father's letter. After our meal, Volodya took me to the police station. I waited while my father's good friend spoke privately to the officer in charge. When the officer finally questioned me, I gave my last name as Renglich instead of Schmer.

As we left the police station, Volodya told me I would receive my documents in about a week.

"Well, are you really as good a tailor as your father says?" Volodya asked.

I assured him that I was.

"Let's go then," he said.

Volodya took me to a small factory which manufactured military uniforms. Only six people worked there. I was hired at once. My new job, sewing pants, was easy by comparison to digging trenches and lugging heavy bales of cotton. Above all, I enjoyed working at my trade again.

Volodya also found me a place to live. My new landlady, Anna, was one of the factory workers. She was about forty-five years old and had an apartment with two rooms. She lived in the larger room with her daughter, Lizavetta, a girl in her early twenties. I was suddenly sharing a house with two beautiful women who, I soon found out, led a complicated existence.

Anna and Lizavetta both had long dark hair, high cheek bones which were always blushing, large dark eyes, and small, shapely noses. They were artists at applying make-up; they always looked like a pair of famous Hollywood actresses. Anna's job at the factory was to sew pockets on pants. Lizavetta was an X-ray technician in a hospital.

At the first opportunity I wrote to Ruchele and told her that I was no longer living at our father's house. I sent her my new address and again asked my sister whether she had heard anything from my wife.

Within a week I received my new papers. My name had finally been legally changed from Schmer to the name I had been born with, Renglich.

Ruchele answered my letter almost at once. She wanted to know why I had moved out of our father's house. Ruchele was sorry to have to tell me that she still had not heard either from Shifra or from Sucher. I wrote back to her and told her everything that happened in our father's house. I also sent a letter to my father, asking him whether he had found out where my wife was.

From Ruchele, I again received a prompt answer. Unfortunately, she still hadn't heard from Shifra. From my father, however, not a word came back.

Anna and Lizavetta soon felt comfortable with me. As I got to know them better, I noticed that even though the mother and daughter treated each other with affection, there was a strange tension between them.

Every now and then one of the two women would fall into a moody silence. When that happened, they would stop speaking. This could last a whole evening. In the morning, when the three of us sat down to breakfast, the two women were the best of friends again, and neither one of them ever mentioned the dark mood that had silenced them the night before.

One evening, when Anna and I were alone she turned to me and asked, "Do you ever wonder why a woman like me is without a man?"

Her directness surprised me. "Aren't you waiting for your husband to return from the war?"

"I waited until about a year ago," Anna said. "My husband was killed at the front. I'm sure he's in heaven right now, looking down and having a good laugh at my expense." She stopped, debating with herself whether to go on. I was quite puzzled by what she had said.

"You're curious," Anna said, smiling. "You're asking yourself, Why would her husband laugh at her from his grave?...I'll tell you if you promise to keep this a secret."

I promised at once.

"It's simple," Anna continued. "I was foolish enough to fall in love a second time. Just three months ago, I met a man who's about my own age. Andre. He's an electrical engineer. I thought he was a fine person. Just a month after we met, he asked me to marry him. I saw no reason to put it off. I said yes and we began to make plans. A month later, he suddenly stopped coming over. I didn't know what to make of it. I gave him two weeks and then I went looking for him. When I asked him what was going on, he tried to put me off with lame excuses. He hadn't been feeling well, he said. Was he sick, I asked? No, not exactly sick. He spoke a lot of nonsense but I thought better not push him. Let him be alone for a few weeks and then let's see how he feels. In the meantime, to keep myself busy, I saw more of my friends. One evening I met an old school mate for dinner. We went to a restaurant near her house. As soon as we sat down, I looked over my friend's shoulder and couldn't believe my eyes. There was Andre sitting at a table with my daughter. I was speechless. As soon as they saw me, they got up and left the restaurant."

"I couldn't go home until very late that night. Lizavetta was already asleep when I came in. I woke her up. 'What's the meaning of this?' I asked her. 'Mother,' she said to me, 'we're very much in love.'

"'For how long? I asked her. 'A month,' my daughter answered. 'I didn't want to hurt you. I didn't know how to tell you.'

305

"I've always loved my daughter. Lizavetta and I have always marvelled at how alike we are. I suppose it shouldn't surprise me that she fell in love with the same man I did; even though I would never have done to her what she did to me.

"I wanted to avoid a scandal. My friend, the one who had been at the restaurant with me, promised not to tell anyone. Somehow the neighbors seem to have found out about it anyway.

"Lizavetta said that she and Andre were going to move away. I don't want to be separated from my daughter, but I agreed that it would be the best solution. They still haven't moved. I'm embarrassed to go out in the street. I keep hoping the two of them will realize their foolishness and break up. If they don't do something soon, I think that I'll pack my bags and I'll be the one to leave."

I listened to Anna's story as if I were hearing a piece of fiction. Nothing in the behavior of the two women towards each other had given me a clue to the depth of the daughter's betrayal of her mother.

I became curious whether Lizavetta, as young, pretty, and intelligent as she was, could really have fallen in love with her mother's fiance, a man twice her age. I watched the two women closely whenever we were together in the evening. Except for the rare times when the dark mood struck one or the other of the women, there was no trace of resentment between them. On the contrary, they enjoyed each other's company. And I enjoyed being with them.

I waited for a chance to speak to Lizavetta alone, to see what I could find out from her. I couldn't let her know what her mother had told me in confidence. I thought, however, that if I could get Lizavetta to speak about love, I might be able to figure something out from her words.

One evening a few weeks after Anna had told me her story, I walked into the kitchen and saw Lizavetta preparing a pot of tea. "Where is your mother?" I asked.

"She's gone out to meet a friend," Lizavetta answered and offered me a cup of tea.

"I'd be delighted to have tea with such a pretty girl as you," I said.

Lizavetta smiled at my compliment. "I've never heard you say such things before. This isn't the first time you've had tea with me."

"But this is the first time we're alone," I said. "Your mother has always been around, and I didn't want to make her jealous."

"That just shows how little you understand us. Mamma would never get jealous about such a thing."

"Not even if she heard me say that I was in love with you?"

I expected Lizavetta to blush at my remark, instead she laughed with delight. "You're a little too late for that," she said as she poured the tea. "I wouldn't have minded it if you'd come a little earlier. I was bored and I could've used a bit of fun. But now, you can just forget it."

I took my cup from her delicate hands. "Why do you say that?" I asked as she poured her own tea.

"Can't you see the nose in front of your face?" Lizavetta asked mockingly. "Then I'll tell you. I'm in love. I've finally found the one man in this world meant for me and no one else. In the last two years, I've had three boyfriends. They seemed nice enough at first, but as soon as we became a little friendlier I found out they were only interested in using me. I'm lucky that I was careful. Then, a few months back, my mother met a man."

Lizavetta threw me a glance to see whether I knew what she was talking about. I acted as if this was news to me.

"He's not young. In fact, he's my mother's age and a bachelor. I used to catch him staring at me and smiling whenever my mother wasn't looking. I had a sense that he was up to no good and I tried to avoid him. Well, soon enough he found out where I worked and every day when I left work, there he was, waiting for me. I told him to get lost. I couldn't do this to my mother. He said that he realized what a terrible thing he was doing to my mother but I had completely charmed him and now he could think of nobody else. He couldn't even eat or sleep. I was always on his mind. He was in love for the first time in his life.

"I couldn't get rid of him. Day after day, he went on like this. He would bring me poems, books, flowers. I had to admit, he was different from the idiots I had dated before. But I still told him to get away from me. There was nothing I could do to discourage him. Rain or shine, when I came out of work, there he stood. Andre, my lovesick engineer. I gave in a little bit. I let him walk with me. Well, in less than a week, he asked me to marry him. I was shocked. 'No,' I told him, 'I will never speak to you again.' He said that if I rejected him, he would kill himself.

"It took another week, and I fell deeply in love with Andre. He never really loved my mother. They would've been miserable if they'd gotten married. This may sound odd, but I saved my mother from a bad marriage. Of course, she wasn't happy when she found out. She's embarrassed by the whole thing, so Andre and I are trying to move to another city. Of course, with this war, it's taking forever to find re-placements for us at our jobs. As soon as they do, Andre and I will get out of Marie and marry. I just don't know how I'll stand it, living without Mother."

The Telegram

IN MARCH OF 1943, I received a letter from the Soviet government. Without warning, I was told to report within three days to a mobilization unit. The letter didn't give a reason for the order, nor did it say where I was being sent, but I feared I was being drafted to dig trenches again, exactly the kind of work which had almost killed me once already.

I took the notice to Volodya Kupsov to see whether a mistake had been made. Perhaps, he could use his influence to help me stay in Marie. Volodya, a serious look on his face, considered the official paper I had laid down on his desk. He wasn't hopeful that he would be able to help me, he said, but he promised to do whatever he could. In the meantime, he urged me to get in touch with my father.

In spite of the many letters I had written to Ashkhabat, I hadn't received a single answer. I looked at the slip of paper with my father's telephone number and decided to call him.

That same evening, I asked Anna if she knew where I could find a telephone. My landlady, aware of the misfortune that had befallen me, took me at once to the apartment of a friend. While the two women talked in the living room, I made my call from the alcove where the black telephone sat on a small table-stand. I listened anxiously as the operator established a connection. Finally, I heard my step-sister's voice in Ashkhabat.

"Could I speak to my father, please?" I asked.

I could tell by her hesitation that she was concocting something. "He can't answer now," she said.

"Marta, I must speak to him."

"He's busy with important guests. There have been problems at the factory."

"Tell him I've got to speak to him for just a few minutes."

"Couldn't you call back another day?"

"No, it's impossible!" I said, my anger rising. "Another day will be too late. I need his help now!"

"Please don't raise your voice to me," Marta said. "I told you that Father has big problems at the factory. He's entertaining some important officials to discuss business."

It was useless. Marta's tongue was wagging quicker than a duck's tail.

"Marta, I beg you. Do me one favor. Tell my father that I'm being shipped out of Marie in two days. If he can do anything to help me, he's got to do it now."

"As soon as he's free," Marta said, "I'll give him your message."

I didn't believe her. But whether she told my father or not, I never heard from him. Volodya couldn't do anything for me either.

It was March when I left Marie and winter had just ended in that part of the country. It never occurred to me, that I was being sent to Siberia. When I arrived in the city of Rubtsofsk, winter was still raging. Dressed lightly, I nearly froze. For the first eight days, I was quarantined along with a hundred other men. After that we were given warm clothing and sent out to do construction work.

On barren fields blasted by icy winds, we carried bricks and dug foundations in soil frozen hard as rock. We were building factories that were to manufacture tanks, tractors, and other heavy machinery for the war. Our 'warm' clothes barely kept us from freezing to death. Huge cast iron stoves had to be kept burning in the fields. Every few minutes we ran to the stoves and huddled as close to the fire as we could get, flapping our arms against our sides. The cold was so harsh that we spent more time trying to warm up than working.

Our foremen soon noticed that they had a worse problem than the cold on their hands. Many of the newly arrived men weren't construction workers. We made so many mistakes that instead of helping we actually held the real workers back. Since the project employed more than ten thousand men, the construction company had set up workshops to provide such items as shoes and clothes for everyone. Just a few weeks after our arrival in Rubtsofsk, those of us who were useless at construction work, but had other skills, were put to work at our trades.

I was sent to a tailor shop. I was also moved from barracks which I shared with twenty men, to barracks which I shared with only four other men. It wasn't a bad setup. I received a ration card for bread; there was a kitchen where I could get a hot meal at government prices, and at the shop, I was paid on piece work—the more I produced, the more I earned. Even though the pay was low, and the distribution of the work wasn't fair, a single person could live. I even managed to save a little money.

One of my new roommates, Menashe Roit, was a co-worker at the tailor shop. He had been working there for over six months and knew everything that went on. He was a little younger than me, hot tempered, and came from Lodz. It was Menashe who explained to me that the shop was really run by the two Haskell brothers: Arie, the tailor, and Mendel, the cutter. What made them different from the rest of us was their membership in the Soviet Communist Party.

The Haskells came from Lodz, where they had spent many years in a famous prison, Kartufbereze, for their communist agitation in Poland. Their reputation had preceded them and when they arrived in Russia, they were invited at once to join the Party. They agreed on the condition that they get credit for their years as Communist activists in Poland. The party leaders of Rubtsofsk didn't have the authority to make such a decision so they turned the matter over to the Kremlin, which eventually ordered that the Haskells be recognized for their political activity in Poland. As a result the Haskells became official members of the Soviet Communist Party.

As people poured into Rubtsofsk to work on the construction project, the tailor shop was flooded with work. Customers had to wait months for a garment. The official policy of the shop was "first-come-first-served." But in fact it was those who greased the Haskells' palms the most who were the first served. The brothers believed in the communist ideal of distribution of wealth enough to share their bribes with our foreman. There were plenty of palm-greasers, too. Almost everyone who worked in a warehouse and could steal had with what to grease: groceries, fabrics, tools, some even used money. Not a single garment left the workshop for which a payment hadn't been made to Arie, Mendel, and the foreman under the table. There were ten people working in that shop. The harder the seven of us worked, the more the other three made in bribes.

As soon as I settled in, I wrote to my sister and father asking for news of my wife. My sister, even though she still hadn't heard from Shifra, wrote back at once. From my father, as usual, there was no answer. I was very disappointed in him. He *was* in a position to help me and yet he did nothing. Even if his wife and daughter were holding him back, I couldn't forgive him for not standing up to them. I was, after all, his son. I began to wish I had never found him. As for Shifra, I didn't know what to think anymore. Whenever I remembered the last time I had seen her in Makhatschkala, pregnant, holding our little Ninale in her arms, I became desperate. I was afraid that something terrible had happened to her and our daughter. Why else hadn't Shifra written to Ruchele's friend in the Urals?

One morning, in May of 1943, the tailor shop's errand-boy came running up to my machine. "A telegram for you!" he said out of breath as he handed me an envelope.

I tore it open. The message was in Russian. I asked Menashe, who sat next to me, to read it. As I looked over his shoulder, Menashe read aloud, "Dear Son, your wife is in Bolotnya, a village near Nova Sibiersk." The letters began to dance before my eyes. "She and two children are in the hospital with dysentery. I wish them a quick recovery. Your Father."

I sank back down into my seat, stared at the piece of paper in my hands, and wondered if I was dreaming. I couldn't understand how my father had performed this miracle, but I was deeply grateful to him. He hadn't forgotten me after all. As soon as I calmed down, I went to see the foreman and showed him the telegram. He told me to drop my work and go at once to Mr. Dubrovin, the director of the construction company.

On the way to the director's office, I stopped off at the telegraph office and sent a message to Shifra at the hospital in Bolotnya. I told her that I wasn't too far away and that I was arranging for us to be together as soon as possible. After Mr. Dubrovin read my father's telegram, he instructed his secretary to write a letter to the military authorities on my behalf.

At the military office, I handed over all my identification papers, my father's telegram, and the director's letter. The officials said they would be in touch with me shortly. Within a week I received a letter from Shifra herself. She had been called to the militia station in Bolotnya and had been given authorization to join me in Rubtsofsk. She even sent me the date and time to pick her up at the train station.

I was besides myself with joy. The first thing I did was look for a place for us to live. Through my foreman, I found a Russian woman who had a room to rent. She was a widow with a twelve-year-old son who lived on her dead husband's pension. The husband had been a high-ranking officer in the Russian Army and the widow received a good pension, but because of the war everything was expensive and she needed to make some extra money. Her apartment had two large rooms and a kitchen. I liked the room she was offering for rent. It was bright and fully furnished, with a closet, chest of drawers, and two beds. The rent the widow was asking was a little too expensive for my salary but I took the room anyway.

In the few days while I waited for my wife to arrive with the children, I cleaned the room, stocked up on groceries, and did everything I could to make them feel as comfortable as possible.

Finally, the day came. Shifra's train was due at ten o'clock in the morning. I left the house at eight to give myself plenty of time. I walked into the station at nine o'clock and the first thing I saw was Shifra sitting on a bench, holding a baby in her arms. Leaning against Shifra, asleep, was Nina.

"Shifra!" I called as I ran up to her.

She looked up at me and smiled weakly. I had never seen my wife so thin and pale. Ninale, two-and-a-half-years old already, looked scrawny and smaller than when I had last seen her nine months earlier. The time we had been separated had taken a heavy toll on my family. My wife couldn't even get up. I sat down next to her and embraced her. I kissed Shifra over and over again. Then I picked up Ninale. My little daughter didn't even seem to know who I was. It broke my heart to feel how light she was. She seemed so fragile in my hands, I was afraid of hurting her. Finally, I looked at the baby in Shifra's arms.

"She was born on the twenty-ninth of October," Shifra said. "Her name is Esther."

"She's so tiny," I said. "All of you look so thin."

"We've been very sick," Shifra said. "Schloime, it's a miracle you found us. We were going under. We couldn't have survived much longer on our own."

"I would've come for you sooner if I'd known where you were," I said. "Why didn't you write to Ruchele's friend Kaile Masler as we had agreed?"

"I lost the address," Shifra said. "I was supposed to travel with Ruchele to the Urals. We signed up together in Krasnovodsk. Then at the last minute they held me back because I was pregnant. Ruchele didn't want to leave me, but they wouldn't let her stay. My life after I got separated from Ruchele was hell. Because of Esther I couldn't work. I've had to depend on what the government gives me. We've been starving. Do you have a room?"

"Yes. I've prepared everything. Come, let me take you home."

"You'll have to carry Nina," Shifra said.

I had my little daughter in my arms and now I grew alarmed at the limpness I felt in her little body. "What's wrong with her?" I asked.

"She can't walk," Shifra said, crying. "The doctors say it's weakness."

"We have to do something at once," I said.

"Food," Shifra said. "She needs good food."

I carried Nina in on one arm. She was so light, I felt that I was holding a small bird. With my other hand I picked up Shifra's suitcase and I took my family home. My happiness and my pain were immense. I cried for joy to have my wife and children back at last and then I cried from pain to see how thin and sickly they were.

While I had been alone, I had saved a little money, and now I made sure to have the best food I could afford in the house. Shifra began to cook. Within a few weeks she and the girls had put on some weight and began to look better. Within a month, Ninale regained strength in her little legs. Shifra and I were deeply relieved one evening when we saw our little Ninale stand up and take a few wobbly steps across the room. We kissed and hugged her all night long. Two weeks later, Nina was running around, getting into trouble just as a two-and-a-half-year-old should.

I wrote to my sister and gave her the good news that Shifra was with me. I also wrote to my father to thank him for everything he had done for us. In my letter, I begged him to keep in touch because we were, after all, family, and the worst thing in the world for anyone was to be alone.

I soon received an answer from Ruchele. She shared my joy that Shifra and I were together again, and that our babies were safe and sound. From my father, I heard nothing.

One evening, when I returned home from work, I found that our room had been divided by a curtain. The landlady had rented the other half of the room to a newly arrived Russian couple in their fifties who also worked for the construction company. I told our landlady that the room was too small for two families.

"Mister Renglich," said the landlady with an air of disdain, "if you're not satisfied with the arrangement, you can move."

I did look for another room awhile but I couldn't find anything else that I could afford and we stayed. After a few weeks we began to get used to our new roommates, Katerina and Sergey. Every now and then, he got a little drunk and we heard muffled arguments across the curtain. Shifra and I weren't happy with this, but they weren't loud, and we lived with it. Everyone has an argument occasionally, we thought. As time went on, however, the couple began to argue more often and more loudly. The husband accused his wife of sleeping around with other men. She accused him of being an insane drunkard. The fights soon grew so vicious that one evening he nearly beat her to death. Between his shouting and her wailing, our children were terrified. Shifra and I quickly bundled up our little daughters and we ran out of the house.

I carried Nina, Shifra held Esther, and we walked around the streets for an hour. When we returned to the apartment, the fight was still raging. And by now all the neighbors had gathered outside.

A friendly couple, seeing Shifra and me with our babies on the street, invited us to spend the night at their flat.

In the morning, after I had made sure that our crazy roommate and his wife had left for work, I brought Shifra and the children back to our half of the room.

Instead of going to work, I went to see the director of the construction company. I told him what had been going on at my apartment and begged him to let me move back into one of the barracks owned by the construction company.

Mr. Dubrovin was sympathetic to my problem. He telephoned the barracks' supervisor and asked him to give me and my wife a separate room. We moved that same day and began to breathe easier. Our new home was again no more than a room. The barracks were dug three-quarters-deep into the earth and the only window was at ground level. We had almost no furniture or appliances. Instead of beds, we had a wide wooden board which ran almost the entire length and half the width of the room. At night, we slept on this board and during the day we sat on it, ate off it, and our children played on it. We also had a small stove for cooking and heat. But what pleased us most about our new home was that we were together and no longer had to worry about the crazy couple.

Our life had almost returned to normal again when the little money which I had saved up was spent. My earnings simply weren't enough to pay the rent and feed a family of four. I knew that if I went to the authorities to ask for help, I would be told to put my children into a nursery and send Shifra to work. My wife and babies, however, had barely regained their strength, and I couldn't endanger their health again. For some time, neighbors who knew I was a tailor had been asking me to do work for them at home. These were people who couldn't afford the bribes to the Haskell brothers to get something done at the tailor shop. Since I didn't own a sewing machine, I had been turning my neighbors away. But as my situation grew desperate, I decided to take on some private work and do it at the shop in the evening after my regular working hours.

Up until then I had no problems at my job. The foreman had always helped me. Now, all of a sudden, he turned against me. As I was working one evening, he walked up to me and asked, "What are you doing? Are you crazy? This is isn't our work!"

"I can't feed my family on what I earn," I said. "What's the big sin if I use the sewing machine for a few hours at night."

"If you want to work overtime," the foreman said nervously, "do it in your own home."

"If I had a machine do you think I'd be here so late at night?" I asked. "I'm not trying to get rich. I'm only trying to keep two babies from starving."

The foreman pulled a chair close to me and whispered, "We're not alone here. Do you understand what I mean?" He looked around. It was late and there was no one left in the shop except for the two of us and yet the foreman continued to whisper. "I don't want to lose my job because of you, and I don't want you to get into trouble." Then he got up and left abruptly. The foreman himself was afraid of doing anything that might anger the Haskell brothers.

I had to stop working nights. I watched Shifra struggle to make ends meet on my meager salary. Meanwhile on Sundays, when I went to the market, I would see Arie's and Mendel's wives selling the goods which their husbands had collected in bribes during the week: sugar, honey, butter, shirts, socks, shoes.

One morning at work, I saw Arie Haskell gloating over a beautiful piece of woolen fabric which he was going to make into a suit for himself. I became incensed when I overheard him bragging to the foreman that he had spent 10,000 rubles on the fabric at the black market. On my salary of about three hundred rubles a month, I could hardly afford to buy bread, which cost one hundred rubles a kilo.

I waited for an opportunity to speak to Arie alone. At lunchtime I walked up to him and asked how could he afford to spend thousands on a piece of cloth while I couldn't earn enough to feed my family.

Ariel looked at me as if I were a flea that had bitten him on the back of the neck and said, "Because you're not Arie Haskell. You're Schloime Renglich."

"Where did you pick up such wisdom?" I asked him. "From Stalin? I don't think they taught such selfishness in the Polish Communist Party."

Haskell stared at me with contempt but he didn't have another smart answer.

"Why can't I work after hours, so I can feed my wife and children?" I asked again.

"If you work nights," Arie said, "you're going to be tired during the day. You see how busy we are. They're tearing the work out of our hands as soon as it's finished."

After that conversation, I decided to go back to working for myself. The following evening, after everyone had left, I sat down at my machine and fixed a pair of pants for a neighbor. I continued to work like this for almost a week without being disturbed, until late one night, the Haskell brothers suddenly appeared at the shop.

"If you don't stop once and for all," Arie said, "we're going to turn you in."

"If you do that," I said, "I'll turn *you* in."

Arie laughed. "Who's going to take your word over mine?"

"Go to hell!" I said. "I have a wife and two small children to feed."

In a few days, I received a letter from the management. I had been sentenced, the letter said, to a month of hard labor for breaking the rules of my workshop. I wanted to go to Mr. Dubrovin, the director, and expose the Haskells for their corruption but Shifra and Menashe talked me out of it.

To serve my sentence I had to report every day for work at a farm about three kilometers from where I lived. By the time I got there, I was dead tired from the walk alone. My hard labor was to grind tomatoes at a mill. All day long, I stood at a large crankshaft and turned a heavy stone wheel. At night, when I got home, I would immediately collapse on the bed.

Two weeks after I had started to serve my sentence, one of the farm managers who knew that I was a tailor, asked me to make him a pair of pants.

"I'd gladly do it," I said, "but I don't have a sewing machine."

"Come to my house," said the manager. "My wife has a machine."

On my first day off, I went to the manager's house. I took his measurements, drew my own pattern, cut the material, and began to sew the pants.

At lunch time, as I sat in the manager's kitchen, he asked me why I wasn't working at my real trade, tailoring.

When I told him how I had been punished for wanting to work a few extra hours to feed my family, the manager became upset.

"Are you telling me that you weren't given the choice of serving your sentence in a tailor shop?" he asked.

"I wasn't given any choice at all," I said. "My sentence was a month of hard labor at the mill."

"Listen to me." the manager said, "Tomorrow morning don't go to the mill. Go instead to the local Secretary of the Party and tell him that Mr. Levitan sent you. Tell him what you just told me. If he doesn't send you right back to the tailor shop, come back and see me immediately! Here in the Soviet Union even when someone is in jail, he still has the right to work at his trade. They had no right to do this to you. What they did is illegal!"

The Remnants

THE NEXT MORNING, I followed Mr. Levitan's suggestion and went to see the local Secretary of the Party. He was a small man, about sixty years old, in trim shape, with a white mustache and goatee. I sat down in his office, a large room in a government building, and told him my story.

"Go back to the tailor shop," the Secretary said when I had finished. "I will telephone them at once."

I was amazed. It was exactly as Mr. Levitan had predicted.

"Mr. Secretary," I said, "couldn't you send me to another tailor shop? I can't work for those people anymore. I'm afraid they're going to push me so far, I'll be forced to send them all to jail for their dirty business."

"You're an experienced tailor?" the Secretary asked me.

"Yes."

"Then I know a shop where they could use a man like you."

I never had to go back to work at the mill again. As soon as I started at the new tailor shop I realized why the Secretary had sent me there. Except for me, the shop didn't have a single experienced tailor. The foreman immediately assigned me the most difficult and important work and began to rely on me heavily. He also allowed me to stay as late as I wanted to do my own work. I finally began to earn enough money to take good care of my family.

When the Haskells found out that I wasn't coming back to work at their factory at the end of my sentence, they sent their foreman to talk to me. I was desperately needed back at my old job, he said. They were willing to pay a little beyond my salary, if I understood what he meant. I would even be welcome to work for myself in the evenings, he said and winked.

I told him to get lost and never mention the Haskells' name to me again. If they tried to force me to return, I would go at once to local secretary of the Party. I knew enough about the Haskell brothers to settle accounts with them once and for all. When the foreman got up from his chair, he was shaken. I didn't think I would be bothered by the Haskells anymore.

My decision to ask the Communist Party for help turned our life around for the better. Within a few months I had saved enough to buy a used sewing machine. I no longer had to spend long hours alone in the factory at night. As soon as I was done with work, I rushed home, ate dinner, and sat down to work in my own room at my own machine.

The war continued to rage. Shifra and I were grateful for our daily bread and roof over our heads. In time, we even managed to move out of the barrack into a normal apartment. It happened when the Communist Party in the city of Rubtsofsk decided to open a large factory to produce clothing and shoes. Since there weren't enough good craftsmen around, the Party asked that each shop send one experienced person to help staff the new factory. I was picked from my tailor shop. It was soon after I started my new job, that I was given a decent apartment. Shifra and the children no longer had to sit, sleep, and eat on the same wooden board. Not only did I get the apartment, I also got a raise in salary, and I was offered an extra sixty rubles a month for every person I taught tailoring. I took on six students and received an extra 360 rubles each month. I could finally stop working at home.

Of course there were problems at this new factory. The cutter, Porfiry Arbutzov, was often drunk and sometimes the cloth was cut either too short or too narrow. I was asked if I wanted to take over the cutter's job. I turned it down because I didn't have much experience cutting. But I suffered more than once because of Porfiry's drunkenness. The worst such occasion was when I had to make a coat for an important member of the Party, a Comrade Bolatov. I warned Porfiry to be careful how he cut the expensive fabric because it was for a high Party official. My warning made no impression on the drunken cutter. When Comrade Bolatov came to try on his coat, he couldn't button it.

"What is this supposed to be," the official huffed, "a coat or a girdle?"

"I'm responsible for the sewing," I said, "not the way the material is cut."

Bolatov realized that the fault wasn't mine. "Can you do something to fix the coat?" he asked.

I promised to try. It was not an easy job, but I did everything in my power to widen the coat.

A few days later when Bolatov slipped on the coat again after I my alterations, a smile broke on his hardened face.

"Ahhh," he sighed with relief. "I don't have to choose between closing the buttons and breathing. I can't give you any money for these alterations, but if you ever need help, knock on my door."

Like Comrade Bolatov, I too breathed easier for having solved that problem. All in all, however, I couldn't complain. I was able to provide for Shifra and our two little daughters. In a world at war what more could I have asked for? And every day Shifra and I prayed, as did every Jewish person in the world, that the heinous German killers would be defeated and that the German atrocities against the Jewish people, the mass murders, the gassing and burning of innocent men, women and children would come to an end.

In time, the fighting on the front turned. The Germans began to loose one battle after another. At long last, the day came when Hitler was forced to surrender. When we heard that the war was over, we felt as if a death sentence had been lifted from our heads. Everyone stopped working. Some people danced and kissed in the streets. Some people got drunk. Some faces were filled with joy. And some people cried as they had not been able to cry before for the loss of fathers and mothers, sisters and brothers, husbands and wives, and children.

Life changed quickly. Almost immediately groceries began to appear in the stores again. We no longer had to buy at the black market.

Towards the end of 1945, I received a letter from my sister. Ruchele still hadn't heard from her husband, but she had run into an acquaintance who told her that Sucher was living somewhere in the Caucasus area. That was the reason, Ruchele wrote, she had decided to return to the city of Naltchik.

In December of 1945, as Shifra and I considered whether to join Ruchele in Naltchik, we found out that Shifra was pregnant. At the same time we received another letter from Ruchele. She had found her husband. A few weeks after her arrival in Naltchik, Ruchele had tracked Sucher down with the help of the military authorities. He had only recently been discharged from the Army. Ruchele wrote that they were planning to go back to Poland.

In Rubtsofsk almost everyone who had come from Poland was also preparing to return home. Although I wanted desperately to find out what had happened to our babies and the family we had left in Warsaw, I wasn't eager to move Shifra and the children back there. I remembered the difficult times we had faced in Poland and I was afraid of what we would find. It had been years since we had heard from Yoinne and Elke. After their few letters asking for food packages, we had never received another word. I didn't, however, want to be separated from my sister. I wrote to my father and told him that Ruchele had decided to leave Russia and that Shifra and I might do the same. A few weeks later, when I didn't get an answer from my father, I tried to telephone. I guessed that his wife and daughter had hidden my letter from my father. Unfortunately it was Marta who answered the telephone when I called. She told me at once that her father was away on a business trip. I asked her to tell him that my sister and I were preparing to return to Poland and if he wanted to see us he would have to contact me soon.

I couldn't wait much longer. Ruchele and Sucher were already on their way to Poland. I still had a commitment to the construction company and I knew that they would try to stop me from leaving. Nevertheless I registered for permission to return to Poland. As I expected, when the management of the garment factory found out that I had applied for emigration, they tried to talk me into staying. One evening, there was a knock on my door. Two policemen in uniform told me they had orders to search my house. I had nothing to hide and let them in. They found some pieces of material, remnants from the days when I was working at home in the evenings, and they accused me of stealing from my shop.

The director of the factory ordered the police to put a stop on my emigration papers. I was told that I would have to face a trial for my crime.

I didn't know where to turn. Rubtsofsk had few lawyers and all of them were swamped with work. I was about to give up hope of finding one when I came into the office of Gregory Papilovitch. The harassed, burly, middle-aged attorney was about to throw me out the door when he heard that I was a tailor.

"Can you make a coat?" he asked.

I told him I could.

Gregory grabbed hold of me by the shoulders and dragged me back to his desk. He threw open a drawer, pulled out a heavy piece of plaid fabric and shoved it into my hands.

"Well," the lawyer demanded, "can you make a coat out of this material by tomorrow or not? If you can't then we're of no use to each other."

"I need to take your measurements."

"The coat's for my wife!" the lawyer shouted.

"How tall is she?" I asked. "And how much does she weigh?"

The lawyer told me his wife's measurements and I ran home with the fabric. I stayed up all night working. In the morning I brought the coat to the lawyer's office.

He looked up in disbelief. "Finished already?" he began to shout. "Are you trying to make my wife look like a clown wearing this rag you've thrown together in a few hours?"

"Have your wife try it on," I challenged him. "If she's not satisfied then you can scream."

"I have a better idea," Gregory said. He ran out of his office and came back instantly dragging a bewildered woman off the street.

"My wife's exact figure," Gregory said. "Throw the coat on her. Quickly!"

"Please, madam," I begged the woman as I handed her the garment, "try it on. My life depends on it."

"What's going on here?" the woman complained as she took off her own coat and slipped on the one I had made.

"It certainly feels very nice," she said after a moment. "Do you have a mirror?"

"Female vanity!" scoffed the lawyer. "Turn around!" he bluntly ordered the poor woman.

When she had done a turn, the lawyer clapped and rubbed his hands together. "It's perfect!" he shouted. "Take it off and get out of here."

I thanked the woman as she returned the coat. She put her own back on and left.

"You kept your part of the bargain," said the lawyer, "and now I'll keep mine. Listen carefully and do exactly as I tell you. Go to the police station and ask to speak to Commander Kamerov. Have you got that name? He was a tailor before he became a useless government official. Tell him that I, Gregory Papilovitch, sent you. Then tell him your story, and ask him what he did with the remnants when he was a tailor."

I looked dumbfounded at the lawyer. I couldn't believe that this was his help; he expected me to go to the police station and question an official.

Gregory laughed when he saw my expression. "Don't worry. You won't get arrested. If I'm sending you to Kamerov, and I'm telling you to use my name, then I must know what I'm doing."

I followed the lawyer's instructions. Commander Kamerov, a man of fifty, with a drawn face and a caved-in chest, listened to my story. When I asked him what he had done with remnants when he was a tailor, he turned an apoplectic red and started to curse me.

I apologized at once and told him that I was only repeating the lawyer's words.

Kamerov calmed down and looked to see if anyone had overheard us. "Your smart-aleck lawyer doesn't know everything," Kamerov whispered. "I can take care of your trial but I'm not sure I can arrange your papers to leave the country. I'll try to do what I can. Go home and be patient."

As I left the police station, I remembered Comrade Bolatov, the party official for whom I had once also made a coat and who had told me to knock on his door if I needed help.

Bolatov, behind his large desk, recognized me as soon as I walked into his office. I explained my situation to him. He laughed heartily when I told him about my lawyer and his solution to my problem. No sooner was I done speaking than Comrade Bolatov was on the telephone to the police station. He spoke for a minute, turned to me and said, "Go back to our friend Commander Kamerov right now."

At the police station, I not only received all my emigration papers, I was given a package with the remnants which had been taken as evidence from my home.

I ran to the factory, showed the managers my papers, and was immediately released from my job. On June 1, 1946, Shifra, our two little daughters, and I left Russia for Poland.

Shifra was beginning her ninth month of pregnancy. The trip was supposed to take no more than a week, and I figured we would have plenty of time to get Shifra to a hospital in Poland. The trains, however, were far from running normally. The tracks were still heavily occupied with the traffic of returning soldiers. We spent more time waiting than traveling. A week passed and we were not even halfway closer to Poland. I began to be afraid that Shifra was going to have the baby on the train.

On June 17, more than two weeks after we had left Russia, we finally arrived on Polish soil.

Everyone in our car was directed to the city of Breslau in Lower Silesia. As soon as we got off the train, I went directly to the Jewish Congregation, explained my situation, and asked for their help. I was told to leave my two little daughters with them and take my wife to the hospital.

After I had made sure that Shifra was well taken care of, I ran back to the Jewish Congregation. They had already found an apartment for us. I picked up my two little daughters and with an official of the Congregation we went to see our new home.

Our apartment, I was amazed to see, had many rooms and was fully furnished. These apartments, I was told, had been deserted by the defeated Germans when they left Poland.

The following morning, I asked my neighbors, a Jewish couple who had also survived the war in Russia, if they could watch my daughters while I went out for a few hours. They told me to leave Nina and Esther with them and not worry. I ran back to the Jewish Congregation and asked the officials if they could help me find out about our two babies who had remained in Warsaw, and the rest of our family. I was led into an office where a survivor from Warsaw asked me where our family had lived. I gave him the address of Uncle Ksiel's basement and the name of everyone who had been there. I could tell at once from the expression in his tortured eyes that no one had survived. He carefully took down all my information and told me not to hope for anything.

After three days in the hospital, on the twentieth of June 1946, Shifra gave birth to a boy. We called him David.

Because of the delay we had faced in leaving Russia, by the time we got back to Poland I had lost track of my sister. I asked the Jewish Congregation as well as the Red Cross for help in locating her. Even though I didn't know where Ruchele was, I knew at least that she and her husband were alive. We also found out through letters from Shifra's Uncle Moishe in Baranovitch that her brothers Khiel and Nachme, and her Uncle Ksiel and his wife were living in Russia. But those of our family who had stayed behind in Warsaw were all murdered by the Germans. My mother, Shifra's mother, Frau Liebe, Yoinne, Elke, their two girls and boy, Ksiel and Lotte's three children, and our own innocent babies, Liebele and Zlatele, had all perished.

At the end of the war Shifra was thirty-one and I was thirty-four. We had survived a Holocaust. We had lost three children, but we had Nina and Esther, who depended on us, we had each other, and we had to go on living.

Two years after our return to Poland, on July 18, 1948, Shifra gave birth to another girl. She was named after my mother, Rosa. Seven years later, on March 16, 1955, our son Henry was born.

Once, as a boy, I had sat the edge of a lake in Lublin and watched a flock of pigeons fly in circles above me. Together they soared up and down, and together they circled left and right, but what amazed me the most was to see that if a single pigeon lost its way from the flock, it was immediately surrounded by all the others and brought back to fly in their midst. After the war, as a man, I remembered this scene every evening when I came home from work, and my five little children ran up to greet me.